Managing Misbehavio

Since the first edition of this book was published, there have been many changes in education. The second edition has been compiled to develop and update the earlier successful book.

Managing Misbehaviour in Schools deals with the theory and practice of managing pupils' behaviour taking into account the effects of the recent Children Act and the 1992 White Paper on Education.

The authors deal first with the theoretical background concerning possible influences upon children's behaviour and the various ways of conceptualizing and understanding behaviour problems. Later chapters consider the effect of pastoral care on behaviour in schools, liaison with other helping agencies, and work with parents. In a wide-ranging final chapter, the editors review the various strands of the book, developed from theory to classroom and school practice, and offer a set of practical guidelines for teachers and students in their daily task of managing pupils' behaviour to enable appropriate learning to take place. Summaries of the main points in recent legislation and reports are given in an appendix. The contributors and the editors – who themselves contribute nearly half the book – are experienced and well-known writers in the field of education.

Tony Charlton is a Research Fellow at the Cheltenham and Gloucester College of Higher Education. **Kenneth David** is a freelance writer and lecturer, and a former Adviser in schools.

Managing misbehaviour in schools

Second edition

Edited by
Tony Charlton and Kenneth David

London and New York

First published 1993
by Routledge
11 New Fetter Lane, London EC4P 4EE

Simultaneously published in the USA and Canada
by Routledge
29 West 35th Street, New York, NY 10001

© 1993 Tony Charlton and Kenneth David

Typeset in 10/12 pt Garamond by J&L Composition Ltd, Filey,
North Yorkshire
Printed and bound in Great Britain by
Mackays of Chatham PLC, Chatham, Kent

British Library Cataloguing in Publication Data
A catalogue record for this book is available from the British Library

Library of Congress Cataloging in Publication Data
Managing misbehaviour in schools / [edited by] Tony Charlton and
Kenneth David. – 2nd ed.
    p. cm.
    Includes bibliographical references and index.
    ISBN 0–415–09287–6
    1. School discipline – United States. 2. School management and
organization – United States. 3. Problem children – Education – United
States. 4. Behavior modification – United States. I. Charlton,
Tony. II. David, Kenneth.
LB3012.2.M356 1993
371.5′0973 – dc20   93–458
ISBN 0–415–09287–6   CIP

Contents

Contributors

Tony Charlton was a Director of English Studies and Head of Pastoral Care in a large comprehensive school and taught in primary and special schools before becoming a part-time tutor at University College, Cardiff. He was then Principal Lecturer and Head of Special Needs at the College of St Paul and St Mary, Cheltenham. This became the Cheltenham and Gloucester College of Higher Education where he is currently Research Fellow in the Faculty of Education and Health. He has published widely on a range of subjects concerned with children's and adults' emotional and behaviour problems, and is co-editor with Kenneth David of *The Caring Role of the Primary School* (1987), *Supportive Schools* (1990) and *Managing Misbehaviour* (1989).

Kenneth David was an army education officer and taught in primary education before becoming principal of a teacher training college and an administrator of schools in Uganda. He then taught in secondary and further education before becoming tutor–adviser in personal relationships, in Gloucestershire, and a general adviser with special responsibility for personal relationships, in Lancashire. In recent years he has been a freelance writer and lecturer, with special links with Cheltenham and Gloucester College of Higher Education. He has published many books and articles on pastoral care, health education, personal relationships and counselling.

Ronald Davie, formerly Professor of Educational Psychology at Cardiff and Director of the National Children's Bureau, is now an independent consultant psychologist. He works in the courts as an expert witness in children's cases, undertakes training on the 1989 Children Act, helps schools in a London Borough with problems of truancy and bullying and continues to have particular interests in the area of children's behaviour and emotional problems. He is currently a Visiting Professor at Oxford Polytechnic and an Honorary Research Fellow at University College, London.

John George is Headmaster of Bettridge School, Cheltenham, which caters for the needs of children with severe learning difficulties. He previously worked in a variety of other special schools providing for pupils with physical and moderate learning/ behaviour difficulties.

Kevin Jones is a lecturer in Special Education at Cheltenham and Gloucester College of Higher Education. His teaching experience spans primary, secondary and special schools and he has served in advisory and support roles. He has published articles on special educational needs and is co-editor with Tony Charlton of *Learning Difficulties in Primary Classrooms* (1992). His research interests include assessment/recognition of learning difficulties and problem behaviours, special educational provision in mathematics and co-operative teaching approaches. He carried out research into the special oral language needs of low-attaining mathematicians which led to an unpublished Ph.D. thesis (University of East Anglia).

Hanne Lambley has taught in special and mainstream schools in both Germany and the UK. After several years of experience in the advisory service for Gloucestershire and as a senior lecturer in teacher education at the Cheltenham and Gloucester College of Higher Education, she is now a freelance lecturer and consultant. She has a particular interest in the training of primary teachers for the teaching of reading, which is the field for her present research.

Mick Lock is a Chartered Educational Psychologist working in private practice in Nottinghamshire. Prior to establishing his own consultancy he worked as an LEA psychologist and as a Head of Year in secondary education. He has a particular interest in short-term problem-solving approaches towards problem behaviour which are conducted jointly with parents.

John Presland trained as an educational psychologist and worked for Warwickshire and Birmingham in that capacity before moving to his present post as Principal Educational Psychologist and Senior Adviser for Special Education in Wiltshire. He has published widely on a variety of educational and psychological topics.

Graham Upton is Professor and Head of the School of Education at the University of Birmingham. He has taught in ordinary and special schools and has been involved in teacher education in Colleges of Education, in a Polytechnic and in two University Departments of Education. In addition to research conducted in conjunction with his own higher degrees, he has conducted large-scale funded research in a number of areas of special education. He has written extensively on behaviour problems in schools and on special education generally.

Foreword

CHALLENGING YEARS

Since the first edition of this book was published four years ago there has been a series of legislative and other changes in education: the developments from the 1988 Education Reform Act; the 1989 Elton Report on discipline in schools; the Children Act of 1989, which will be followed by many other developments in due course; and recently the 1992 White Paper on Education, with its radical reassessment of the whole structure of education. All these, directly or indirectly, will have varied effects on behaviour in schools, and this book considers them now in a considerably revised and updated version of the successful *Managing Misbehaviour* published in 1989.

Not only do the new and revised chapters take account of the legislative changes, but the opportunity has been taken to introduce new writing: recent academic studies have been included in references and bibliography and the editors have added to their own reflections on behaviour in schools in the final summarizing chapter and the appendix. More than half of the present book is new or considerably revised work.

Teachers continue to be assailed by a major public challenge of their professional competence, as well as their moral leadership. This challenge has come from the media as well as from government, and has occasionally been merited although frequently it has been undeserved and ill-informed. Teaching continues to be an increasingly demanding and difficult profession, and teachers will continue to need academic and other support, rather than constant criticism, in their work of caring for their pupils and in their tasks of developing and controlling young people, tasks which are increasingly being subjected to public evaluation and scrutiny, fair and unfair.

This book is therefore concerned with the everyday business of teaching, and particularly with the skills of managing behaviour in classrooms and the wider school to ensure that effective learning can take place.

We are attempting to help practising and student teachers:

1 to enhance and reflect upon their knowledge and understanding of the many factors which may affect pupils' behaviour in school;
2 to develop techniques, strategies, skills and attitudes which can be used effectively to manage pupils' behaviour in school.

Our contributors have been invited to reflect, with us, on these aspects of pupil behaviour, with consideration of the recent substantial changes in education. Our presentations move gradually from the theoretical stance of the earlier pages to a more practical approach in later ones.

Throughout the book the writers make wide-ranging contributions to the understanding of possible causes of behaviour problems in schools, and to the ways in which teachers can deter problems, and manage them if they arise.

The contents are directed towards the behaviour of children in mainstream primary and secondary schools as well as special schools, though on occasions the discussions may be more pertinent to a particular type of school. All the theoretical viewpoints referred to, the biological and environmental factors examined and the management policies and practices discussed, have as much relevance for pupils in mainstream schools – including those deemed to have special educational needs, with or without formal statements – as for children in special classes and schools.

This diversity is important. The traditional divide between children with special educational needs and others is being eroded both in policy and practice (though we and some of our colleagues are concerned about the possibility of 'sink' schools being created by opting out arrangements). The once distinct and divisible populations are now much more amalgamated – though not necessarily integrated – and mainstream teachers as well as their colleagues in more specialized schools have become more sensitive to pupils' emotional and behavioural needs.

We greatly value the contributions of our expert colleagues in this updated review of behaviour in schools, and in the final chapter, after considering their varied experiences and recommendations, the editors attempt a personal set of guidelines for practising and student teachers.

Part I

The theoretical background

In Chapter 1, 'Ensuring Schools are Fit for the Future', Tony Charlton and Kenneth David reflect on the influence of schools and of teachers on the behaviour of pupils, and discuss what exactly is meant by misbehaviour – how it can be defined and what the extent of misbehaviour is in actual fact. The link between teachers' perceptions of bad behaviour, the quality of teaching and the ethos of the school are considered. There are then many factors which combine to make essential a 'whole school' approach when considering the behaviour of pupils.

Tony Charlton and John George in Chapter 2 consider the development of behaviour problems. They emphasize the intricate interaction between factors, internal and external to pupils, which influence aspects of the pupils' behaviour, and argue for the effect of specific situations on much behaviour. They discuss the range of biological and environmental factors which have been shown to influence pupils' behaviour at home, in school and elsewhere, and consider and update the considerable research which has taken place.

Ronald Davie continues to develop the theoretical basis for behaviour problems in Chapter 3, 'Assessing and Understanding Children's Behaviour'. He considers the link between assessment and the process of dealing with behaviour problems in school, in the classroom and elsewhere. He then clearly describes the major theoretical models which attempt to provide explanations of children's behaviour problems. He questions how far they are mutually inconsistent and incompatible and the practical implications of this. Finally he questions the efficacy of basing practice on a single theoretical model, or on a more eclectic approach.

Chapter 1

Ensuring schools are fit for the future

Tony Charlton and Kenneth David

SCHOOLS MAKE A DIFFERENCE

The increasing challenge to schools is to examine what they are offering their pupils, how it is offered and whether it meets the needs of the pupils and the public. This is reflected in the demands of the National Curriculum and the assessments at different ages now being required by the Education Reform Act of 1988. Inevitably linked with this is the question of behaviour in schools. Numerous studies, such as those by Coleman *et al.* (1966) and Rutter *et al.* (1970), show that most children present behaviour problems in school or at home, but not necessarily in both. Behaviour is therefore *specific to situations*, which suggests that misbehaviour can best be resolved in the situation where it occurs. It is seldom satisfactory then always to look outside the school when considering misbehaviour in school.

Much evidence clearly shows that schools do affect their pupils' behaviour within school (Hargreaves 1967; Rutter *et al.* 1979; Galloway and Goodwin 1987; Reynolds and Cuttance 1992). What schools offer, and how they offer it, helps determine whether pupils respond in desirable or undesirable ways, and the reasons for pupils' misbehaviour may have as much (if not more) to do with their experiences at school as those they encounter in the home, or with aspects of their personality. Factors which seem to affect the influence of schools have been researched in many studies including Mortimore *et al.* (1988), and are explored in later chapters.

Frude and Gault (1984), commenting on school-based causes of behaviour problems, reported:

> Many of the incidents reported to us indicated some weakness in the school organisation, sometimes relating to the use of

buildings, sometimes in the curriculum, or timetable, and sometimes in the teaching or pastoral context.

(p. 36)

Along similar lines Galloway *et al.* (1982) suggested that:

knowledge of a school's policies and its teachers' attitudes is often as important in understanding disruptive behaviour as knowledge about family stress and intellectual weakness.

(p. 63)

Obviously not all behaviour problems in schools emanate from within the school. Pupils from disadvantaged homes can, of course, bring their problems with them, though it is very risky to link disadvantaged homes with disturbed children, for some who are extremely disturbed come from good homes and have parents, as Stott (1972) reminds us:

whom one has to rate not only as stable and affectionate, but as having shown almost superhuman patience and tolerance.

(p. 43)

He also points out that many well adjusted and successful pupils come from extremely adverse backgrounds.

LOOKING AT OURSELVES

Many readers will remember with affection the cartoon showing a large and fearsome teacher towering over a miscreant, bellowing:

Some people will blame your genes, some people will blame your environment, some people will blame your teachers, but I blame you, Wimpole, pure and simple.

Many of us become defensive and irritated when confronted by pupils' misbehaviour, and find it difficult to look hard at ourselves and our methods and attitudes. But if we take pride in the successes that we know of when we affect pupils' attitudes, feelings, actions and academic achievements, then we must logically accept that the reverse can happen – we can affect pupils in unacceptable or undesirable ways, for perfection eludes many of us. Lawrence and Steadman (1984) noted in their research that:

Many teachers are understandably reluctant to acknowledge that the reasons for pupils' misbehaviour may be found as often in their teaching as in the pupils' inability or failure to learn.

(p. 24)

The most effective way of managing behaviour problems must surely be to work to prevent them arising, and to minimize their occurrence. In a well-known study Kounin (1970) reported that when attempting to differentiate between more and less successful teachers, he found no difference between the two groups in terms of their effectiveness in *dealing* with behaviour problems, but successful teachers were seen to be far more adept at *preventing* them.

Much of the stress of teaching is related to problem behaviour in the classroom. Sometimes these problems manifest themselves as physical or verbal abuse, yet more often they present themselves as minor yet disruptive behaviour. In the Elton Report (DES and Welsh Office, 1989), 97 per cent of primary and secondary teachers reported they were called on to deal with behaviour such as 'calling out' and 'distracting others by chattering'. Lawrence and Steadman (1984) reminded us that disruptive behaviour of this type is often:

> frustrating, irritating and stressful, in extreme cases it may lead to complete breakdown of the classroom order and, more seriously, of the teacher's health.
>
> (p. viii)

From another perspective HMI (1987) stress:

> Good behaviour is a necessary condition for effective teaching and learning to take place, and an important outcome of education which society rightly expects.

Society is expecting good order and good results from teachers, and will be increasingly impatient and lacking in understanding if we do not provide them. So looking hard at ourselves, our teaching, our institutions, our rituals and our effect on pupils is becoming obligatory rather than just advisable, as we seek to eradicate or prevent pupils' behaviour problems by various forms of intervention.

THE EXTENT OF MISBEHAVIOUR

Public concern about pupil misbehaviour in school is often widespread. The popular media has not been slow to disseminate (and, at times, misrepresent) this concern to its readership. This type of publicity, which has been paralleled in literature from teachers' unions and – to a lesser extent – in educational journals, has brought unprecedented levels of debate among the teaching profession, parents and the wider public. Prominent in such debate has been the controversy as to whether or not current levels of 'misbehaviour' in school have increased significantly during recent years.

Those convinced that the incidence of pupil misbehaviour has escalated have argued the need for a variety of resources, additional to those already available in schools, to meet both the behavioural needs of practising (and potential) miscreants and the professional needs of those who teach them. However, with reference to disruptive pupils Galloway (1987) comments that there is no evidence to suggest an increase in such behaviour even though:

> It is a standard piece of educational folklore that such pupils have increased in numbers, and that the problems these pupils present have become more severe.
>
> (p. 29)

In a similar vein Hargreaves (1989) remarks that:

> there is little to suggest that there is a major problem of pupil misconduct on a large scale in our schools or that the situation has deteriorated in recent times. Most teachers have (and always had) routine problems of class management and meet the occasional difficult child who cannot easily be contained.... It seems, then, that it is a small number of individual teachers, who have substantial problems in relation to pupil misbehaviour.
>
> (p. 3)

More moderate opinion considers the concern over misbehaviour in school to be a reaction to a perennial problem in society itself. Human nature being what it is, individuals are expected to differ from each other in a plethora of ways including the extent to which they practise behaviours deemed to be acceptable, or unacceptable, according to the demands and expectations of the particular community/society within which they function. Supporters of this thinking recognize the existence of misbehaviour in school but contend, for example, that an unequitable focus upon the misbehaviour of a few ignores and obscures the acceptable behaviour practised by the vast majority of children and youngsters attending school.

DEFINING MISBEHAVIOUR

It is unfortunate that at least some of the controversy has arisen from semantic confusion concerning the term 'misbehaviour'. This imprecision about behavioural description has been responsible, at times, for generating confusion and misinformation among the public and – to a lesser extent – the teaching profession.

To some the term has been construed as analogous with maladjustment; a term of limited value, as Galloway and Goodwin (1987: 31) admit, which 'is neither a clinical diagnosis nor even a descriptive term but an administrative category'. Others have perceived it as behaviour (usually bereft of the excessive 'disturbing' or 'disturbed' connotation attached to the first interpretation) manifested verbally, or physically, which overtly challenges – to varying degrees and in a variety of ways – the authority of the teacher or school. At variance with their colleagues are those who define it for the most part as a catalogue of comparatively minor misdemeanours which, whilst not immediately challenging the authority of the teachers, demand the expenditure of inordinate amounts of teacher time and energy.

Clearly a need exists for yet more research to be undertaken in order to clarify what teachers construe as 'misbehaviour', and to ascertain the extent to which those misbehaviours prevail both in classrooms and the broader school context. Whilst it is logical, and defensible, to argue that any enquiry investigating the nature, and extent, of school misbehaviour should consult closely with teachers, it is of paramount importance that such investigations are bereft of methodological flaws such as those which have often characterized enquiries undertaken by teachers' professional associations (see Jones 1989).

TEACHERS' PERCEPTIONS OF MISBEHAVIOUR

In March 1988 Lord Elton led an enquiry into discipline in schools in England and Wales and made recommendations in the light of his committee's findings. As part of their enquiry the Elton Committee commissioned the Educational Research Centre, at the University of Sheffield, to examine teachers' perceptions and concerns about discipline. The results from this research (DES and Welsh Office 1989) provide an absorbing and much-needed insight into the nature and extent of the problem behaviours reported by primary- and secondary-school teachers. Contrary to the beliefs of some teachers' unions the most 'disturbing' misbehaviours encountered by teachers were not found to be physical or verbal abuse but, in accordance with the last of the definitions referred to earlier, a variety of minor – but nevertheless 'disruptive' – incidents including:

- talking out of turn
- hindering other pupils
- making unnecessary noises
- calculated idleness or work avoidance
- not being punctual
- getting out of seat without permission

The survey also found that teachers did encounter problem behaviours of a more serious nature such as:

- verbal abuse towards teachers
- physical aggression towards teachers
- physical aggression towards other pupils
- physical destructiveness

However, by comparison with the 'minor' misbehaviours previously referred to, these more serious incidents were encountered with far less frequency. Just over 2 per cent of primary-school and 1 per cent of secondary-school teachers, for example, reported that they had experienced physical aggression directed towards them during the week in which the survey took place. In contrast 97 per cent of both primary- and secondary-school teachers admitted that they were called upon to deal with behaviour such as 'calling out' and 'distracting others by chattering' during the survey period. These findings are not disputed by more temperate opinion within the unions. de Gruchy (1989), for example, speaking on behalf of the NASUWT, commented:

> I cannot speak for other teacher organisations including those who chose the dubious company of the *Daily Express* to produce reports on this issue. A careful reading of the NASUWT literature produced down the years would show that the Association is in agreement with the Committee's findings that violent attacks whilst deplorable and traumatic are not necessarily the greatest problem. For the majority of teachers it is constant petty disruption which does so much to damage the quality of lessons.
>
> (p. 13)

THE QUALITY OF TEACHING

Reflections upon our own childhood and adolescent experiences are unlikely to reinforce notions that classrooms and schools in the past were filled with halcyon days devoid of troublesome incidents. Is it not true that we behaved impeccably with some teachers whilst we behaved less acceptably with others? Did we not learn a great deal which was desirable and healthy in some classrooms whilst others were intellectual wildernesses? For the most part what determined the nature of the behaviour practised, and the associated learning which took place, was the quality of the pedagogy offered to us.

Our own reminiscences, for example, conjure up vivid images of stereotyped teaching and management styles; all of which affected classroom behaviour. We recollect the strict teacher with a penchant for administering a variety of corporal – and other – punishments which quelled the misbehaviours of even the more rebellious amongst our peers. Invariably, however, this system of control fuelled the tendency for misbehaviour to emerge in the lesson which followed; particularly if the teacher then involved was less punitive. Similarly, we remember the ineffective 'communicator' whose inability to arouse academic endeavours from the class actively encouraged the expenditure of available time and energy on a variety of misdemeanours. Thankfully, there were others who succeeded in 'breathing life' into their teaching, and by healthily arousing their pupils' appreciation of the material being taught left no time – or inclination – for deliberations upon, or the actual demonstration of, misbehaviour.

Other more recent memories (from the other side of the desk) recall a school where the general atmosphere (which we now term 'climate' or 'ethos') was what can only be called 'depressed'. Dissension in the staffroom was conspicuous, and recriminations for the school's shortcomings (when not disingenuously cast upon 'other colleagues') were surreptitiously thrown backwards and forwards between the headteacher's study and the staff room. Morale was low, particularly among the younger teachers and others less well equipped to cope, and misbehaviour was (also) rampant elsewhere in the school. The staff's time and energy appeared to be sapped more by the demands of internal strife among the staff than those apportioned to the educational needs of the pupils.

If pupils' interests are not aroused and capitalized upon, if the teachers' classroom organization skills are inadequate to manage pupil behaviour healthily, if there is conspicuous inconsistency between staff in the ways in which they interpret and enforce school rules, and if relationships between colleagues are fractious and non-supportive, then it is likely that (and certainly not unreasonable if) pupils behave in ways which are deemed unacceptable by teachers.

It is only in recent years that research enquiries have assembled evidence supportive of the above experiences and associated reasoning.

A CHANGED FOCUS

Currently, there is an increasing trend within education which focuses upon a more realistic and equitable perspective of the causes of pupil (mis)behaviour in school. This movement, called the systems' approach, has moved away from the individual (pupil and teacher) towards an institutional focus. Additionally, it has recognized the futility of establishing a punitive regime to control pupils' behaviour. In the old tripartite system, for example, the grammar schools could abrogate responsibilities towards recalcitrant youngsters by transferring them to a secondary modern school. Secondary schools could resort to a number of sanctions such as corporal punishment or exclusion or, to a lesser extent, transfer to a special school.

Whilst the threat, or practice, of such sanctions often appeared successful they were too often inequitable, unhelpful and counter-productive. They were inequitable where pupils were labelled as disruptive when it might have been more honest to label their teachers (individually or collectively as a staff) as lacking in professional competence. They were often unhelpful where they only suppressed the misbehaviour without exploring the root causes of it. Additionally, actions such as labelling a child as 'disruptive' or using inordinately other punishments (including expulsion, suspension or transfer to another school) were counterproductive in the sense that they actively de-skilled the teachers concerned. Where practices of this type prevailed the existing 'climate' was one where problems could be satisfactorily explained away by the teacher, or school, by placing blame solely upon the child concerned, or with his or her home background, or by transferring the 'problem' elsewhere. With foresight it would have been more productive if a school's philosophy (or policy) and practices had included a recognition – as is currently prevalent – that the reasons for pupils' misbehaviour may have as much (if not more) to do with their experiences at school as those they encounter in the home, or with aspects of their personality.

THE SCHOOL'S RESPONSIBILITY: WITHIN A SYSTEMS PERSPECTIVE

In explaining misbehaviour, and offering strategies for preventing its future occurrence, the systems' approach retreats from an unreasonable and unjust preoccupation with a 'within-child' deficit perspective of problem behaviour in favour of a broader – more contextualized – approach which Ronald Davie recognizes in Chapter 3, that:

> each individual child is embedded in a number of systems, notably family and school, and that the individual's behaviour can only meaningfully be viewed in that sort of context.

A corollary of this thinking is that the quality and range of the experiences which schools provide affect not only children's academic performances and attainments but also their social and emotional functioning.

Over the last decade a number of research enquiries have identified school characteristics which appear likely to influence positively (directly or otherwise) pupil behaviour (e.g. Rutter *et al.* 1979; Reynolds 1984; Mortimore *et al.* 1988). These include:

1 good leadership by senior management in consultation with colleagues and sensitive to the opinion of parents and pupils;
2 shared staff policy on academic and behaviour expectations, which are meaningful to pupils and consistently (though not necessarily inflexibly) enforced;
3 a curriculum which is matched to pupils' present and future needs;
4 academic expectations which are high, though not unreasonable;
5 an emphasis upon effective use of rewards for good behaviour and good work, rather than the application of punishments;
6 high professional standards by staff in terms of planning, setting and marking work and starting and ending lessons on time;

7 pedagogical skills which arouse pupils' interest in the subject material and motivate them to work well;

8 classroom management skills which help prevent problem behaviours from arising;

9 healthy supportive and respectful relationships between teachers, between teachers and pupils, between pupils, school and parents and between the school and outside agencies;

10 opportunities for pupils to become involved in, and share responsibilities for, the running of the school; and

11 an effective system of pastoral care.

WHOLE-SCHOOL APPROACH

Thinking of this kind suggests that where problems arise in the school it is probable that they can be best understood, and action best taken to resolve them (and help prevent their re-occurrence), within the same setting. Along these lines Galloway (1987) argues a need for schools and teachers to 'overcome their preoccupation with the behaviour of individual pupils and individual teachers' (p. 33) and to recognize that school responses to disruptive behaviour are likely to be more effective where they are organized at the institutional level, using a whole-school approach. Along these lines the Elton Committee (DES and Welsh Office 1989) recommended that:

> headteachers and teachers should, in consultation with governors, develop whole school behaviour policies which are clearly understood by pupils, parents and other school staff.
>
> (R21, p. 100)

The Committee contended that it is the satisfactory construction, implementation and ongoing evaluation of such a policy which underpins the school's overall effectiveness. They noted also that research findings had stressed that a punitive regime (where school rules consist of a long list of prohibitions, where punishments outnumber rewards and where rewards are open only to a select few) was unlikely to create a good school climate and therefore promote good behaviour. The Committee therefore envisaged that the central purpose of such a policy should be the encouragement of good behaviour rather than the application of punishments towards bad behaviour. More specifically, they made clear, for example, the need for schools to help ensure that:

- they assemble a small number of essential school rules – expressed in positive terms, wherever practicable – derived from, and consistent with, the principles upon which the behaviour policy is based (R. 22);
- rules are applied judiciously and consistently by all members of staff (R. 25);
- their practices emphasize the use of rewards for a range of academic and non-academic achievements, and that contact with parents should communicate aspects of pupils' achievements as well as their problem behaviour (R. 23);
- they avoid both the injudicious use of group punishment for infringement of rules where the innocent as well as the guilty are punished (R. 26), and public punishment which humiliates individuals (R. 27).

TO CONCLUDE

To speak of a whole-school policy in dealing with (mis)behaviour requires us to look not only at classroom incentives and punishments, at school philosophy and associated rules, at the various internal/external communication systems, at staff liaison and at pastoral responsibilities; we shall also inevitably be looking at the quality and effectiveness of school leadership and management systems, at teacher assessment/appraisal and staff development, at the meaning of professionalism and at the purpose and effectiveness of the manner in which the curriculum is organized and delivered. Equally we need to explore ways of assessing, and perhaps changing, the school 'climate'. The importance of the school climate was stressed repeatedly by the Elton Report. They contended, for example, that:

> When we visited schools we were struck by the difference in their 'feel' or atmosphere. Our conversations with teachers left us convinced that some schools have a more positive atmosphere than others. It was in these positive schools that we tended to see the work and behaviour which impressed us most. We found that we could not explain these different school atmospheres by saying that the pupils came from different home backgrounds. Almost all the schools we visited were in what many teachers would describe as difficult urban areas. We had to conclude that these differences had something to do with what went on in the schools themselves.
>
> (DES and the Welsh Office 1989: 88)

Favourable responses to these views should be within the capabilities of each school. Whilst research enquiries have indicated that some schools have much to accomplish 'to place their house in order', the same investigations have noted that other schools have already made successful moves to improve the quality of their offerings. Perhaps schools should capitalize upon the achievements of others. As Docking (1989) comments:

> since it also appears that in all kinds of behaviour there are wide variations between schools with similar intakes, the right question to ask is not so much, 'Is there a problem?' but 'Where is the problem and where is there not', and therefore is there something we can learn from 'good practice' from the schools which are not experiencing serious indiscipline.
>
> (p. 13)

It is unlikely that anyone can argue against the benefits of observing and scrutinizing good practice with the intention of modelling that which is deemed to be of relevance and value. Nevertheless, such benefits may not always be obvious to, or welcomed by, all staff. Here lies, perhaps, the greatest obstruction to initiatives to devise whole-school policies on behaviour. Arguably, in their attempts to develop an effective whole-school policy, the most important attributes for a school to hold are first, a consensus of opinion among staff that, individually and collectively, they exert (for better or for worse) considerable influence over the ways in which their pupils respond in school; and, second, that it has a positive commitment from its staff to explore ways in which they can improve the quality of the content and delivery of their work.

Given that the whole-school policy, during the planning implementation/evaluation stages, receives active and genuine support from school staff (in the broadest context), governors, pupils and parents then the school community can only benefit. The policy, by clarifying the school's aims and objectives and by constructing a code of expected behaviour for the whole community (which derive from the policy), makes clear the responsibilities of, and expectations for, individuals and groups (teachers and pupils alike). We all need to know what we are planning to undertake; as we need to know what our responsibilities are and what is expected of us. Such knowledge within the school community has much to offer. It can enhance a sense of 'community', help provide a healthy learning environment and help build a positive school ethos.

The challenge confronting schools is consistent with current trends towards increased accountability, evaluation and appraisal. As a society, as teachers, pupils and parents, our expectation is that we require schools to clarify what their aims really are and to specify how those aims can be, and will be, achieved. Similarly we wish to know how schools intend to evaluate the extent to which those aims become realized. Whilst the challenge is a righteous one, only the uninformed and unenlightened will underestimate the magnitude of the task which confronts some schools. Nevertheless, the task has to be undertaken in order to help ensure that our schools really are 'fit for the future'.

REFERENCES AND FURTHER READING

Best, R. (1988) 'Care and control – are we getting it right?', *Pastoral Care in Education* 7 (4).

Barton, L. (1991) 'Teachers under siege: a case of unmet need', *Support for Learning* 6 (1).

Charlton, T. and David, K. (1989) *Managing Misbehaviour*, Basingstoke: Macmillan.

Coleman, J.S., Campbell, E.Q., Hobson, C.J., McPartland, J., Mood, A.M., Weinfold, F.D. and York, R.L. (1966) *Equality of Educational Opportunity*, Washington, DC: US Government Printing Office.

DES and Welsh Office (1989) *Discipline in Schools*, Report of the Committee of Enquiry chaired by Lord Elton.

de Gruchy, N. (1989) 'Elton Report lets Baker off the hook', *NASUWT Career Teacher Journal*, Summer, 12–13.

Docking, J. (1989) *Control and Discipline in Schools: Perspectives and Approaches*, New York: Harper & Row.

Frude, N. and Gault, H. (1984) *Disruptive Behaviour in School*, London: Wiley.

Galloway, D. (1987) 'Disruptive behaviour in school', *Educational and Child Psychology* 4 (1): 29–34.

Galloway, D. and Goodwin, C. (1987) *The Education of Disturbing Children*, London: Longman.

Galloway, D., Ball, T., Blomfeld, D. and Seyd, R. (1982) *Schools and Disruptive Pupils*, London: Longman.

Hargreaves, D.H. (1967) *Social Relationships in a Secondary School*, London: Routledge.

—— (1989) 'Introduction', in N. Jones (ed.) *School Management and Pupil Behaviour*, London: Falmer Press.

HMI (1987) *Education Observed 5: Good Behaviour and Discipline in Schools*, Stanmore: DES.

Jones, N. (1989) *School Management and Pupil Behaviour*, London: Falmer Press.

Kounin, J. (1970) *Discipline and Group Management in Classrooms*, New York: Holt, Rinehart & Winston.

Lawrence, J. and Steadman, R. (1984) *Disruptive Schools: Disruptive Pupils*, London: Croom Helm.

Mortimore, P., Sammons, P., Ecob, R. and Stoll, L. (1988) *School Matters – The Junior Years*, London: Open Books.

Peagram, E. and Upton, G. (1991) 'Emotional and behavioural difficulties and the Elton Report', *Maladjustment and Therapeutic Education* 9 (3).

Ramasut, A. (1989) *Whole School Approaches to Special Needs*, London: Falmer Press.

Reynolds, D. (1984) 'The delinquent school', in Hammerslee, H. and Woods, P. (eds) *The Process of Schooling*, London: Routledge.

Reynolds, D. and Cuttance, R. (1992) *Effective Schools*, London: Cassell.

Rutter, M., Tizzard, J. and Whitmore, K. (1970) *Education, Health and Behaviour*, London: Longman.

Rutter, M., Maughan, B., Mortimore, P. and Ouston, J. (1979) *Fifteen Thousand Hours: Secondary Schools and their Effects on Pupils*, London: Open Books.

Stott, D.H. (1972) *The Parent as a Teacher*, London: University of London Press.

Tattum, D.P. (ed.) (1986) *Management of Disruptive Pupil Behaviour in Schools*, Chichester: Wiley.

Wolfendale, S. (1987) *Primary Schools and Special Needs: Policy, Planning and Provision*, London: Cassell.

Chapter 2

The development of behaviour problems

Tony Charlton and John George

THE COMPLEXITY OF BEHAVIOUR

The more we investigate human behaviour the more we appreciate its complexity, and how difficult it often is to explain precisely why individuals behave as they do. We know only too well that the manner in which, and extent to which, children and adults learn behaviours and that whether (and, if so, which of) those behaviours will be practised are affected by a whole range of variables, usually in combination.

These variables can be usefully construed as being either internal or external to the individual. *Internal* variables include biological factors such as the state of the nervous system and certain glandular functions, heredity and other genetic considerations. They also encompass psychological factors which refer to aspects of the individual's affective and cognitive states (e.g. levels of self-concept, anxiety, intelligence and motivation). *External* variables are represented by an array of environmental influences of which the family, school and peer group appear to be the most influential. It is the intricate interaction between such variables which affects how (and what) we think, feel and act.

BEHAVIOUR PROBLEMS: DIFFERING PERSPECTIVES OF CAUSATION

Where behaviour problems arise in school, or elsewhere, it may be difficult to determine precisely which – or how – internal and external factors combined to generate them. One way of helping to clarify the complexity of this difficulty is to think in terms of predisposing, precipitating and reinforcing causes.

Research findings, although not conclusive, have suggested, for example, that particular types of temperament may *predispose* young children to later maladjustment (Thomas and Chess 1977). Predispositions of this type include under- and over-activity, poor adaptability, tendency to withdrawal, irregularity of sleeping and irritability. Such patterns of 'aggravating' behaviour – particularly where they persist into adolescence – are more likely to arouse negative than positive responses from care-givers, and others. Responses of this kind may create unhealthy feelings within the child (e.g. of rejection, lowered self-esteem) as well as generate overt responses of a kind unlikely to improve the situation (e.g. hostility, aggression). It is fairly conclusive, also, that certain adverse temperamental characteristics may render children more vulnerable to environmental stress (Graham *et al.* 1973).

On other occasions behaviour problems may be *precipitated* by certain happenings in the environment. Teachers preoccupied with berating pupils when they misbehave, yet ignoring them when they behave, may be precipitating the very behaviours they are attempting to eradicate. Children, like adults, need attention. It is unfortunate that some pupils find that their only route to secure this attention is to misbehave. Problems become compounded when children learn that such attempts are successful; for their subsequent misbehaviour is often then *reinforced*, though unintentionally, by the teacher.

Unfortunately for those who try to assist in the prevention and resolution of children's behaviour problems, the subject of causation is often far more complex than the previous paragraphs perhaps imply and involves intricate interactions amongst a host of contributory factors (as the later case studies illustrate).

However complex the cause-and-effect association may be, a paramount task confronting teachers is to determine ways in which appropriate management skills can be directed towards the amelioration or prevention of behaviour problems. On many occasions this can only be accomplished where teachers are sensitive to the differing causal mechanisms which may be operating in a given instance. Without this knowledge the assessment 'picture' may be incomplete and any action taken unlikely to be effective.

Another perspective on causation refers to the particular theoretical model within which the behaviour is examined (e.g. psychodynamic, humanistic, behavioural). Different models not only hold disparate perspectives on the aetiology (causation) of behaviour problems, but also on the skills which are required to address them. There are, of course, many models of human behaviour which speculate about how behaviour is fashioned. However, of the major theories referred to in Chapter 3, the three upon which later chapters primarily focus are the *behavioural*, *psychodynamic* and *humanistic* models. These are selected for purely practical reasons; arguably, of all the theories they are of most use to classroom practitioners in helping them to understand causes of problem behaviours as well as acquire the skills to manage them. Nevertheless, for reasons which Ronald Davie makes clear in the next chapter, both the systems approach and labelling theory are taken into account when discussing the other three theories.

THE COMPLEXITY OF CAUSATION: CASE STUDIES

The following extracts from case histories highlight how on occasions numerous factors (some related, others seemingly not) may combine to create, or exacerbate, behaviour problems which young children and teenagers experience or present.

PHILIP was found by the science teacher to be one of the most disruptive pupils he had ever met. He was constantly off-task, often annoyed other pupils by interrupting their work with silly comments and was frequently rude to the teacher. Philip's home life seemed a good one. The parents were interested in his work and very supportive to his school. When the parents questioned Philip about his misbehaviour in school, he replied that he only 'played up' in science lessons. He did this, he explained, because the lessons were so boring.

CLIVE, a 15 year old, attended a residential special school for children with emotional/behavioural problems. His unmarried mother had abandoned him when he was two. During the next ten years he spent time in two children's homes, and with three sets of foster parents before transfer from a day special school to one with residential provision. As he became older his behaviour progressively deteriorated. Adults in both the children's and foster homes, and the teachers in the day school, found his behaviour increasingly disruptive and disturbing to the other children around him. When he was 12 an educational psychologist's report showed him to be seriously under-functioning in all basic skills' areas, frequently depressed and experiencing difficulties building – with even greater difficulties sustaining – relationships with peers and adults.

CLAIRE, born with both cleft palate and a double cleft lip, did not receive the last of the corrective surgery until she was in her late teens. In the primary school her poor articulation elicited hurtful comments from her peers. In response she rarely spoke in class and, where practicable, gradually withdrew from all social situations. Despite repeated attempts by teachers, parents and more helpful peers to involve her with her peers she became more and more withdrawn. When the teacher attempted to involve her in group discussions, or other group work, she became embarrassed, highly anxious and reluctant to become involved. As a result she found it difficult to make friendships and became both more and more isolated and increasingly unhappy.

RICHARD came from a large family. Shortly after Richard's eighth birthday, his father (a violent character with a long history of convictions – and prison sentences – for GBH and burglary) left home to live with his wife's sister. When Richard was nine the mother, unable to cope with her seven children, sent Richard to live with aged maternal grandparents some miles away. Right from the start teachers at his new school found him almost impossible to contain. While occasionally he was affable, on most occasions he was not. At the age of 9 he had a reading age of 6.1. Apart from being boisterous and aggressive with his peers – to such an extent that most of the children became frightened of him – he also had a short attention span and quickly became frustrated when confronted with problems in his academic work. In such instances he would fling his books away, storm out of the room and then out of the school. Usually it took the headmaster to entice him back within the school, where he would spend the rest of the day quietly working in the Head's study. On following days, however, the pattern was likely to repeat itself.

According to his mother, STEWART, who was asthmatic and suffered from eczema, had always been difficult; even his birth had been difficult and prolonged. As a baby he had irregular sleep patterns, did not feed properly, was rarely quiet and was constantly active. At primary school the teachers found him pleasant, but highly distractful and easily distracted. He was rarely able to work quietly and his boisterous and hyperactive behaviour frequently upset his peers. After transfer to secondary school, Stewart became increasingly agitated before going to school and was frequently referred by teachers to the Head of House because of his poor attention span and habitual bouts of disruptive behaviour.

The parents of JANE were adamant that her transfer to the local comprehensive school was the cause of all her problems. At the small village primary school she made reasonable progress in all school subjects, was quiet but friendly, never seemed worried and always enjoyed going to school. When she was 7 it was discovered that she suffered from petit mal, although the seizures seemed infrequent and slight. Upon transfer, matters soon changed. Each morning the mother had to contend with persistent tantrums during which Jane screamed that she wasn't going to school. Towards the end of her second term at secondary school her attendance became, at first, erratic and then was followed by more prolonged absences. Letters from the school and visits by the educational welfare officer initially failed to improve the situation. Only finally, at the end of her second year at school when the local education authority threatened legal action, did her attendance improve slightly. Her behaviour, however, deteriorated. At school she became insolent and disobedient and was finally suspended, pending the outcome of a case conference, for stealing money from a member of staff. In the home she became sullen, uncooperative and eventually beyond the control of the parents.

The case studies emphasize a number of points. First, they indicate that when more serious problems become manifest in school it is more than likely that whatever intervention is required will need to refer to a range of so-called causal factors. Additionally, a number of the helping professionals outlined in Chapter 9 may need to become involved. These professionals will be equipped with the expertise and experience to deal with aspects of the problem which the school cannot.

Second, because more serious problem behaviours usually demand more time, energy and greater expertise than lesser ones, it seems more sensible, wherever practicable, to prevent problems arising, or less serious ones escalating. Just as there is much that can happen in classrooms and schools which increases the likelihood (and severity) of problems arising, so there is much that can be done to help prevent problems from occurring or escalating. This latter point is a recurrent theme in the chapters within Parts II and III of this book.

Third, within any case description (and even with access to the complete files) it is difficult – if not impossible – to isolate a *single* factor which was the sole cause of *all* the problem behaviours. While it may be possible to point to one particular factor which triggered the problem initially, others were certainly contributory.

Finally, how the problem is rationalized, or explained, in terms of causation, will depend upon which theoretical perspective is used. Each perspective focuses upon differing facets of the case histories and explains the behaviour problems in differing ways. In Richard's case the behaviouristic model could see problems in the context of maladaptive behaviours being learned (e.g. through reinforcement or modelling of undesirable behaviours) and adaptive behaviours or competencies not being learned. The psychodynamic model would be more concerned with Richard's inner experiences; the extent to which a succession of rejections (by father, mother and other adults) posed as a threat to his ego, and generated anxieties; and the manner in which he handled those anxieties. Similarly, the humanistic model's focus would be upon the manner in which he perceived those experiences and the impact of the perceptions upon his developing 'self' (i.e. self-concept, self-esteem) and consequent behaviour.

FACTORS ASSOCIATED WITH THE DEVELOPMENT OF BEHAVIOUR PROBLEMS

In the rest of this chapter the intention is to look at some examples of factors, internal and external to the individual, which:

- are often associated with behaviour problems
- may exert adverse influences (either separately or in combination) upon children's behaviour

Biological factors

While it has long been recognized that the individual is the product of genetic inheritance and sociological and psychological influences, it is the nature of biological differences among people which, until recently, has received the least attention. One difficulty is the complexity of analysing biological factors and the consequent shortage of research. Another problem is that some biological abnormalities may not be visually apparent and the observer has no immediate clues to their existence, other than the abnormal behaviour of the child. For example, the child with a visual defect may be immediately recognizable by his performance, whereas the child with a specific food intolerance may pass undetected except for concern over his abnormal behaviour.

We can start to explore the biological influences on human behaviour by examining the nature of the building blocks of the human body, for any imperfections which occur at the foundation level are likely to have far-reaching consequences as development proceeds.

Nervous systems

One of the most important underlying features in determining behaviour is the integrity, or quality, of both the central (nerves in the brain and spinal cord) and peripheral (nerves from the brain and spinal cord to other parts of the body) nervous systems. Inevitably, *serious* damage to either system usually manifests itself in gross physical and/or performance abnormalities, the effects of which can be quite marked.

The young child's developing brain is particularly sensitive and vulnerable to damage from a number of agencies. Damage may occur during pregnancy as a consequence of the mother's exposure to certain diseases, e.g. rubella, toxoplasmosis, AIDS and syphilis, the effects of which may be transferred to, and affect the nervous systems of, the unborn child. More recently, attention has focused on the harmful nature of certain drugs, alcohol abuse, smoking and excessive radiation during pregnancy. Similarly, placenta insufficiency, toxaemia and poor maternal nutrition may cause conditions of low birth weight which, in turn, may increase the vulnerability of the very young child.

Complications during the birth process itself can result in direct damage to the brain or may limit or prevent the flow of oxygen. As brain cells are particularly sensitive to a lack of oxygen, any interruption of supply may result in widespread and irreparable damage.

Infections of the brain such as meningitis and encephalitis can also have a marked effect on the performance and behaviour of the victims, as can any direct or severe injury to the head. Not surprisingly Barker (1981) suggests that from evidence provided from research there is an increased incidence of a wide variety of behavioural disturbances in children following such traumas. However, more subtle or minimal damage to the nervous system may create conditions in children which, at first, are not so obvious and may include auditory and visual perceptual disturbances which disrupt the processing of information and form the basis of cognitive and psychomotor learning problems.

Clumsy children constitute such an enigma. Some researchers see such a problem as a consequence, primarily, of a developmental disorder and outline several factors including genetic and environmental influences which may produce the atypical clumsy child (e.g. Gordon and McKinlay 1980). Difficulties may appear in large-muscle activities and balance or equally as an impairment of fine motor movements. Exposure of such children to situations which amplify their problems, such as the games field or PE lesson, may lead to the development of secondary emotional problems and increasing social isolation.

Endocrine glands

The nervous system does not work in isolation to other body functions and its total coordination is assisted by the secretion of various hormones into the bloodstream by the endocrine glands. Such hormones are important in determining levels of growth, motivation and response, emotional behaviour and some aspects of personality.

Of the two most important glands, *adrenal* glands play a vital role in neural functioning and in preparing the body to tolerate the effects of stress, and the *pituitary* gland produces a large number of different hormones and controls the activity of several other endocrine glands, such as the thyroid glands, sex glands and those which control the timing and amount of body growth. It therefore follows that any malfunction in the operation of these glands can have far-reaching effects on individual development.

Heredity

All behaviour is the result of the complex *interaction* between heredity and environment. The characteristics of each parent are passed on to their children by a special code – the genetic code, a blueprint for the child which is carried in each cell of the body and which plays a specific role in psychological, emotional and physical development. While inherited physical characteristics are perhaps some of the first features to draw comment from the parents of newborn infants, later developing intelligence and special abilities, such as musical or artistic talent, also appear to have a hereditary component and some differences in temperament appear to be innate. It follows, therefore, that any errors which occur in the transmission of inherited information can have a direct effect upon the quality of development and behaviour.

Chromosomes

Most of the body cells have a nucleus in which there are special filaments called chromosomes. Each of these cells contains forty-six chromosomes arranged in pairs. One chromosome of each pair comes from each parent in a system of automatic reduction as the cells divide into twenty-three pairs. Twenty-two of these pairs are perfectly matched, but the twenty-third pair determines our sex and is known as the sex chromosomes. In the female they are perfectly matched (XX), but in the male they are unequal (XY). Occasionally, something goes wrong with the process of reduction and each cell may contain an extra chromosome or 'trisomy' which may be linked to certain developmental or behavioural features. For example, an extra chromosome on the twenty-first pair results in the condition known as Down's syndrome (1.8 per 1,000 live births).

Very rarely only some of the cells have an extra chromosome which is known as 'mosaicism', and partial trisomies may exist where extra chromosome material is present. In these cases the abnormal chromosome pattern may cause low intelligence rather than bring about emotional disturbance, although an emotional disorder may also be present.

Some conditions exist, however, where abnormal chromosome formation may produce a deficiency in the ability to absorb essential vitamins and minerals. In Down's syndrome, for example, the changes in the structure of the wall of the intestine brought about by the presence of the trisomy create a condition of poor absorption. In recognition of this biological abnormality, the prescription of vitamin supplements to complement the diet of such children has received considerable support in recent years.

Sex chromosome abnormalities also occur on rare occasions where, for example, the female may have only one X chromosome (Turner's syndrome) or where the male may have an extra Y chromosome (XYY). Similarly, Fragile X (1 per 1,000 live births) where the X chromosome appears affected is a complex chromosomal disorder believed to be the most common cause of inherited mental handicap.

Attempts have been made in the past to suggest a causal relationship between sex-linked chromosome abnormalities and certain behaviour disorders, but the evidence has been lacking and inconclusive. It does seem reasonable to suggest, however, that some basic features of personality are genetically determined.

Genes

Each chromosome is made up of hundreds of small units known as genes, each of which plays a specific role in the development of the body. In some cases a single abnormal gene can arise spontaneously and have a marked effect on the way in which development proceeds. For example, in 1986, scientists identified the gene that carries Duchenne Muscular Dystrophy where in the majority of cases the gene is carried by the mother. In other instances two abnormal genes may be present, one from the father and one from the mother. These are known as recessive genes. A number of syndromes associated with intellectual retardation are due specifically to abnormal genes (e.g. Rubinstein–Tabi's syndrome, tuberous sclerosis, microcephaly).

Gene defects can also cause errors in metabolism such as phenylketonuria, in which there is an error of amino-acid metabolism characterized by an abnormal buildup of damaging chemicals which require treatment with a diet low in phenylalanine. Untreated, phenylketonuria has strong associations with severe intellectual retardation.

Recent research into autism includes an exploration of the role of essential fatty acids and the secretion of hormones in the creation of this condition which, with an incidence of 4:10,000, is a mental handicap which affects the ability to use senses to the full. Although no specific neurological or neurochemical abnormalities have been consistently identified in autism, its biological base is no longer in doubt and it is suggested by Aarons and Gittens (1991) that autism is linked to certain physical disorders including viruses and to some inherited conditions such as Fragile X syndrome.

Similarly, it has been suggested by Stevenson (1987) that dyslexia has genetic causes. As a condition which affects the brain's general coding capacities it tends to run in families and is more common in boys than girls by four to one. Excess of the hormone testosterone appears to influence the growth of ectopias (brain warts) which have been found in abnormal quantities in the brains of deceased people known to have had reading and writing difficulties.

What is clear at this point is that researchers are becoming far more aware of the need fully to explore the biological bases of many conditions in the increasing knowledge that subtle biochemical imbalances, whether genetically or environmentally initiated, do have a significant effect upon individuals' behavioural performance.

Hyperactivity

Many children are hyperactive from birth (often also *in utero*). They present as restless and fidgety, sleep for only three to four hours in twenty-four and cry incessantly. They will not feed properly and may also suffer from asthma and eczema. As they grow older, such children may destroy furniture and toys, have poor communication and may resort to self-injurious behaviour. Parents are often exhausted by the stress and continual crises of coping with the excessive demands of such a child, as are teachers when these children enter schools.

Several attempts have been made to isolate factors which may cause such a condition to occur. Feingold (1975) was one of the first to focus international attention on the relationship between diet and behaviour. Prior to this there had been too great a willingness to ascribe a psychosocial aetiology to children's behaviour disturbances when the cause often stemmed from adverse responses to certain environmental factors such as food or chemicals. Crook (1980) contended that on the basis of recorded evidence and his own experience he was certain that a child's intake of food could determine whether he was dull, stupid or hyperactive. However, Vass and Rasmussen (1984) suggested that foods are not the only environmental factors implicated in allergy, but that many other products of modern technology are commonly incriminated (e.g. pollution).

Allergic responses in young children are thought by some researchers to stem from a vulnerability to foreign chemicals at a time when the mechanisms that provide protection against these substances are absent or not fully developed. The lower efficiency of young children in metabolizing some chemicals may cause them to accumulate such chemicals to excessive levels at a time when sensitivity to toxic effects is critical, and therefore most detrimental to balanced growth. In a review of possible causes of hyperactivity, Shreeve (1982) suggests that hyperactive children have abnormally low levels of essential fatty acids, and are in this respect biologically different to non-hyperactive children. Such a defect in metabolism allows hyperactive children to become extremely susceptible to certain substances, the result of which is an observable deterioration in behaviour.

Morley (1985) describes those whose behaviour is affected by food as having a 'food intolerance', and she distinguishes between a non-allergic mechanism or food idiosyncrasy and a food allergic disease, where there is a measurable *allergic* response.

More recently, attention has been paid to the quality of the daily diet, not so much from the perspective of restricting artificial additives, but from a realization that many young people eat huge amounts of 'junk food' much of which is deficient in vitamins and minerals which are essential for healthy living and efficient mental functioning. The results of early pilot studies in Britain and America indicate that children who receive a sufficient daily intake of vitamins and minerals are in a better position to profit from learning experiences than their peers, who languish almost daily in a state of dietary deficiency.

A general and positive spin-off from such research can be seen in the increasing efforts being made to produce healthy eating habits across the nation, and in particular by the schools' catering services, and an awareness of the dangers of eating and drinking indiscriminately. However, Swinson (1988) warns against the danger of believing that, when faced with a badly behaved child, all that needs to be done to improve his or her behaviour is to change his or her diet. His message directs teachers and parents to improve their behavioural management rather than merely rely on restricting the consumption of additives.

Epilepsy

The exact size of our epileptic population is not easily determined but it is suggested by the British Epilepsy Association that over 100,000 children and young people in the UK have some form of epilepsy, the majority of whom receive their education in ordinary schools. Less than 1 per cent actually attend the six schools for children with epilepsy.

Epilepsy is caused by brief disruptions in the normal electro-chemical activity of the brain which can affect people of all ages and intellect. It is not a disease or illness but may be a symptom of some physical or metabolic disorder which, although not always obvious, is an elusive condition, the existence of which many individuals and families may choose to conceal. It has been suggested by Stedman (1973) that social rejection of children with epilepsy is still apparent in many schools and, coupled with the risk of overprotection and anxiety by parents and staff, can create a climate in which the child is prevented from fulfilling his or her real potential.

Epilepsy causes people to have fits or seizures which fall into broadly different categories according to their nature and severity. Major fits or tonic clonic seizures often last for several minutes during which the child may fall to the ground and lose conscious-ness, salivate, jerk violently and may pass water. The child may blink his eyes or appear to be day dreaming or staring inattentively. Often during this confused period, sensory messages are not received by the child and learning may be seriously impaired. For example, if a teacher says to a child, 'Andrew, sit down here and (put those books away before you) go to the toilet', and Andrew has an absence for the duration of the words in parentheses, the teacher's communication will make little sense and could provoke a quite disturbing reaction from the child!

Psychomotor fits or complex seizures occur when only part of the brain is affected and may lead to a child making involuntary movements such as twitching and being unable to communicate although being conscious. Unobserved fits or subclinical seizures may be suspected if a child's attention, work or attainment level suddenly drops for no apparent reason. Such fits impair a child's ability to receive, retain and recall information and can have a devastating effect upon progress and learning. Small 'absences' and 'blank spells' should arouse the suspicion of teachers who should then seek professional support and advice. About 2.5 per cent of people with epilepsy have 'photosensitive epilepsy', and are affected adversely by flickering lights, faulty televisions and strobe lights.

Medication given for the treatment of epilepsy is designed to build up chemical resistance to stimuli that can trigger or precipitate a fit. When correctly balanced with need, the use of medication can be most effective. Surprisingly, however, little is known about the side-effects of medication given to children with epilepsy and imbalances sometimes occur which manifest themselves in the child by drowsiness or an increase in seizures. Such changes should be closely monitored, and reported.

There is evidence to suggest a higher incidence of behaviour disorders among epileptic children than among normal children but, as long ago as 1957, Halstead concluded that there was no such thing as the 'Epileptic Personality'. However, Stedman (1973) identified an unusual scattering of abilities from the results of intelligence tests on epileptic children with a particular imbalance on subtests concerning language and spatial skills. This can lead to very uneven educational profiles compounded by the fact that on some occasions epileptic children may be unteachable for days at a time due to fluctuations in their ability to attend and respond to their environment.

Further information about epilepsy is available in the form of a schools information pack from The British Epilepsy Association, Anstey House, 40 Hanover Square, Leeds LS3 1BE.

Asthma

A number of children attending both ordinary schools and special schools suffer from varying degrees of asthma. Asthma is a non-infectious disease of the chest which causes a narrowing of air passages of the lungs with resulting difficulty in breathing and wheeziness. Attacks may be brief, occasional and mild or may be more severe, resulting in the need for absence from school and, in extreme cases, treatment in hospital. The start or 'trigger' of an attack may be different for individual children and occurs because of the extreme sensitivity of the air passages to environmental changes. Such changes may be physical, e.g. exposure to strong strains such as excitement or prolonged laughing. Alternatively, infections and activity which is too vigorous or prolonged may also induce an asthmatic attack.

Allergy is a special form of sensitivity in which substances normally innocuous to most people provoke attacks of wheezing in asthmatics. Allergens may be airborne, such as pollen, dust, hair or fur, and therefore inhaled, or may be taken as food where, for example, there may be a measurable allergic response to cheese, eggs, milk etc. Such allergens may not always produce wheezing but instead may cause other responses such as running eyes and nose, sneezing and itching. It is not uncommon to find that some asthmatic children also have eczema, the condition of which can also be affected by similar factors.

Minor attacks are usually coped with by the child ceasing the activity in hand and administering one of the medical treatments available. Once this treatment has proved effective the child may continue with normal activities. Severe attacks usually occur after treatment that is normally effective fails to work and the child becomes acutely distressed, often becoming blue around the lips and finding it extremely difficult to exhale. At this stage urgent medical attention should be sought without delay as the need for additional treatment is required immediately.

Two different forms of medication are available to help control the effects of asthma and to help affected people to live a normal life.

1 Preventive treatments (usually sprays or tablets) taken regularly attempt to increase the resistance to factors which may trigger attacks, by reducing the sensitivity of the air passages.
2 'Bronchodilators' (often taken as a spray) open up the narrowed bronchial tubes of the lungs to give immediate relief.

Teachers should ensure that they have a thorough knowledge of the child's condition, preferably by contact and discussion with parents, and that within the classroom setting asthmatic children are not exposed directly to animals, materials, foods etc. which are known to cause problems for them, and that sympathetic consideration is given to the child's individual needs in matters relating to games and PE.

It is often possible for all but the most severely affected asthmatic children to participate in a wide range of physical activities, but the type of sport and level of participation will be critical. Most asthmatic children will prefer to cope with short bursts of moderate exercise in an atmosphere which is warm and moist and may need to take additional doses of inhalant before they start. It is important for teachers to take seriously the need for a child to have an inhaler constantly available, and not to dismiss the condition as merely a nervous disorder.

This information, and more, is readily available for teachers from National Asthma Campaign, 300 Upper Street, London N1 2XX.

Environmental factors associated with behaviour problems

Behaviouristic, psychodynamic and humanistic models of behaviour all recognize that the *environment* affects human behaviour; although, as mentioned earlier (and as Ronald Davie discusses in the next chapter), they have differing ways of conceptualizing how that influence works. The major environments which exert this influence are the *home*, the *peer group* and the *school*.

Family factors

Of the major environments within which children grow and develop the parental home (in most instances) generates the earliest influences upon their behaviour. Consequently, the range, duration and quality of family experiences are likely to make significant contributions, adversely or otherwise, to children's behaviour.

Separation experiences is one such area which has attracted much interest and some controversy. As early as 1946, Bowlby contended that early and prolonged separation of young children from their mothers was a prime cause of 'delinquent character development and persistent misbehaviour' (p. 41). His contention derived from his observations of institutionalized children, most of whom were denied the facility to develop close interpersonal relations with a care-giver. Similar discoveries were later reported by Beres and Obers (1950) with their sample of thirty-eight adolescents who had been institutionalized between the ages of three weeks and three years. At the time of their enquiry all but 7 per cent of the adolescents were diagnosed as psychotic, having a character disorder, neurotic or mentally retarded.

Underpinning the concern of studies in this area has been the 'disruption of bonding' between mother and infant; a concept which has been criticized by Rutter (1972). He argued that bonding need not take place only with the biological parent (whether father or mother) but can take place with a surrogate parent, or care-giver. What appears to be of primary importance where protracted periods of separation take place is that the child has someone available with whom he or she can form a stable relationship. Along these lines Upton (1983) makes the valid point in his summary of the research that:

> neither separation *per se* nor separation from the biological mother or 'permanent mother substitute' are key factors.

Rather, it seems that the quality of substitute care is of major importance.

(p. 49)

Bowlby's findings also generated concern about the effects of other separation experiences, such as hospitalization, upon young children's later behaviour. While Rutter (1980) argued that although emotional distress may arise from such experiences it was unlikely to persist, others showed that the impact of hospitalization experiences seems to depend upon the child's age upon admission, length and frequency of stays, temperamental characteristics and prior relationships with the mother (Stacey et al. 1970; Douglas 1975). Stacey et al. confirmed earlier findings that the crucial time is between six months of age and the child's fourth or fifth birthday, and suggested that children who were under stress at home, who were highly dependent upon their mothers or who felt insecure upon admission were the most vulnerable. The two previously mentioned studies also found that repeated admissions and more long-term stays were associated with increased risks of later behaviour problems.

Parental deprivation as a consequence of the bereavement of a parent may also have an impact upon children's emotional and behavioural functioning. The extent, duration and levels of severity of any consequent problems seem to depend upon a plethora of factors including the age of the child when the bereavement occurred (Rutter 1966), the manner in which the remaining parent discusses the death with the child (Marsden 1969) and the quality of prior parental relations (Anthony 1973). The post-bereavement 'health' of the family is also an important factor (see Finer Report 1974).

During the past twenty years or so there has been a rapid increase in divorce rates. In 1961 25,000 divorces were granted; a figure which rose to 74,000 in 1972 and 180,000 in 1986. More contemporary marriage and divorce statistics show that for every two marriages in 1990 there was almost one divorce; and that 55 per cent of divorced couples had at least one child under the age of 16 (HMSO 1992). With the majority of divorces taking place during the early years of marriage a considerable number of young and vulnerable children are involved. Rutter (1971) found that children between the ages of 2 and 3 seem to be particularly vulnerable to the separation of their parents, particularly to the loss of the parent of the same sex. In line with a number of enquiries Douglas (1975) found a significantly higher risk of later delinquency among boys, and illegitimate births among girls, where parental separation occurred before they were 6. Experiences leading up to, and those following, separation may precipitate stress, feelings of rejection and insecurity within offspring (Mitchell 1987). However, it must be noted that not all children of divorced parents develop behaviour problems; indeed, as Jobling (1976) noted in her research review, behaviour problems are often not generated by the divorce itself but by prior turbulent parental relations, and the act of separation 'may actually benefit the child by bringing relief from inconsistent discipline, constant quarrelling and tension' (p. 1).

While the types of separation referred to so far are indicative of one type of deprivation (i.e. that resulting from permanent or temporary separation from parents, the death of a parent or the loss of a parent consequent to divorce) another is concerned with inadequate parenting. An enquiry by Bullard *et al.* (1967) identified a 'failure to thrive' syndrome; a condition arising from 'parental neglect and variable forms of maternal "deprivation"' (p. 689). A follow-up study completed after neglected children had been removed from the home revealed that two-thirds of the children evidenced growth failure, mental retardation or emotional disorder. Ribble's (1944, 1945) earlier studies had already shown that children who were exposed to maternal rejection, indifference and frequent punishment later became tense, unsatisfied and negativistic. In a similar vein Rutter and Madge (1976) found that symptoms of emotional disturbance were most common in children who had failed in early childhood to form stable attachments with an adult.

Coleman (1976) made reference to children's behaviour problems which he perceived as being consequential to adverse influences arising from conditions existing *among* the family, as well as their *relationships with* either or both of the parents. He perceived problem behaviours stemming from inadequate, disturbed and anti-social families; though these categories are by no means exclusive. The inadequate family (for a number of reasons including immaturity, lack of education and mental retardation) lacks the competencies to cope with ordinary day-to-day living and the responsibilities and problems associated with them. Any neglect which children incur in these instances derives from the parents' inability, rather than unwillingness, to exercise reasonable care over them. A characteristic of the anti-social family is a set of values inconsistent with those held by the wider community. These values often lead to marital and other family problems as well as conflict with the law, and similar circumstances which lead to the presence of unsatisfactory models for children and youngsters. Loyalty *within* such a group usually contrasts with its *absence* to the wider society. Members of the disturbed family, because of personal instability, interact with the people around them in ways which are destructive to themselves as well as the others. The constant quarrelling, bickering and conflict within the family unit is additional to the tension and anxiety which it generates.

Concern about child abuse has been well documented in recent years in both research investigations (e.g. Furniss 1987) and the wider media. The NSPCC (1974) showed that children from violent families often manifested withdrawn or disruptive behaviour which retarded their development and impeded their progress in school. While some children become withdrawn 'to keep themselves inconspicuous in a situation of conflict' (Hart 1976: 1), others model parental behaviours and become aggressive themselves. In the latter instances there is the distinct likelihood that, in time, abused children become abusers of their own children (Rutter and Madge 1976). This modelling characteristic is emphasized by Jones (1976) who wrote that:

> There is increasing evidence from retrospective data on the backgrounds of parents who abuse their children, husbands who seriously assault their wives, and murderers, that physical violence featured prominently in their childhood experiences.
>
> (p. 10)

Addressing the consequence of child abuse in a wider context, Kempe (1981) identified three categories of possible long-term effects upon children who were victims of child abuse:

> namely, psychological problems such as neurosis, psychosis, depression and low self-esteem; problems in sexual adjustment including dysfunction during intercourse, promiscuity, prostitution, homosexuality and sexual molestation of children; and interpersonal problems such as conflict with marital partner, parents or in-laws, and social isolation.
>
> (p. 111)

Clearly, research evidence supports the notion that children with more serious behaviour problems often come from homes characterized by parental conflict, psychiatric illness or family disturbance:

> that often eventuates in divorce, absence of prosocial standards of behaviour in the parents as evidenced by high rates of parental delinquency, and a failure to communicate standards of behaviour to the child.
>
> (Suran and Rizzo 1979: 344)

While most of the families referred to so far represent a minority of troubled or troublesome family groups, there are other occasions when, perhaps for the very best of reasons, parents in otherwise healthy families act in ways which generate emotional problems within their children. Teachers are often well aware of pupils whose anxiety has been caused by parents demanding 'perfection' from their children. By holding unrealistic expectations about their offsprings' performance in school, and elsewhere, by being continually dissatisfied with their performances and habitually telling them that they should do better, they may precipitate fears and anxieties within them which cause untold misery and unhappiness.

Overpermissive parents can also create anxieties in their children. Children require boundaries or guidelines within which they can act and feel secure. Homes which fail to provide reasonable structure and where 'environmental predictability is lessened and uncertainty heightened' (Clarizio and McCoy 1983: 63) may leave children feeling insecure and anxious.

Social class differences

Inconsistencies are evident amongst studies investigating the association between social class and behaviour. While some reports have indicated that behavioural difficulties are found more frequently in children from families in the lower social classes (Rutter *et al.* 1970; Davie *et al.* 1972), others have either found no such differences (Miller *et al.* 1974; Newson and Newson 1976) or have reported a greater incidence of problems amongst children from social class I groups (Moore 1966). Some writers have drawn attention to the imbalance between upper and lower class children attending special schools for children with behaviour problems. In a study by Ford *et al.* (1982) it was noted that the overwhelming majority of children on roll at four schools for the maladjusted came from social classes IV or V. Similarly, Galloway and Goodwin (1987) concluded that 'While it would be an overstatement to say that children from middle-class and professional homes are never placed in special schools or units, it is certainly true that this happens very seldom indeed' (p. 45).

In his review of the literature Upton (1983) added a cautionary comment which emphasized that 'the relationship between social class status and behaviour problems is neither consistent nor proven' (p. 35). Additionally, he explains the contradiction (though not inconsistency) between findings in the following way:

> Explanations of a higher proportion of problems amongst lower class groups have commonly focussed on the extent to which criteria of adjustment and problem behaviour are based on middle class norms. Conversely, a greater proportion of behaviour problem children amongst higher social class groups can be explained in terms of an increased interest among upper class groups in psychiatric problems . . . and greater strains of brittle middle class nuclear family existence.
>
> (p. 35)

Social disadvantage

The National Child Development Study has made major contributions to our understanding of the impact of home characteristics upon children's health, educational progress and behaviour. Wedge and Essen's (1982) study, for example, revealed that 5.8 per cent of children were socially disadvantaged at either 11 or 16 years of age. The criteria for this group were that children grew up in families which:

1 had a single parent/large family, *and*
2 were poorly housed, *and*
3 had a low family income.

The writers questioned what it must:

> be like for a child in the late twentieth century to have grown up in a family that lives on the poverty line and is overcrowded? Or to have lived with only one parent in a household which lacks basic amenities and depends on a subsistence income provided by the state?
>
> (p. 27)

Later in the book the writers give a graphic account of some of the answers to these questions. They talk of the children, at the time of birth, as 'already facing substantially diminished prospects of normal development' (p. 48) and progressing through childhood experiencing (compared with their non-disadvantaged peers) more health problems, increased rates of accidents requiring medical treatment, weighing less and being shorter, behaving less acceptably – as well as performing academically less well – in school, leaving school earlier and holding lower aspirations for further education. Along similar lines the NCB (1991) talks of lone parent families – and the 1.6 million children involved – constituting 17 per cent of all families in Britain. Reference is made also to the links between lone parent families and poverty; links which are particularly strong for those families with young children. The plight of children in homeless families is also highlighted in a number of reports and research articles (e.g. Audit Commission 1989; HMI 1990). The dilemma of raising a family alone on a limited budget exposes the youngsters to a range of adversities which increases the likelihood of physical, mental, educational and health problems arising (Storie 1990).

Lask and Lask (1981) made the pertinent comment that:

> Poverty is likely to be associated with other socio-cultural factors such as poor housing and unemployment, family factors such as increased tension and disharmony, and such biological factors as poor nutrition, inadequate ante-natal care, and increased susceptibility to disease.
>
> (p. 19)

More recently, Graham (1988) has provided a similar and cogent explanation of the association between overcrowding/lack of sufficient living space and housing amenities/low income and both emotional and behaviour problems in childhood as well as later delinquency.

While the notion that children from such homes *will* develop behaviour problems must be expunged, they clearly are exposed to conditions and experiences which may render them more vulnerable to the onset of such problems than their more advantaged peers.

Peer group influences

As children grow older so the influence of their peer groups becomes stronger and more pervasive. As they attach themselves to a group it usually becomes incumbent upon them to accept, and behave according to, what Frude (1984) refers to as the 'consensus attitudes of the peer group' (p. 32). Peer groups often have their own sets of values and norms and where these conflict with, or are radically different from, those of the individual's family or the wider society, he or she has to determine which of the conflicting or differing expectations to adhere to. The behaviour of children who come from home backgrounds where little concern or interest is expressed about their 'out of home' activities, and who find satisfaction from becoming involved with a high status delinquent group, is likely to be more strongly influenced by the peer group than the home. Similarly, in school, pupils are likely to:

> form small sub-cultures with shared views about school, teachers, and attitudes to discipline and disruption. The existence of such groups is widely recognised by the children themselves and, to a lesser extent, by those who teach them.
>
> (Frude 1984: 32)

Hargreaves (1967) suggests that 'pressures towards conformity to the peer group will be especially powerful after the third year in secondary school with the onset of the "adolescent syndrome"' (p. 183). Similarly, Morris (1976) talks of school as:

> a place where only the fittest survive socially. Those who don't measure up find themselves left out, and pressure to be 'in' and fear of being 'out' can cause far greater emotional strain than the academic pressure parents typically worry about.
>
> (p. 103)

The outcomes of Hargreaves' (1967) enquiry in a Manchester boys' secondary school suggested the existence of two distinct pupil-cultures linked to social class (one conformist and the other oppositional). The school's policy and organization seemed responsible for helping to differentiate the two groups whereby the oppositional, or delinquent, subculture became status deprived and were allocated poorer teachers. Conscious of their inferior status within the school the subculture established its own 'autonomous and independent peer culture' (p. 172) which Hargreaves claimed:

> is unlikely to encourage a boy to strive towards academic goals, since the pressures within the peer group will confirm and

reinforce the anti-academic attitudes . . . and the climate within the low streams will be far from conducive to academic striving.

(pp. 169, 170)

School factors

Only in recent years have research enquiries, to any great extent, begun to explore the impact of school-based experiences upon children's behaviour. The findings from these enquiries have tended to confirm what most teachers have always believed: that the range and quality of these experiences (in varying ways and to differing degrees) affect not only children's academic performances and attainments but also their social and emotional functioning. This is hardly surprising. Numerous studies had already shown that much behaviour is determined by, and confined to, specific situations. This is not to deny that occasions do arise when children endure experiences (usually traumatic in nature) which adversely affect their behaviour across all, or at least most, of the areas of their lives. Most of us can recollect unpleasant happenings (at home, school or elsewhere) which generated anxieties, unhappiness or fears which were omnipresent within us for short, or more protracted periods of time.

As teachers we sometimes feel it difficult to accept that there are limitations to the extent to which we can intervene, directly or indirectly, to improve the quality of our pupils' experiences at home. We can derive some comfort, however, from research which provides strong indications that there is much that we can accomplish to enhance the range and quality of services which we make available to children in school. This optimism is stressed within the comment by Galloway and Goodwin (1987: 135) that:

the consistency with which behaviour at school has been found to be relatively independent of the pupils' families and social backgrounds could be seen as extraordinarily encouraging for teachers.

The study by Burt and Howard (1974), for example, listed a number of school experiences or conditions significantly associated with maladjustment, including:

1 teachers who were uncongenial, unsympathetic or lacked understanding;

2 uncongenial pupils, a reference to pupils who bullied, teased or generally made life difficult for their peers;
3 absence from, or a change of, school;
4 placement in a class where the work was too difficult.

In support of their contention that the above factors, separately or collectively, help precipitate or exacerbate pupils' problem behaviour, they referred to a large number of their own case studies, spanning a period of twenty years, where transfer to another school or class (and in most instances a change to a more congenial teacher) was 'followed by a complete and apparently permanent disappearance of every overt sign of maladjustment' (p. 130).

Some writers have cited an inappropriate curriculum as a major source of pupil disaffection (Hargreaves 1967; Charlton 1986; Reynolds 1988). Reynolds (1988), for example, referred to two large comprehensive schools both of which offered their pupils a traditional academic, grammar school curriculum which had adverse 'consequences on the bottom two-thirds of the ability range who entered a pressured, academic and alienating school atmosphere' (p. 68). Understandably, it is difficult for (and unreasonable to expect!) pupils to engage in, and sustain, good behaviour when their school days are filled with material and presentations which fail to arouse their interest and industry.

Other enquiries have focused upon variations in schools' delinquency rates. As early as 1967 Power et al. reported large differences between the delinquency rates of a London borough's twenty secondary schools: differences which they contended could not be accounted for in terms of variations between the schools' catchment areas, selection processes, intake characteristics such as ability, sex or ethnic composition, school size or the age and type of buildings used. Their findings, supported by later studies (e.g. Gath et al. 1977; Rutter et al. 1979), pointed to 'within school' factors which help determine delinquency rates and led to their suggestion that:

> some schools may be successful in protecting children from the risk of delinquency, though they live in neighbourhoods where many children come before the courts. Conversely, other schools may be exposing children who live in delinquency-free neighbourhoods to such a risk.
>
> (p. 542)

For some time a strong association has been recognized between truancy, or persistent school absenteeism, and behaviour problems (Galloway *et al*. 1982; Tattum 1982). In more general terms Rutter *et al*. (1979) found that secondary schools varied markedly with regard not only to their pupils' behaviour, examination successes and delinquency rates, but also to pupils' attendance rates, even after 'taking into account differences in their intakes' (p. 205). Understandably the incidence of truancy has been a major concern of other professionals. Thornbury (1978) provided an indication of the magnitude of the problem in one region, Lambeth, where 'police estimated that one-third of all secondary school children in the locality played truant' (p. 183). The remarkable expansion of special provision for truants in both mainstream schools and elsewhere provides a salient indication of local authorities' current concern.

An indication of the link between truancy and behaviour problems is given by Reid (1984) who revealed that one in three of his sample of absentees in a South Wales comprehensive were rated as disruptive (anti-social) by their teachers. A similar – though hardly scientific – finding was encountered by the first of the present two writers when meeting the staff of another comprehensive school in South Wales. Staff reported that on any one school day they anticipated one in three of the children on roll being absent; they then declared that if the 'missing' third (many of whom they regarded as disruptive) returned *en bloc*, then the staff would walk out.

Some studies have attempted to explore reasons for the truancy–behaviour problem link and have noted that schools which have fewer behaviour problems also tended to have more favourable school attendance patterns. Others have reported differences between secondary schools' truancy rates which were not a consequence of variations between their intakes (Reynolds 1976; Gath *et al*. 1977; Rutter *et al*. 1979). The consensus of opinion seems to be that many absences from school are for neither medical nor other acceptable reasons, but a response to unpleasant or unattractive conditions or experiences within school. It is worth noting that while some pupils may be absent from school because they are fearful of attending, others elect not to go because they have found alternative less arduous and less boring activities to engage in away from school. Jones (1980), for example, argues that absenteeism is often a response to an unstimulating curriculum administered through the use of boring and uninteresting teaching methods. Supportive to this reasoning was Charlton's (1986) comment that those:

> who are disinterested in, or disenchanted and dissatisfied with the educational programmes schools offer to them, may well direct their interest and energies away from school tasks towards a variety of maladaptive behaviours (e.g. non-involvement in academic work, truancy, abuse towards teachers) which facilitate an excitement and involvement unavailable elsewhere in school.
>
> (p. 56)

In a similar vein Reynolds (1984b: 15) stresses truancy 'may be the rational reaction of a psychologically normal child to an institution which is not using his talents'. Additionally, he points out that schools often fail to investigate the 'root' cause of poor attendance rates by restricting their efforts mainly to 'get the truants to attend, rather than attempt to see if the child is being misused by the institution' (p. 15). Reid (1984) gives a salient reminder of negative school practices of this type where there is a tendency to punish non-attenders rather than give positive attention to attenders.

However, Carlen *et al.* (1992) caution against the above thinking on the grounds that much of the truancy literature is 'unconnected to a wider sociological analysis' (p. 71) and ignores social, economic and political contexts. Nevertheless, regardless of the causes of truancy, when schools' attendance rates are published for the first time in 1993 many will reflect upon HMI's (DES 1989) claim that a school's attendance rate can be regarded as a significant indicator of its performance. (It is worth reflecting that, for a period in the eighteenth century, teachers' salaries were related to pupils' attendance. Perhaps there is a lesson to be learned from past policy!)

Nearly two decades ago Rutter (1976) was stressing that there was a paucity of information about particular school factors which encouraged/discouraged desirable pupil behaviour. Indeed until the 1970s research in the USA (e.g. J.S. Coleman *et al.* 1966) had insinuated that schools had a marginal impact upon pupils' performance. Understandably, comment of this type provided meagre comfort to teachers in their endeavours to improve pupils' personal, social and educational performance.

Fortunately, the decade and a half following Rutter's comment produced an explosion of 'effective schools' research which accentuated schools' influence upon their pupils. Of particular interest were the findings from two major research enquiries in Britain; findings which contradicted earlier contentions from the USA. Investigations within secondary schools (Rutter *et al.* 1979) and primary schools (Mortimore *et al.* 1988) yielded results supportive of notions that differences in pupil outcomes between schools could not be explained by socioeconomic factors alone; in other words pupils' home background on entry to school did not explain variations in outcomes between schools. The inference from these discoveries was that 'the school was much more important than background in determining the progress of pupils' (Stoll 1991); that pupils' learning and behaviour in school was influenced more by school processes than their social, economic and ethnic background (though more recent comment cautions against presumptions that school influences might be as large as family or community influences). Interestingly, final preparations for the delivery of the manuscript of the book to the publishers have coincided with the publication of the much awaited 'exam league tables'. Concerns have been broadcast in Parliament, and the media, that the raw, unadjusted data used in the tables do not take into account the widely varying social conditions that different schools serve. Intriguingly the raw, unadjusted data appear to be offering some measure of support to findings from the enquiries led by Rutter and Mortimore. Wide variations have been noted within the league table in terms of the performance of schools serving similar areas.

In preparing its report to the Secretary of State for Education, the Elton Committee provided a pragmatic response – to what it perceived to be the positive conclusions drawn from contemporary research and extant beliefs relating to school effectiveness – by commenting that:

> The message to heads and teachers is clear. It is that they have the power, through their own efforts, to improve standards of work and behaviour and the life chances of their pupils.
>
> (DES and Welsh Office 1989: 88)

Having warmed to the notion that 'schools do make a difference' research activity then probed to unveil the precise nature of within-school ingredients likely to affect learning and behaviour. An early work by David Reynolds (1984b) speculated upon factors which hinder 'good' school influences. The indentification of these hindrances not only endorses characteristics to be discouraged or evaded, but also alludes to contraconditions as guidelines for good practice. In attempting to explain the genesis of a high-vandalism and high-disaffection school he refers to the following as probable causal factors (1984b: 174):

1 a highly coercive regime where control was more concerned with physically punishing, rather than seeking the root cause of, deviant behaviour, where many rules prevailed and were inflexibly enforced;
2 relationships between teachers being marked by friction;
3 the headteacher and staff apportioning the blame for school problems upon each other;
4 a high turnover of staff;
5 a paucity of pupil involvement in running the school;
6 classroom management practices which included public ridicule of miscreants and the administration of class punishment for individual rule breaking;
7 an unwillingness to welcome parents into the school;
8 an iniquitous investment of staff expertise, time, energy and other resources into A streams, and a consequent low, or inferior, investment into other classes;
9 negative staff perceptions of pupils who were seen as 'irredeemable' and as having irremedial problems, stemming from apparent deficiencies in primary socialization.

Contraconditions drawn from the above list are comparable with those derived from the earlier work of Rutter *et al.* (1979) in their enquiry into twelve London secondary schools. From their research Rutter and colleagues identified the following eight factors which they argued were important determinants of school effectiveness:

1 a reasonable academic balance (of more and less able pupils);
2 working conditions which were appropriate and befitting;
3 effective use of homework;
4 ample employment of positive reinforcement, with prudent use of punishment;
5 competent classroom management;
6 firm leadership with involvement of staff;
7 teachers acting as models of good behaviour;
8 involvement of pupils in running the school.

A concluding comment by the researchers contended that children:

> benefit from attending schools which set good standards, where teachers provide good models of behaviour, where they are praised and given responsibility, where the general conditions are good and where the lessons are well conducted.

(p. 204)

Similar findings/recommendations were identified through the Junior School Project conducted by Mortimore *et al.* (1988) in fifty London junior schools. At the end of their enquiry the project team asserted that 'the school makes a far larger contribution to the explanation of progress than is made by pupil background characteristics, sex and age' (p. 204). On this occasion twelve organizational/interpersonal pointers towards school effectiveness were identified:

1 purposeful leadership of the staff by the headteacher;
2/3 involvement of the deputy head and other teachers in running the school;
4 consistency among teachers;
5 structured, well organized lessons;
6 intellectually challenging teaching;
7 work-centred focus in lesson;
8 limited focus within lessons;
9 maximum dialogue between teachers and pupils;
10 good record keeping (personal/social/academic);
11 parental involvement;
12 positive climate.

In combination these characteristics appear to prevail in schools which are seen:

> as being inviting, supportive environments, led by headteachers who are not afraid to assert their views and yet are able to share management and decision-making with the staff. Class teachers within effective schools provide a structured learning situation for their pupils, within which freedom and personal responsibility are encouraged. Through the flexible use of whole class and individual contacts, they maximise communication with each pupil. Furthermore, by limiting their focus within a session, teachers' attention is less fragmented, and the opportunities for presenting challenging work to pupils are increased.

(Stoll 1991: 73)

Whilst the majority of these characteristics are hardly novel, in the sense that they present as logical conditions for helping to maximize pupils' learning and behaviour, the notion of a positive school climate or school ethos – and the insinuation of its importance to school effectiveness – is more innovative. Whilst 'ethos' and 'climate' notions have permeated the lexicon of education over the last few years, they have retained a mystical semblance. In this context Robinson (1989) talks about ethos (and by implication, climate) being felt but not measurable and being sensed but unseen. In a similar vein the Elton Committee admitted when they visited some schools that they were 'struck by the differences in their "feel" or atmosphere' (DES and Welsh Office 1989: 88). Furthermore, they confessed that the schools with a positive feel tended to be those where they were most impressed with pupil behaviour and learning. Whilst research enquiries are providing fairly clear directions for schools to follow in their endeavours to become more effective, the ethos factor is still elusive; elusive in terms of defining and measuring it as well as prescribing resource to enhance it. Nevertheless, in terms of its genesis and effects within the school it seems likely that ethos plays a role in both reflecting and stimulating pursuit of other effective school characteristics. On occasions a positive school ethos may emerge as a response to a school acquiring those types of positive characteristics previously referred to, whilst on other occasions it may help act as an agent for those types of changes to take place.

Recently there has been a swing away from a research pre-occupation with wider institutional influences upon pupil perform-ance towards an amplified focus upon the classroom and the teacher. Regarding earlier beliefs concerning school effectiveness, it seems that 'early simplistic assumptions . . . are now no longer tenable' (Reynolds 1991: 95) and that 'the great majority of variation between schools is due to classroom variation' (Reynolds and Packer 1992: 173). Mindful of the inextricable links between the school and its classrooms, the logical and pragmatic response to this change is to accept both as being influential in affecting pupils' learning and behaviour as well as providing foci for change to take place. The aims and content of this book reflect this trend. Whilst parts of this book focus upon ways in which the wider school environment can effect – and be modified to exert – favourable influences upon behaviour in school, more of the chapters' contents are concerned with ways in which teachers can develop their classroom management skills in ways which help them to prevent misbehaviour arising (where this is practicable) and to resolve it on those occasions when it does arise.

CONCLUSION

In this chapter discussion focused upon examples of a range of factors located within – as well as outside – the child, which may interact to affect his or her behaviour in unhelpful or unhealthy ways. It was stressed that where problems arise it may be necessary to search for problem causes from a multifactorial perspective. A failure to undertake this could result in an incorrect assessment of a child's needs and, consequently, the formulation and implementation of intervention strategies unable to meet those needs satisfactorily. Attention was drawn, also, to varying ways of conceptualizing the impact of those factors upon behaviour, with particular reference being made to the differing causal, and intervention, perspectives of behavioural, humanistic and psychodynamic models.

The latter part of the chapter was preoccupied with school effects upon pupil behaviour, and concluded in an optimistic vein by noting that whilst aspects of school organization and classroom experiences have been shown to be strongly associated with a range of pupil misbehaviours, there is evidence available which strongly suggests that schools and their teachers can do much to minimize the occurrence of behaviour problems, and successfully help manage them when they do arise.

REFERENCES

Aarons, M. and Gittens, T. (1991) 'Autism as a context', *Special Children* 50: 14–17.

Ainscow, M. (1991) *Effective Schools for All*, London: David Fulton.

Anthony, E.J. (1973) 'The syndrome of the psychologically invulnerable child' in Anthony, E.J. and Koupernik, C. (eds) *The Child in his Family: Children at Psychiatric Risk*, New York: Wiley.

Audit Commission (1989) *Housing the Homeless: the Local Authority Role*, London: HMSO.

Barker, P. (1981) *Basic Child Psychiatry*, London: Granada.

Beres, D. and Obers, S.J. (1950) 'The effects of extreme deprivation in infancy on psychic structure in adolescence' in Eissler, R.S. *et al.* (eds) *The Psychoanalytic Study of the Child*, vol. 5, New York: International University Press.

Bowlby, J. (1946) *Forty-four Juvenile Thieves: Their Characters and Home Lives*, London: Balliere, Tindall & Cox.

Bullard, D.M., Glaser, H.H., Heagarty, M.C. and Pivchek, E.G. (1967) 'Failure to thrive in the neglected child', *American Journal of Orthopsychiatry* 37: 680–90.

Burt, C. and Howard, M. (1974) 'The nature and causes of maladjustment among children of school age', in Williams, P. (ed.) *Behaviour Problems in School*, London: University of London Press.

Carlen, P., Gleeson, D. and Wardhaugh, J. (1992) *Truancy. The Politics of Compulsory Schooling*, Buckingham: Open University Press.

Charlton, T. (1986) 'A special need in the curriculum: Education for life', in Charlton, T., Lambley, H. and Jones, K. (eds) *Educating Children with Learning and Behaviour Problems: Some Considerations*, Faculty of Education Monograph 1, Cheltenham: College of St Paul and St Mary.

Clarizio, H.F. and McCoy, G.F. (1983) *Behaviour Disorders in Children*, New York: Harper & Row.

Coleman, J.S., Campbell, E., Hobson, C., McPartland, J., Mood, A., Weinfeld, F. and York, R. (1966) *Equality of Educational Opportunity*, Washington D.C.: National Center for Educational Statistics.

Coleman, J.C. (1976) *Abnormal Psychology and Modern Life*, Dallas, Tex.: Scott, Foresman.

Crook, W.G. (1980) 'Can what a child eats make him dull, stupid or hyperactive?', *Journal of Learning Disabilities* 13: 53–8.

Davie, R., Butler, N. and Goldstein, H. (1972) *From Birth to Seven*, London: Longman.

DES (1989) 'Attendance at school: a report of Her Majesty's Inspectorate', *Education Observed 13*, London: DES.

DES and Welsh Office (1989) *Discipline in Schools*, Report of the Committee of Enquiry chaired by Lord Elton.

Douglas, J.W.B. (1975) 'Early hospital admission and later disturbance of behaviour and learning', *Developmental Medicine and Child Neurology* 18: 358–68.

Feingold, B.F. (1975) *Why is your Child Hyperactive?* New York: Random House.

Ferri, E. (1976) *Growing up in a One-Parent Family*, Windsor: NFER.

Finer Report (1974) *Report of the Committee on One-Parent Families*, London: HMSO.

Folstein, S. and Rutter, M. (1977) 'Infantile autism: a genetic study of 21 twin pairs', *Journal of Child Psychology and Psychiatry* 18: 297–321.

Ford, J., Mungon, D. and Whelan, M. (1982) *Special Education and Social Control: Invisible Disasters*, London: Routledge.

Frude, J. (1984) 'Frameworks for analysis', in Frude, N. and Gault, H. (eds) *Disruptive Behaviour in Schools*, Chichester: Wiley.

Furniss, T.H. (1987) 'An integrated treatment approach to child sexual abuse in the family', *Children and Society* 1 (2): 123–35.

Galloway, D. and Goodwin, C. (1987) *The Education of Disturbing Children*, London: Longman.

Galloway, D., Ball, T., Blomfeld, D. and Seyd, R. (1982) *Schools and Disruptive Pupils*, London: Longman.

Gath, D., Copper, B., Grattoni, F. and Rockett, D. (1977) *Child Guidance and Delinquency in a London Borough*, London: Oxford University Press.

Gordon, H. and McKinlay, I. (1980) *Helping Clumsy Children*, Edinburgh: Churchill Livingstone.

Graham, P. (1988) 'Social class, social disadvantage and child health', *Children and Society* 2 (1): 9–19.

Graham, P., Rutter, M. and George, S. (1973) 'Temperamental characteristics as predictors of behaviour disorders in children', *American Journal of Orthopsychiatry* 43: 328–39.

Halstead, H. (1957) 'Abilities and behaviour of epileptic children', *Journal of Mental Science* 103: 28–45.

Hargreaves, D.H. (1967) *Social Relationships in a Secondary School*, London: Routledge.

Hart, D. (1976) *Violence, Disruption and Vandalism in Schools – A Summary of Research*, London: National Children's Bureau.

HMI (1987) 'Behaviour and Discipline in Schools', *Education Observed 5*, London: DES.

—— (1990) *A Survey of the Education of Children Living in Temporary Accommodation*, London: HMSO.

HMSO (1992) *Marriage and Divorce Statistics 1990*, London: HMSO.

Jobling, M. (1976) *The Abused Child: An Annotated Bibliography*, London: National Children's Bureau.

Jones, A. (1980) 'The school's view of persistent non-attendance', in Hersov, L.A. and Berg, I. (eds) *Out of School*, Chichester: Wiley.

Jones, C. (1976) 'Children in violent families', *Therapeutic Education* 4 (2): 8–12.

Kempe, H. (1981) 'Recognition of child sexual abuse in the United Kingdom', in Mrazek, P. and Kempe, H. (eds) *Sexually Abused Children and Their Families*, London: Pergamon.

Kounin, J. (1970) *Discipline and Group Management in Classrooms*, New York: Holt, Rinehart & Winston.

Lask, J. and Lask, B. (1981) *Child Psychiatry and Social Work*, London: Tavistock Publications.

Lawrence, J., Steed, D. and Young, P. (1984) *Disruptive Children – Disruptive Schools*, London: Croom Helm.

Marsden, D. (1969) *Mothers Alone: Poverty and the Fatherless Family*, Harmondsworth: Allen Lane Penguin.

Miller, F.J.W., Court, S.D.M., Knox, E.G. and Brandon, S. (1974) *The School Years in Newcastle-upon-Tyne*, London: Oxford University Press.

Mitchell, A. (1987) 'Children's experience of divorce', *Children and Society* 1 (2): 136–47.

Moore, T.W. (1966) 'Difficulties of the ordinary child in adjusting to primary school', *Journal of Child Psychology and Psychiatry* 7: 17–38.

Morley, C.M. (1985) 'Food and behaviour', paper presented at a one day conference on Nutrition and Behaviour on 13 July 1985 at John Radcliffe Hospital, Oxford.

Morris, C.G. (1976) *Psychology: An Introduction*, Englewood Cliffs, N.J.: Prentice Hall.

Mortimore, P. (1980) 'Misbehaviour in schools', in Upton, G. and Gobell, A. (eds) *Behaviour Problems in the Comprehensive School*, Faculty of Education, University College, Cardiff.

Mortimore, P., Sammons, P., Stoll, L., Lewis, D. and Ecob, R. (1988) *School Matters: The Junior Years*, Shepton Mallett: Open Books.

NCB (1991) Homeless Families, *Highlight No. 99*, London: National Children's Bureau.

Newson, J. and Newson, E. (1976) *Seven-year-olds in the Home Environment*, London: George Allen & Unwin.

NSPCC (1974) *Yo Yo Children. A Study of 23 Violent Matrimonial Cases*, School of Social Work, London: NSPCC.

NSPCC (1986) *The Forgotten Children*, London: NSPCC.

Power, M.J., Anderton, M.R., Phillipson, C.M., Shoeberg, E. and Morris, J. (1967) 'Delinquent schools?', *New Society* 10: 542–3.

Reid, K. (1984) 'Disruptive behaviour and persistent school absenteeism', in Frude, N. and Gault, H. (eds) *Disruptive Behaviour in Schools*, Chichester: Wiley.

Reynolds, D. (1976) 'The delinquent school', in Hammerslee, M. and Woods, P. (eds) *The Process of Schooling*, London: Routledge.

—— (1984a) 'The school for vandals: a sociological portrait of a disaffection-prone school', in Frude, N. and Gault, H. (eds) *Disruptive Behaviour in Schools*, Chichester: Wiley.

—— (1984b) 'Creative conflict: the implications of recent educational research for those concerned with children', *Maladjustment and Therapeutic Education* 2 (1): 14–23.

—— (1988) 'Changing comprehensive schools', *Children and Society* 2 (1): 68–77.

—— (1991) 'Changing ineffective schools', in Ainscow, M. (ed.) *Effective Schools for All*, London: David Fulton.

Reynolds, D. and Cuttance, P. (1992) *School Effectiveness*, London: Cassell.

Reynolds, D. and Packer, A. (1992) 'School effectiveness and school improvement in the 1990s', in Reynolds, D. and Cuttance, P. (eds) *School Effectiveness*, London: Cassell.

Ribble, M.A. (1944) 'Infantile experience in relation to personality development', in Hunt, J.McV. (ed.) *Personality and the Behaviour Disorders*, vol. 2, New York: Ronald.

—— (1945) 'Anxiety in infants and its disorganizing effects', in Lewis, N.D.C. and Pacella, B.L. (eds) *Modern Trends in Child Psychiatry*, New York: International University Press.

Robinson, P. (1989) *Exploring Educational Issues. Unit 16. Course E208*, Milton Keynes: Open University.

Rutter, M. (1966) *Children of Sick Parents: An Environmental and Psychiatric Study*, Maudsley Monograph No. 16, London: Oxford University Press.

—— (1971) 'Parent–child separation; psychological effects on the children', *Journal of Child Psychology and Psychiatry* 12: 233–60.

—— (1972) *Maternal Deprivation Reassessed*, Harmondsworth: Penguin.
—— (1976) 'Sociocultural influences', in Rutter, M. and Hersov, L. (eds) *Child Psychiatry: Modern Approaches*, Oxford: Blackwell Scientific.
—— (1980) *Changing Youth in a Changing Society*, Oxford: Nuffield Provincial Hospitals Trust.
Rutter, M. and Madge, N. (1976) *Cycles of Disadvantage*, London: Heinemann.
Rutter, M., Tizzard, J. and Whitmore, K. (1970) *Education, Health and Behaviour*, London: Longman.
Rutter, M., Maughan, B., Mortimore, P. and Ouston, J. (1979) *Fifteen Thousand Hours: Secondary Schools and their Effects on Children*, London: Open Books.
Sharron, S. (1987) 'Asthmatic children: victims of ignorance', *Special Children* 13: 8–9.
Shreeve, C.M. (1982) 'A state of perpetual motion', *World Medicine* 17 (15): 87–93.
Silva, P.A., Kirkland, C., Simpson, A., Stewart, I.A. and Williams, S.M. (1982) 'Some developmental and behavioural problems associated with bilateral otitis media with effusion', *Journal of Learning Disabilities* 15 (7): 417–21.
Stacey, M., Deardon, R., Pill, R. and Robinson, D. (1970) *Hospitals, Children and their Families*, London: Routledge.
Stedman, J. (1973) 'Epilepsy: a barrier to learning', *Times Educational Supplement*, 3 March.
Stevenson, J. (1987) 'Report of a one day conference', *Special Children* 8: 5.
Stoll, L. (1991) 'School effectiveness in action: supporting growth in schools and classrooms', in Ainscow, M. (ed.) *Effective Schools for All*, London: David Fulton.
Storie, J. (1990) *Bed, Breakfast and Social Work*, Social Work Monographs 86, University of East Anglia.
Suddaby, A. (1987) 'A temporary phenomenon', *Special Children* 8: 22–3.
Suran, B.J. and Rizzo, J.V. (1979) *Special Children: An Integrated Approach*, Dallas, Tex.: Scott, Foresman.
Swinson, J. (1988) 'In praise of chemical food', *Special Children* 18: 6–7.
Tattum, D. (1982) *Disruptive Pupils in Schools and Units*, Chichester: Wiley.
Thomas, A. and Chess, S. (1977) *Temperament and Development*, New York: Bruner/Mazel.
Thornbury, R. (1978) *The Changing Urban School*, London: Methuen.
Upton, G. (1983) *Educating Children with Behaviour Problems*, Faculty of Education, University College, Cardiff.
Vass, M. and Rasmussen, B. (1984) 'Allergies: the key to many childhood behaviour abnormalities', *Elementary School Guidance and Counselling*, 242–50.
Wedge, P. and Essen, J. (1982) *Children in Adversity*, London: Pan Books.

Chapter 3

Assessing and understanding children's behaviour

Ronald Davie

INTRODUCTION

In this chapter we shall consider three questions which are at the heart of the professional task of meeting the needs of pupils whose behaviour is giving cause for concern. The issues involved are relevant whether the child has a statement of special educational need (SEN) or whether the concern is less extreme than this but is nevertheless a matter needing attention and decision.

The first of these questions centres on assessment including the day-to-day task for the teacher of reaching a decision about responding to an apparent problem. This question is set in the wider context of educational assessment, since many of the issues overlap.

The second question, which takes up most of the chapter, is how far the major theoretical models which attempt to explain the children's behaviour actually aid teachers' understanding of that behaviour. Lastly, we examine the extent to which any of these models can be seen as offering the 'right' explanations, and consider how the teacher can best make use of them in the school and in the classroom.

PROBLEM CHILDREN OR PROBLEM SCHOOLS?

Before embarking on a consideration of any of the above questions, however, it is necessary briefly to clarify one point, although it will be looked at in more detail later. As we consider assessment below, it may be thought that it is the child who is the focus of the assessment, because in some sense he or she is where the behaviour problem lies. This is not necessarily the case and no such assumption should be made.

Research evidence for some time has been confirming what common knowledge indicates, namely that schools make a difference to their pupils' behaviour – for better or for worse (see Galloway and Goodwin 1987; Mortimore *et al.* 1988; Reynolds 1989). For example, schools from very similar areas can have very different prevalences of delinquency or behaviour problems. Therefore, in some instances the 'problem' may lie with the school and not the child.

This understanding, sometimes termed an 'interactionist' perspective, has now been incorporated into circulars to schools from the Department of Education and Science (DES/DH 1989: paragraph 17) and from the National Curriculum Council (1989). The latter, for example, pointed out (paragraph 5) that: 'Special educational needs are not just a reflection of pupils' inherent difficulties; they are often related to factors within schools which can prevent or exacerbate some problems.'

ASSESSMENT – CHANGING CONCEPTS AND PROCESSES

For the teacher in the classroom, changing ideas and changing practice in relation to assessment may at first sight appear a little esoteric. Not so, as we shall see. Certainly for the teacher in the senior management team or the pastoral care team it is vital to be aware of the movement in this field if his or her role is to be discharged responsibly and with professional competence.

In this short section, we shall first identify some of the recent legislation which bears on the topic of assessing children, not simply in relation to their behaviour but more generally. Second, we shall compare 'one-off' assessments, which outside agencies and professionals often carry out, with the more dynamic notion of continuous assessment. The latter is much closer to the way in which most teachers implicitly or explicitly operate. Lastly, we shall look at multi-professional assessment, which may occur with referrals to, say, the educational psychology, health or social services.

The last ten years or so have seen substantially increasing interest in the topic of assessing children's needs. This has been evident in discussion on the different concepts of assessment and the processes involved and also in the various legislative frameworks within which assessment is embedded. Some of this interest has focused on assessing children in the context of SEN, both within the UK (e.g. Wolfendale 1993) and internationally (Cline 1992). This field has also attracted more political interest in the UK because assessments of SEN (statements) under the 1981 Education Act have come under some critical review (e.g. Audit Commission/HMI 1992; DFE 1992). As a result, new guidelines are planned on the process of statementing; and new legislation is foreshadowed in relation to appeals against statementing decisions and on parents' rights to choose a school.

However, the 1988 Education Act has produced much more public interest, turbulence and controversy, for example, on issues surrounding assessment and testing in the National Curriculum, notably 'standard assessment tasks' (SATS). This Act has also spawned more professionally focused debate and analysis, for instance, on 'curriculum-based assessment' (Frederickson 1992) and on the 'formative' and 'summative' aspects of the assessment process (Norwich 1990).

The above developments in relation to assessment have arisen as a result of legislation in the education sector. However, a third piece of legislation – quite as radical in its own way as either of the above two Education Acts – is the 1989 Children Act, which raises new issues and new possibilities in the area of assessment, some of which have particular potential relevance to children's behaviour, as we shall see below.

STATIC AND DYNAMIC FORMULATIONS OF ASSESSMENT

For teachers in schools, of course, these pieces of legislation are backcloths against which their professional practice is played out. For most of their purposes, most of the time, assessment is an ongoing process, either in terms of marking written work and responding in an oral situation or in terms of being part of the pedagogical process of encouraging/discouraging/shaping pupils' behaviour as it emerges in the classroom, the corridor or the playground.

Some of the time, the assessment is literally made minute by minute; sometimes the timescale is in months or years, as the teacher observes the growth of knowledge, understanding and skill or the development of personal relationships in individuals and in whole groups.

It is important that teachers hold on to that dynamic, developmental concept and process of assessment, because without it assessment is in some danger of being 'hijacked' by 'experts', who can only appear infrequently and work on a model of assessment which is based more on the snapshot than on the moving film.

The rhetoric of government circulars and of official reports leaves no apparent room for doubt that assessment, at least of children's special needs (but extending to 20 per cent of the school population) should be seen as continuous. Thus, 'The monitoring and assessment of each child's progress are continuous processes' (DES/DH 1989: paragraph 19). And yet a little later in the same paragraph, we read, 'Where the support provided by the school does not seem to meet the child's needs, the school will need to refer the child for assessment'.

The possible confusion created by such mixed messages is semantic in a sense. No one can dispute that from time to time a school will need to seek another professional perspective from outside the school as part of the process of assessing a child's needs. Such a referral *per se* does not invalidate or undermine a process of continuous assessment, any more than the ability to 'freeze' a frame of a video film destroys the film's essential motility.

Nevertheless, this is not simply a semantic quibble, because ways in which ideas are expressed can influence ways in which they are perceived. And inferential messages such as the one contained in the second sentence quoted above from the government circular can be more powerful in their effect than more straightforward assertions such as in the first quotation. This is especially so when the more subtle, inferential message is reinforcing an existing stereotype, namely that by and large assessment is carried out by 'experts' who bring to bear their superior skills and experience onto a problem. Their prescription or diagnosis (note how the medical terminology comes readily to mind here) is then taken forward by people with rather lesser skills who implement the recommendations.

The alternative formulation put forward, for example by Davie (1983), is that assessment and 'treatment' should be seen as 'indivisible parts of a continuous cyclical process'. As indicated above, this does not imply that the same people should be involved all of the time. Part of the essential feedback and monitoring process may be carried out by people with particular skills who may only appear rarely, maybe only once, in the cycle. However, the 'assessment' is not then attributed to them alone.

Most of the same issues arise in child care (see Fuller 1985), where assessment was traditionally carried out at 'assessment centres' and is still seen primarily as a decision-making event carried out at a point in (perhaps extended) time rather than as a continuous process (Grimshaw and Sumner 1991).

The importance of this issue is not a theoretical one. There are two very practical reasons why assessment should be seen as continuous and not the 'territory' of an outside group. First, in the 'external model' the quality of information flowing into and out of the system is almost inevitably flawed because of the separation between the decision makers and those who know the child best. Second, the external model has a tendency to devalue and de-skill those closest to the child, be they parents, teachers or careworkers.

MULTI-PROFESSIONAL ASSESSMENT

If the above discussion has dwelt upon some of the dangers inherent in the use of outside professionals or services in the assessment process, the balance must now be redressed.

No professional can work effectively as 'a one-man team' (Young-husband *et al*. 1970). The various facets of children's development are inextricably linked (Davie 1993 (b)) and therefore it is vital in assessing and responding to their pupils' behaviour that teachers are fully aware of the possibility that emotional, social, intellectual or physical factors may be affecting the behaviour. In some situations, of course, a formal process of multi-professional involvement has to be invoked, where the possibility of a statement of SEN is to be considered. However, there are many more instances where a child's behaviour is causing concern – especially if the behaviour is untypical of the child, or where it is extreme or persistent – when another professional view will be appropriate.

This is not – to recap on our earlier discussion – to hand over the assessment to someone else because one has 'failed' to find the answer. Rather, it is to seek out complementary skills and perspectives, because some of the dimensions of the situation may be outside the field of one's professional competence. The continuous nature of the assessment process can best be maintained if outside referrals are built into a system which has been thought through carefully and becomes part of the whole-school policies and procedures. There is no one 'right' way of achieving this but its main characteristic is a cyclical flow of information and feedback.

THE 1989 CHILDREN ACT

It is impossible to leave the topic of multi-professional assessment without referring briefly to the 1989 Children Act. Generally speaking, this Act is not yet well known by teachers – understandably perhaps in view of the all-consuming appetite of the National Curriculum – but this is not the place to remedy the situation. However, in the particular context of the assessment of behaviour and the interface between social services and education, two new terms from the Children Act should be mentioned (see also Davie 1993 (a)). The first is 'a child in need' and the second is 'significant harm'.

The definition of 'a child in need' has some similarities with that of 'special educational need', as set out in the 1981 Education Act. In both cases the child is seen to be in need of provision over and above that which is normally available. Furthermore, the criteria of 'need' in the Children Act include whether a child is unlikely to achieve or maintain a 'reasonable standard' of mental health or development (including emotional, social or behavioural aspects) without the provision of additional local authority services. The Act (Schedule 2, part 1, section 3) also gives specific encouragement to local authorities to carry out joint assessments of need under both the Children Act and the 1981 (or now 1993) Education Act, when this seems appropriate.

The second new term introduced by the 1989 Children Act which is of special relevance to teachers and to assessment is 'significant harm'. This supplants the old concept of ill treatment (or child abuse). Its relevance derives from the fact that the new wider concept covers not only abuse (of any kind) but also situations where a child's mental health or development (defined as above) is being impaired, or is likely to be impaired, as a result of the care he or she is receiving.

In respect of the various forms of child abuse, the teacher's role is largely one of surveillance and screening. Even this kind of role, of course, must carry an element of assessment but the teacher's responsibility normally ends at the point where the possibility of abuse has been drawn to the attention of some other designated person or agency. Any further contribution by the teacher is likely to be directed to helping the child to cope in whatever outcome emerges.

However, as Davie (1993 (a)) points out, when there is a

decision to be made on the wider question of whether a child's development is being significantly impaired, the teacher should be an important if not central part of the process of assessment. This is especially the case when the court (where appropriate) is considering – as the Children Act requires it to do – the child's development in relation to other, 'similar' children (e.g. others of the same age, sex or social group).

The implications of some of these issues for teachers and schools, and for collaborative working between education, health and social services, have scarcely been broached, far less thought through. However, the outcomes of these considerations may well have far-reaching consequences for procedures which will involve teachers' assessments (especially of children's intellectual, social, emotional and behavioural development). In particular respects, or for particular teachers, this new non-educational legislation could transform some educational roles.

FIVE MODELS

We now turn our attention to a brief review of five of the major theoretical models encountered in this field, which are used to understand or explain children's behaviour problems. Many of these models are dealt with in some detail in the following chapters, so that our purpose here is to set them out in broad outline and to make some initial comparisons.

The order in which they are presented is not fortuitous. It happens largely to be a chronological order. More importantly, however, it follows a trend which has been evident and gathering momentum over the past twenty to thirty years in our thinking about children and about the structuring of our services for them, discussed elsewhere by Davie (1982). In the context of children's behaviour and development, this period has seen a movement from a narrow psychological perspective to a broader, contextualized, at times sociological, approach. It might be characterized as a 'movement from an individualised to a systems approach, from the atomistic to the holistic, occasionally from the micro to the macro' (Davie 1986).

At the professional level, one can see this movement in most of the relevant sectors. Educational psychologists, for example, saw themselves until the 1970s largely as psychometricians, dealing mostly with the assessment of individual pupils, albeit having an important role as a link between the child guidance team and schools. Since that time, however, they have increasingly seen themselves as working in a consultative capacity, perhaps as 'agents of change', with teachers and with whole schools (see Gillham 1985; Davie 1991).

A not dissimilar trend can be seen in social work over the same timescale. The concept of 'community social work' emerged in and around the time of the Seebohm Report (DHSS 1968) and was extensively discussed in the Barclay Report (1982). This concept did not replace the idea of individual or family casework but it moved the profession towards a wider view of its role. Another example of this trend was the emphasis given in the Court Report on child health services to the role of the community paediatrician (Court 1976).

These parallels cannot be coincidental, although no one as yet has attempted to analyse in depth the common factors which lie behind them. It is clear nevertheless that the movement was – and is – not confined to professional development but is to be traced in academic writing both in Britain and in the USA (Davie 1982).

The psychodynamic approach

Hence, in reviewing the theoretical models we shall start with arguably the most individual of them all, namely the one which originated with Sigmund Freud. Strictly we should be speaking of models here rather than a single model because of the number of important differences of approach within the general orientation (e.g. Adler, Bowlby, Erikson, Klein, Redl, Winnicott etc.). However, for present purposes within this chapter we can group them together as sharing certain common features and beliefs; and we shall refer to this common ground as the 'psychodynamic model' (Chess and Hassibi 1986).

Brown and Pedder (1979) distinguished five common features or assumptions which can be found in the work of all theorists and practitioners adopting this model, namely: unconscious processes; anxiety and psychic pain; defence mechanisms; motivational drives; and developmental phases. Both the general framework of the psychodynamic model and the significance of these five principles are so familiar as to require no substantial restating here. They are now part of western cultures, appearing frequently in art, literature and drama as well as in everyday language and allusions.

Perhaps the most central and the most widely known feature of this model is the assumption of the unconscious: that inner, psychic world, not normally accessible to conscious thought but exerting a powerful influence upon our feelings and our behaviour. Much of this unconscious material, it is assumed, has been repressed because it is associated with feelings of guilt, conflict or anxiety, too painful to be held at the conscious level. If this inner conflict or pain becomes intolerable for the individual, it can emerge as unacceptable or sometimes debilitating behaviour. However, it will be noted, this overt behaviour is essentially a symptom of the underlying, unconscious conflict (see Chapter 5). Thus, to concentrate on removing or suppressing the symptom without tackling the underlying problem can be seen as at best of limited value, because some other symptoms may take its place; at its most dangerous, it can be thought to be taking away the safety valve which alone is safeguarding the individual's mental health. Thus:

> the aims of many of the psychodynamic procedures in teaching and therapy are primarily concerned with the provision of opportunity for acceptable outlets of the internal pressures ('letting off steam', 'getting it off your chest'). . . . In addition to finding release, it is also seen as important to gain understanding of some of the causes of the internal pressures and problems.
>
> (Gobell 1980)

Behaviour modification

The second model for us to consider goes back almost as far as the psychodynamic one but comes from a very different stable. While Freud, as we all know, developed his theory and his practice out of his work with patients, our second model has its modern origins in the laboratories of experimental psychologists working largely with animals. These 'behaviourists' developed, in a much more rigorous and scientific way, a body of empirical evidence which was subsequently brought together as a theory of learning.

Although it has quite a long history, this behavioural model has only in more recent years had any major impact or practical relevance for work with people. In this context it is usually referred to as social learning theory; and the clinical techniques employed are known as behaviour modification. The principal and most obvious contrast with psychodynamic theory is that the behavioural model makes no assumptions about unconscious or inner processes. Its quintessential principle is that behaviour which is reinforced, whether by accident or design, tends to recur or gain in strength, while behaviour which is not reinforced tends to disappear (see Herbert 1987, 1991).

The simplicity and universality of this principle is one of its attractions both in relation to its practical uses and also in theoretical scientific terms, where the law of parsimony applies. Furthermore, there is no room for doubt about the effectiveness of the approach in changing behaviour (Leach 1990). Indeed, its effectiveness has given rise to some ethical concern about its use, not unlike the anxiety sometimes expressed about the use of drugs to help modify or influence behaviour. The difficulty about sustaining ethical objections to behavioural techniques is that parents and teachers have been utilizing the same basic principles since time immemorial, albeit with less success!

The behaviourist, then, is concerned largely with the here and now and the observable rather than with any distant aetiology or unconscious mental conflicts. He does not therefore assume that the behaviour problem is a symptom of some underlying mechanism. It would be wrong to say that he actively rejects that possibility; it just does not enter his scheme of things. As far as he is concerned, the behaviour in question must have been learned, which implies that it must have been, and still is being, reinforced. His first concern is to carry out a 'behavioural analysis', which is a precise and detailed description and analysis of the behaviour which is causing concern. How does it manifest itself? What circumstances precede it and accompany it? Who else is involved and in what way? The second stage of the analysis is to identify what it is that is reinforcing the behaviour. Paradoxically, the attention which a behaviour problem may attract from adults attempting to deal with the problem can be the reinforcement for an attention-seeking child. The teachers' or parents' current solutions therefore may actually be making the position worse! The third stage is to seek ways of changing the situation so that the problem behaviour is not reinforced and − if at all possible, too − so that some more acceptable pattern of behaviour is reinforced.

This is a very simple description of what can be quite a complex and time-consuming process. In fact, the time involved can be an important inhibiting factor in considering the use of this approach, especially in mainstream schools. However, this has to be weighed against the time taken, disruption and distraction caused and pressure exerted by even a single pupil with a significant behaviour problem. Furthermore, an understanding of the basic principles involved can often help teachers prevent a problem occurring, or assist them to analyse a situation in a way which will suggest a constructive way forward without any elaborate and time-consuming programmes.

Humanistic psychology

Our third theoretical model is much less well known than the two already discussed. It could be said, as we shall see below, to be a reaction against earlier models. It is usually referred to as humanistic psychology or, when related to the education process, as humanistic education. Its principle proponents and architects in the 1950s and 1960s were the Americans Carl Rogers and Abraham Maslow. Nye (1992) contrasts the psychology of Rogers with that of Skinner, the behaviourist, and that of Freud.

The model is in some ways more difficult to characterize than the others included in this chapter but in other ways it is simpler. Humanistic psychology can be seen as a reaction against the positivism of the empirical sciences. It therefore rejects 'mechanistic' explanations of human behaviour or generalizations about causal processes. For the humanistic psychologist, the individual is unique. At the centre of this theoretical model, therefore, is the individual's perception of himself (his self-image) and his unique perception of others and of the world around. The model also stresses the relevance and the integrity of the whole person and resists attempts to split off and deal with bits of behaviour or life experience.

Writers and practitioners espousing this model tend to stress empathy, in the same sense of being able to put or feel oneself in someone else's place (Visser 1983). Hence, they emphasize the validity of a person's perception or interpretation of events rather than any attempt at an 'objective' description of the events themselves. In the USA, some therapists refer to this approach as 'client-centred' (see Johnson et al. 1986: 124–34).

Gobell (1980) emphasizes the above points as central to the humanistic model and highlights some of the practical implications for teachers. Worster and Bird (1980) in the same publication usefully describe a number of specific techniques emanating from this model which can be utilized in schools. They highlight the value of working in small groups in a pastoral care group situation, developing the interpersonal skills of listening and sharing. The benefits of such activities, they claim, are cognitive as well as affective. The overall objective is to encourage respect for others' perceptions, others' points of view, others' feelings. In the process of doing this, pupils gain in respect for their own perceptions, points of view etc. because of the positive feedback they are obtaining from other group members. Hence, their self-image is improved, they benefit as a whole person and this is reflected in their behaviour and their school work.

Humanistic education seeks to involve the students in experimental learning and self-discovery methods. Also 'the teacher is characterised as a helper who provides a climate in which the student can feel free to develop emotionally' (Burns 1982).

Behaviour and environment

At this point, we pause briefly to consider a group of researchers who have much in common with each other but are not sufficiently close theoretically to be described as adopting the same model in the way in which we have been using that term in this chapter. Nevertheless, their evidence is often cited in the literature on behaviour problems, so they should be mentioned.

This group shares the same scientific paradigm and its members are all broadly interested in the relationship between behaviour problems in children and environmental factors in the home, the school and beyond. Most of them could be described as epidemiologists. Amongst the factors they have measured, analysed and correlated with behaviour problems (as you will already have noted in Chapter 1) are social class, family size and composition, family pathology, sex, poor housing and overcrowding, educational attainment, birth factors (including maternal smoking in pregnancy) and parental–child relationship. Upton (1983) in reviewing these workers' findings points to the considerable degree of agreement in their results. At the same time their methodology is mostly designed to establish correlations rather than to prove causation. Their principal value for the practitioner, therefore, is to increase his general awareness of the range of environmental factors which may be impinging upon the behaviour and adjustment of individual pupils.

Best known amongst this group in Britain is Rutter (e.g. 1983), whose work since the 1960s has included most of the above variables and whose later research has also examined the relationships between school characteristics and pupils' behaviour and adjustment (Rutter *et al.* 1979). Many of the contributors to Reid's two edited volumes (1989) on *Helping Troubled Pupils in Secondary School* draw on this paradigm in developing their practical strategies, although some fit more readily into our next section on systems approaches.

At the outset of this second section of the chapter we foreshadowed moving along a continuum in terms of the models we are examining, both chronologically and also from the psychological to the psychosocial perspectives. Of course, such directional movements are never exact. As we have seen, the humanistic model was something of a reaction against prevailing approaches and could be said to be the most individually based of all the models we are reviewing. However, as we move to our penultimate model, we reach well past any notional centre point of the continuum.

A systems approach

The model we now examine is rooted in systems theory, implicitly or explicitly, and therefore in an educational context embraces 'whole-school' approaches and institutional change strategies, while on the therapeutic front it includes family therapy. In essence, the systems model takes the view that each individual child is embedded in a number of systems, notably family and school, and that the individual's behaviour can only meaningfully be viewed in that sort of context. There are some elements of this in all of the models we have reviewed, of course. From the psychodynamic standpoint, the context is largely historical, although it is the present inner state which is of central concern. The behaviourist on the other hand is interested in the immediate context, the precipitating factors, the reinforcers and so on. The humanist is perhaps furthest from this point in that he tends to reject any notion of the individual being caught up in a system outside of himself. However, it is notable that the techniques described by Worster and Bird (1980) involve working in groups, developing listening skills and respect for others' perceptions.

Nevertheless, the systems model is a far cry from these other perspectives. From a theoretical viewpoint, the model like most others can become quite complex and the practical or treatment techniques, too, are often elaborate, but the central core of the approach is simple. Man is a social animal and his behaviour is essentially defined in social terms. Therefore, if a child's behaviour is a cause for some concern, it is highly likely to be related in some way to the matrix of relationships around him. It is a familiar concept that a child may be 'scapegoated', for example, and there are many other circumstances where behaviour may be clearly seen to be directly related to some external factor. Even where the genesis of a problem is found to be an identifiable medical condition, the way in which the problem manifests itself, the reactions to it by others and the child's reaction to those reactions are often influenced by the pre-existing relationships in a particular system. Furthermore, the nuclear systems (family, school, peer group etc.) are related to each other in ways which may be important in understanding an individual child's problem.

In discussing family therapy, for example, Speed (1983) explains that 'working with families . . . is not an adjunct to the main business in hand (treating the individual), rather it is central to the whole enterprise of therapy'. A similar movement can be discerned in educational circles. Thus Davie (1980a, b) describes and later evaluates (Davie et al. 1984, 1985; Phillips et al. 1985) an in-service course for experienced and senior teachers which is concerned with institutional change in schools as a way of responding to behaviour problems. This approach has subsequently gathered momentum nationally in different forms and has also widened to cover the whole field of special educational needs. Muncey and Ainscow (1986), for instance, describe a scheme developed in Coventry which involves the selection and training of a teacher in each school who is responsible for assisting the school as a whole to respond to its pupils' special educational needs. Faupel (1990) examines an approach to building emotional, social and behavioural development into the school curriculum.

Labelling theory

The final model for us to consider shares with systems theory a rejection of the idea that individual behaviour (or problems) can meaningfully be viewed out of context. However, this last model goes further in challenging the very concept of individual deviance. The theory is usually attributed to the American sociologist Becker

(1963). He argued that deviance is not something intrinsic to the individual; it is created by society. Thus, our social system sets up certain rules or has certain expectations of people; when these rules are broken or expectations confounded, deviancy is created. Another concept and term which forms part of this theoretical model is that of labelling (hence, 'labelling theory'). It is pointed out, for example, that the same overt acts carried out by, say, Oxbridge undergraduates and young football club supporters may be seen as boisterous high spirits in the former and hooliganism in the latter. Henry (1989) specifically examines the accounts by students of their deviant behaviour.

Labelling theory represents, like humanistic psychology, a rejection of the determinism and positivism of conventional empirical science. Both models also place great emphasis upon the personal, subjective perspective as against attempts to measure objective reality. The former is often referred to as a 'phenomenological' approach. Hargreaves *et al.* (1975) contrast the difference between the kinds of questions posed by empirical scientists and labelling theorists. The scientists set out to establish measurable criteria by which, say, a 'behaviour problem' may be identified and classified. They then ask about causal factors and associated relationships. Finally, they seek to find out how to predict, prevent, control or cure the condition. The labelling theorists on the other hand ask what the circumstances or conditions were which led to a pupil being categorized as a behaviour problem. How have other people's (and pupils') attitudes or actions changed as a result of that categorization? How has the pupil reacted to being cast in that role? and so on.

In educational contexts this model – sometimes also called the interactionist approach – would lead the practitioner to ask whether the pupil was a problem all of the time and with all teachers. If not, the practitioner would further explore the nature of the interactions which were presenting the difficulty. He would also be especially vigilant to ensure as far as possible that the mere attribution of a label was not itself adversely affecting the situation. The dangers of self-fulfilling prophecies are well known (Furlong 1985).

FROM INDIVIDUALS TO SYSTEMS

We have now reviewed five different theoretical models. Each of them offers a different way of understanding, explaining or construing children's behaviour problems. In consequence, each of them may suggest different ways of responding to, or treating, such behaviour. We shall return to the implications of these differences shortly. Before doing this, however, we should spend a moment to consider any implications of the broad direction which the models are taking, namely the suggested continuum from an individual/psychological perspective to a social/sociological one.

First, we may note, as we did earlier in another context, that the reality in such things is often not neat and tidy. The idea of a continuum does not imply a straight line without deviations; nor should it be taken to mean that there is only one dimension to the issue. Furthermore, the swing from a micro to a macro perspective is by no means new in the history of knowledge. In many fields, one has seen, and can see, movements which focus more narrowly or in a more detailed fashion on particular areas of knowledge, followed by subsequent movements to broaden the knowledge, sometimes for the purpose of generalizing it, or else to temper it in the light of a wider perspective.

To take an educational example of this phenomenon, there are periods when schools and education generally seem very concerned with curricular matters, with standards or teaching methods in literacy and numeracy, with the training of teachers, and so on. In contrast, at other times the field appears much more outward looking with talk of 'whole school approaches', of community schools and of partnership with parents and with other services. Although such trends are much more evident at a national level and in the area of policy developments and debate, they can also be discerned in the individual school.

No doubt then, there is an element of this general phenomenon in the directional trend identified in the continuum along which our five models are ranged. This is not to seek to reduce the significance or importance of the trend but to place it in a wider context. Furthermore, although in many of these movements, there is often an element of fashion – a 'bandwagon' effect – there is also a serious, underlying reason for the trend. The pendulum may swing back but it rarely returns to its former position.

In terms of the perspectives we have been examining in this chapter, the directional trend is an important area to consider. If the individual professional is to be in full command of his professional situation or task – rather than be blown by winds of change he does not recognize, far less understand – he needs to grasp the significance of this movement. The major implications are twofold. First, there has been some tendency in the past to concentrate on the individual child and his personal history without fully taking into account the potential relevance and importance of external forces and perceptions and systems. On the other hand, there is also the danger of ignoring the individual and overstressing the system. The danger – in both directions – exists to some extent in the construction of theoretical models but, more importantly for most professionals, it also exists in terms of how a particular child or situation is perceived or handled.

The second major implication is the impact of the trend on professional training and professional roles. Most teachers enter their profession – as do psychologists, and psychiatrists, for example – because of an interest in individuals. It is not a difficult step for them to grasp, accept and utilize the concept that the child's immediate contexts to a greater or lesser extent affect his behaviour, his performance etc. However, the wider the contextual view becomes, the more difficult it is for an individual teacher or school to pursue it in any practical sense.

If he does try to pursue it, there are twin dangers. Let us take, for example, poverty, poor housing and unemployment. All of these factors, as we know, impact upon educational performance, if not directly then in the consequential effects on the morale, aspirations, mental and physical health etc. of families and communities. A teacher faced with these consequences may be tempted to blame families or the local authority or central government for the performance or behaviour of children in the school. This is especially dangerous if, as a result, he ignores what the school could or should be doing.

The opposite temptation is for a teacher within and outside school to spend an inappropriate amount of time and energy on welfare matters and on community work to the detriment of his pedagogic role. For some teachers, political or industrial action is seen as a relevant and appropriate response to the wider, contextual view.

This leads us into issues beyond the scope of this chapter, or this book. Suffice it here to put a marker by this more distant terrain because when one opens up the more social and societal perspectives it becomes ever more difficult to draw a firm line around the professional role.

WHICH MODEL TO BELIEVE?

We now reach the final section of our chapter and confront the issues raised by having a variety of different models. Each of them has extensive literature and, albeit in varying degrees, a strong following. More problematically, they are in several important respects mutually incompatible. Does this matter?

To those who are concerned primarily to build theories and/or to carry out scientific research, the discrepancies are not problematic. On the contrary, they could stimulate experimental work designed to test alternative hypotheses, drawn from different theories. In reality, this potential advantage is not often seen because most researchers have insufficient familiarity with a range of theoretical models and their associated research literature to be able to design such critical experiments. They tend instead to confine their work and their interest to one model. Where any kind of comparative work is attempted, the results are not definitive enough to permit the rejection of a major theoretical tenet. Therefore, in summary, the incomparability between theoretical models does not pose a problem for the theorists, mostly because they are not often interested in theories other than their own except perhaps to use them as straw men! Potentially, the discrepancies could be valuable scientifically, although this seems rarely to happen.

THE PRACTITIONER'S DILEMMA

Experienced practitioners in the specialized field of emotional and behaviour difficulties have often tended to take a position similar to the theorists, namely they have espoused one model and eschewed the others. Indeed, some of the most distinguished practitioners have themselves written extensively on theoretical aspects.

However, this position has been changing in recent years for a number of reasons. First, the number of credible, well-documented theoretical models with their associated practical skills and techniques has increased. Behaviour modification, for example, and family therapy have both made giant strides in the past twenty years. Their impressive results are difficult for intelligent, uncommitted new entrants into the professions to ignore. Second, there has been a tendency over a similar period to move towards multidisciplinary teams in this context as in many others; and this, too, has led to significant erosion of the single-model approach (Rutter 1991). It is true, of course, that child guidance and child psychiatric teams were quite common fifty years ago and more but they were on the whole dominated by the psychiatrist or medical director who would determine the treatment model. Today's clinical teams are much less hierarchical professionally, therefore allowing different approaches to be introduced more readily. Furthermore, non-clinical teams (i.e. without a medical base) are now much more common in this area; and the 1981 Education Act with its move-ment towards integration in mainstream schools and the growth of a community orientation in social services will continue that trend.

What might at first sight, then, appear to be a dilemma for the practitioner is on further scrutiny much less so. The problem only remains if the question to be answered is: which of the theories is right? As we have already seen, the definitive evidence to validate one model and discredit another is not in sight; and it is unlikely ever to emerge in quite that way. Much more probable will be some formulation which incorporates two or more of the models together within an overarching framework.

The answer to the above question may therefore be that all of the theories may be right in their own way. Each one takes a different point of departure in terms of its mainspring: its conceptual or professional framework; the evidence it seeks in order to verify or modify its direction; and the outcomes it expects which will justify its continued existence. Thus, to say that each model gives us a partial glimpse of the truth, is not to imply that they are all deficient but merely that in the present state of our knowledge the truth appears to have a number of faces, which shine in a certain light, as it were.

AN ECLECTIC STANCE

Without wishing to venture further down this metaphysical path, we can accept from a practical standpoint that there is no necessity to make any absolute choice between different and even conflicting explanations. The range of possible interpretations in the individual case, or situation, may readily be scanned in order to determine which is likely to be the most productive. However, this is not seen as a process of attempting to assemble a number of possible solutions. For example, for an individual child with a *prima facie* problem we might start by asking whether we are quite sure that there really is a problem. Does everyone who interacts with him see him as a problem? And does everyone have the same perception of the situation? If not, why not, and how do they differ? What could be reinforcing this particular behaviour? Would it be useful, or practical, to bring the whole of the child's family together or all of his teachers etc. to consider the situation? Is the behaviour likely to be a symptom of some underlying problem in the family? Is it therefore a cry for help? Is it attention seeking?

By concentrating on the questions, one is in a sense trying out different formulations of 'the problem' in order to judge which of them may suggest further enquiry or action. The great virtue of such an approach is that options are kept open, and several possible lines of enquiry or action usually emerge. Furthermore, no assumption is made that somewhere, somehow, *an* answer will be found. This is because in the individual case more than one of the theoretical models may very well be relevant.

Thus, it is not difficult to conceive of a child who, because of some changed situation at home (a new baby arrives, mother remarries), is feeling unwanted or rejected. Whether that situation were to be fairly straightforward, or complex, it could result in some attention-seeking behaviour at school. If misbehaviour proved to be the only – or the easiest – way of obtaining that attention, it would be reinforced. Furthermore, if he were new to the school, he might be identified (labelled) as a 'difficult' child. This might become self-fulfilling if the school were to complain to the parents, who then were to chastise the child, making him feel further rejected, and so on.

The example is a facile one, but it illustrates the point. Several of the questions suggested earlier would have thrown some light on such a situation. It also illustrates that there is no single 'cause', which can necessarily be identified and removed, thus providing a solution. It further demonstrates that if, in this hypothetical instance, the child's teacher had intuitively sensed some need for attention and provided this, the whole 'problem' might have melted away in months if not weeks.

DIFFICULTIES IN ECLECTICISM

The adoption of this kind of eclectic stance, however, is not entirely without difficulty. Its first potential shortcoming might be the creation of a shallow, professional dilettantism, which would militate against sound judgement from an adequate knowledge base. This might best be prevented by structuring the professional situation on a team basis. This, as we have seen, is a growing trend anyway but a structured, eclectic approach would perhaps necessitate different members of the team electing to familiarize themselves with particular models, if there were significant gaps in the team's collective expertise. Beyond this, it is difficult to generalize because the detailed structure and level of expertise needed would be very different, depending on the institutional context, for example mainstream school, special unit, day or residential special school, clinic team etc.

However, there is one other potential difficulty which has particular relevance to special schools and units. There has been some tendency, as was mentioned earlier, for special schools to base their whole ethos on one theoretical approach. The psychodynamic model in particular has provided a framework in which many of the best known residential schools or communities for children with emotional and behavioural difficulties have operated and this still applies to a lesser extent. Behaviourism, too, more recently has been the model on which a number of schools have based their education and care.

Dealing with disturbed and disturbing children in a segregated setting, especially if this is residential, is recognized to be extremely demanding and stressful work. Perhaps these demands incline some practitioners to develop a strong identification with, and faith in, a particular set of beliefs about children's behaviour and adjustment. If this is the case, eclecticism may be found wanting on this plane. It is rather more cerebral than inspirational. In difficult and stressful situations there is great comfort and support to be derived from an inner conviction that one knows the way, the truth and the light! Indeed, religion in some circumstances may provide that support. Eclecticism, however, explicitly demands a rejection of such an approach. There is no royal road. Judgements need to be weighed, options kept open.

A TEAM APPROACH

The special school context, of course, especially the residential situation, applies only to a minority of children who need professional help. However, whatever the context, there is growing evidence of the efficacy and attractions of the multi-disciplinary team approach (e.g. Woodcock and Frances 1981; Rutter 1991), and although this is not synonymous with eclecticism, there must be a great deal of common ground in terms of group dynamics and team building. It is no easy option, but it offers a way forward which can be adapted to many different situations – including the use of outside consultants, for example, to a school – and which has much to commend it.

REFERENCES

Audit Commission/HMI (1992) *Getting in on the Act – Provision for Pupils with Special Educational Needs*, London: HMSO.

Barclay, P. (1982) 'Social workers: their role and tasks', *Working Party Report*, London: Bedford Square Press.

Becker, H. (1963) *Outsiders: Studies in the Sociology of Deviance*, New York: Free Press.

Brown, D. and Pedder, J. (1979) *Introduction to Psychotherapy*, London: Tavistock Publications.

Burns, R. (1982) *Self-Concept Development and Education*, London: Holt, Rinehart & Winston.

Chess, S. and Hassibi, M. (1986) *Principles and Practice of Child Psychiatry*, New York: Pergamon.

Cline, T. (ed.) (1992) *The Assessment of Special Educational Needs: International Perspectives*, London: Routledge.

Court, S.D.M. (Chair) (1976) *Fit for the Future: Report of the Committee on Child Health Services*, London: HMSO.

Davie, R. (1980a) 'Behaviour problems in schools and school-based in-service training', in Upton, G. and Gobell, A. (eds) *Behaviour Problems in the Comprehensive School*, Cardiff: Faculty of Education, University College.

—— (1980b) 'Promoting school adjustment', in Pringle, M.K. (ed.) *A Fairer Future for Children*, London: Macmillan.

—— (1982) 'Child development in context', *BPS Education Section Review*, 6: 1–12.

—— (1983) 'Testing and assessment', in Upton, G. (ed.) *Educating Children with Behaviour Problems*, Cardiff: Faculty of Education, University College.

—— (1986) 'Understanding behaviour problems', *Maladjustment and Therapeutic Education* 4 (1): 7–15.

—— (1991) 'Educational psychologists and the Act', *Children & Society* 5 (1): 40–7.

—— (1993 (a)) 'Interdisciplinary perspectives on assessment', in Wolfendale, S. (ed.) *Assessment and Special Needs*, London: Cassell.

—— (1993 (b)) 'Developing Warnock's multi-professional approach', in Upton, G. and Visser, J. (eds) *Special Education after Warnock*, London: Fulton.

Davie, R., Phillips, D. and Callely, E. (1984) *Secondary Schools Research*

Project: Evaluation of INSET Course on Behaviour Problems, Cardiff: Welsh Office.

——, —— and —— (1985) *Change in Secondary Schools*, Cardiff: Welsh Office.

DES/DH (Department of Education and Science and Department of Health) (1989) *Assessments and Statements of Special Educational Needs: Procedures within the Education, Health and Social Services*, Circulars 22/89, HN(89)20, N(FP)(89)19 and LASSL(89)7, London: HMSO.

DFE (Department for Education) (1992) *Special Educational Needs: Access to the System*, a consultation paper, London: DFE.

DHSS (1968) *Report of the Committee on Local Authority and Allied Personal Social Services* (Seebohm Report), London: DHSS.

Faupel, A. (1990) 'A model response to emotional and behavioural development in schools: the place of emotional, social and behavioural development within the curriculum', *Educational Psychology in Practice* 5 (4): 172–82.

Frederickson, N. (1992) 'Curriculum based assessment: broadening the base', in Cline, T. (ed.) *The Assessment of Special Educational Needs: International Perspectives*, London: Routledge.

Fuller, R. (1985) *Issues in the Assessment of Children in Care*, London: NCB.

Furlong, V.J. (1985) *The Deviant Pupil*, Milton Keynes: Open University.

Galloway, D. and Goodwin, C. (1987) *The Education of Disturbing Children*, London: Longman.

Gilham, B. (1978) *Reconstructing Educational Psychology*, London: Croom Helm.

—— (1980) *Problem Behaviour in the Secondary School: A Systems Approach*, London: Croom Helm.

Gillham, B. (1985) 'School organisation – the control of disruptive incidents', in Frude, N. and Gault, H. (eds) *Disruptive Behaviour in Schools*, Chichester: Wiley.

Gobell, A. (1980) 'Three classroom procedures', in Upton, G. and Gobell, A. (eds) *Behaviour Problems in the Comprehensive School*, Cardiff: Faculty of Education, University College.

Grimshaw, R. and Sumner, M. (1991) *What's Happening to Child Care Assessment?* London: NCB.

Hargreaves, D.H., Hester, S.K. and Mellor, F.J. (1975) *Deviance in Classrooms*, London: Routledge.

Henry, S. (ed.) (1989) *Degrees of Deviance: Student Accounts of Their Deviant Behaviour*, Aldershot: Avebury Gower.

Herbert, M. (1987) *Behavioural Treatment of Children with Problems*, London: Academic Press.

—— (1991) *Clinical Child Psychology: Social Learning, Development and Behaviour*, London: Wiley.

Hollins, S. (1985) 'The dynamics of team work', in Bicknell, J., Craft, M. and Hollins, S. (eds) *Mental Handicap – a Multidisciplinary Approach*, Eastbourne: Bailliere & Tindall.

Johnson, J.H., Rasbury, W.C. and Siegel, L.J. (1986) *Approaches to Child Treatment*, Oxford: Pergamon.

Leach, D.J. (1990) 'Home-based reinforcement for changing children's school behaviour', in Gupta, R.M. and Coxhead, P. (eds) *Intervention with Children*, London: Routledge.

Mortimore, P., Sammons, P., Ecob, R. and Stoll, L. (1988) *School Matters: the Junior Years*, Salisbury: Open Books.

Muncey, J. and Ainscow, M. (1986) 'Meeting special educational needs in mainstream schools: a transatlantic perspective', *International Journal of Special Education* 1 (2): 161–76.

National Curriculum Council (1989) *Implementing the National Curriculum – Participation by Pupils with Special Educational Needs*, Circular No. 5, York: NCC.

Norwich, B. (1990) *Re-appraising Special Needs Education*, London: Cassell.

Nye, R.D. (1992) *Three Psychologies: Perspectives from Freud, Skinner and Rogers*, Monterey, CA: Brooks/Cole.

Phillips, D., Davie, R. and Callely, E. (1985) 'Pathway to institutional developments in secondary schools', in Reynolds, D. (ed.) *Studying School Effectiveness*, London: Falmer Press.

Reid, K. (ed.) (1989) *Helping Troubled Pupils in Secondary School*, two volumes, Oxford: Blackwell.

Reynolds, D. (1989) 'Effective schools and pupil behaviour', in Jones, N. (ed.) *School Management and Pupil Behaviour*, Lewes: Falmer Press.

Rutter, M. (1983) *A Measure of our Values*, London: Quaker Home Service.

—— (1991) 'Services for children with emotional disorders: needs, accomplishments and future developments', *Young Minds Newsletter* 9: 1–5.

Rutter, M., Maughan, B., Mortimore, P. and Ouston, J. (1979) *Fifteen Thousand Hours: Secondary Schools and their Effects on Pupils*, London: Open Books.

Speed, B. (1983) 'Systemic family therapy and disturbing behaviour', in Upton, G. (ed.) *Educating Children with Behaviour Problems*, Cardiff: Faculty of Education, University College.

Upton, G. (1983) *Educating Children with Behaviour Problems*, Cardiff: Faculty of Education, University College.

Visser, J. (1983) 'The humanistic approach', in Upton, G. and Gobell, A. (eds) *Behaviour Problems in the Comprehensive School*, Cardiff: Faculty of Education, University College.

Wolfendale, S. (1993) 'Involving parents in assessment', in Wolfendale, S. (ed.) *Assessment and Special Needs*, London: Cassell.

Woodcock, M. and Frances, D. (1981) 'The nine building blocks of team effectiveness', in Woodcock, M. and Frances, D. (eds) *Organisational Development through Team-Building*, Aldershot: Avebury Gower.

Worster, A.D. and Bird, E.G.E. (1980) 'Social skills training in a pastoral care group', in Upton, G. and Gobell, A. (eds) *Behaviour Problems in the Comprehensive School*, Cardiff: Faculty of Education, University College.

Younghusband, E., Birchell, D., Davie, R. and Kellmer Pringle, M.L. (1970) *Living with Handicap*, London: NCB.

Part II

Theory and practice

In Chapter 4 Hanne Lambley explores the complex relationship between learning and behaviour problems, the subject of many research studies. She reviews these studies and examines the educational practices which underlie the framework for intervention. She discusses a balanced approach for assessment and intervention. The chapter includes an observation plan to provide data for appropriate provision for pupils' needs.

Graham Upton, in Chapter 5, discusses the dynamics of emotional and behavioural difficulties. Commencing with a serious and ugly incident observed, he explores dynamic psychotherapy, the life-space interview and the role of the teacher, and considers aspects of the teacher's approach, including attitudes and values.

Part II concludes with Chapter 6 where John Presland asserts that behavioural approaches are interpreted as arising from a combination of behavioural and humanistic views of behaviour. He describes a sequence of stages during which problem behaviours are defined and measured and intervention programmes are planned, administered and evaluated. Illustrative examples are given, the range and scope of behavioural approaches are discussed and training methods outlined.

Chapter 4

Learning and behaviour problems

Hanne Lambley

CONCEPTS OF SPECIAL EDUCATION WITHIN THE EDUCATION SYSTEM

Concern for pupils' learning has by definition always been at the heart of education. As the education system has developed, consideration for those individuals who showed problems with learning has increasingly become a priority. Gradually a segregated sector of special education emerged to provide an appropriate education service for a small identified proportion (2 per cent) of handicapped pupils. Developments during the 1970s and 1980s expressed in a government report (DES 1978) and legislation (DES 1981) led to a widening of special education by the introduction of the concept of special educational needs and the abolishment of existing categories of handicap. The resulting concept of special educational needs relates now to all pupils in special schools (2 per cent) together with those encountering significant difficulty with learning (approximately 18 per cent) in ordinary schools. This revised statutory framework removed special education from its former isolation and established it as a central concern of *all* teachers and *all* schools. In continuing this development the 1988 Education Reform Act requires that 'all pupils share the same statutory entitlement to a broad and balanced curriculum, including access to the National Curriculum' (DES 1989a).

A survey of teachers (Wragg *et al*. 1989) and other educationalists such as Wedell (1988) expressed reservations regarding the suitability of the National Curriculum for pupils with special educational needs. However, the advantages associated with a move from the previously restricted curriculum to a common curriculum for all children is increasingly recognized (Lewis 1991).

The Warnock Committee (DES 1978) suggested a continuation of the use of certain existing terms of disability to identify particular groups of children who require special educational provision. Additional to descriptions for physical/sensory disabilities and maladjustment, the term 'children with learning difficulties' has been retained for children who were previously categorized as educationally subnormal and for those with educational difficulties who are often the concern of remedial services.

There is considerable variation in, and some confusion about, the definition of the concept of 'learning difficulty' as an umbrella term. Over the years children with learning difficulties have been described as educationally retarded, slow learners, remedial, dyslexic, minimally brain-damaged and perceptually handicapped.

Amongst professionals the term 'learning difficulty' is used in a descriptive manner, as suggested by the Warnock Committee, and the ensuing discussion is based on the same understanding.

Learning difficulties were originally believed to be organic in origin and interpreted in terms of causes centred within the child. Recent thinking has abandoned the theory of internal deficiency by placing learning difficulties within the context of the environment in which the child lives and learns.

Bloom (1976) developed a model for school learning which identified three major influences on pupil performance:

• cognitive entry behaviour (thinking)
• affective entry characteristics (feelings and attitudes)
• quality of instruction (teaching)

He states that the manipulation of these three components can reduce the individual differences which lead to variation in school achievement. In schools it is 'part and parcel' of teachers' responsibilities to help ensure that the above variables are manipulated so as to optimize pupils' learning and behaviour performances. A failure to do so may mean that a pupil encounters learning or/and behaviour problems.

There still exists considerable uncertainty and controversy regarding the causes of learning difficulties but it is now well established that many children with learning difficulties suffer from associated emotional or behavioural problems. Difficulties in the affective area range from severe maladjustment to slight emotional problems (e.g. minor anxieties or a low self-concept). Their main characteristic, however, is that they *may* constitute an emotional blockage to successful learning.

The concept of 'maladjustment' was introduced in the 1920s and first used in 1945. It was defined in the 'Handicapped Pupils and School Health Service Regulations' as 'emotional instability or psychological disturbance', requiring special educational treatment in order to effect personal, social or educational readjustment. The terms maladjustment, behaviour problems, emotional difficulties, conduct disorder, psychiatric disorder, disturbed behaviour and personality disorder are often used in the literature interchangeably, a practice which frequently creates some confusion.

As a basis for the following discussion it is therefore helpful to define learning difficulties as an 'academic achievement deficit' and behavioural problems as those 'unhealthy emotional or behavioural conditions which arise from or/and contribute to learning difficulties'.

THE RELATIONSHIP BETWEEN LEARNING AND BEHAVIOUR PROBLEMS

Any teacher of children with behaviour and learning difficulties will be able to describe their lack of attention and motivation, as well as their possible anxiety, distractibility and aggressiveness. It is no new observation that these characteristics are concomitants of both behaviour and learning difficulties, and an insight into their existence will help illuminate the principles underlying their influence.

Croll and Moses (1985) analysed pupils' activities in class and suggest a 'slow learning behaviour pattern' (p. 126) which is characterized by children with learning difficulties and behaviour problems spending more time distracted and fidgeting than other pupils. The amount of fidgeting was double that of the control group. Interestingly, the distraction does not always involve inter-action with other pupils but can consist of 'solitary distraction'. With less time spent on curriculum tasks, this often leads, under-standably, to underachievement. Hunter (1982) suggests a matrix framework for teachers to diagnose inappropriate learning strategies responsible for reading difficulties. Within a hierarchy of pupils' difficulties, attention problems occur more frequently than other difficulties cited (e.g. memory, sequencing, rhythm and context). She suggests that 'attention relates to apparent concentration difficulties, fluctuation in energy, or interest level characterised by apparent lack of motivation' (p. 148). Rutter and Yule (1972), in a comparison of poor and good readers amongst anti-social boys, state that 'over half the poor readers (52.9 per cent) showed very poor concentration compared with only 13.6 per cent of the good readers' (p. 104). Why do underachieving pupils with behaviour problems lack attention and motivation? While it is not possible to state with precision what has caused these unfavourable attitudes towards school learning, it is widely accepted by psychologists that behaviour is determined by the world in which we live and that the outcomes of behaviour weaken or strengthen that behaviour (see Chapter 6). Our behaviour is reinforced by successful actions. The emotional concomitants of learning difficulties, therefore, could be a reaction to school failure and in turn could cause further underachievement. Gulliford (1985) contends that 'A significant feature of learning failure is that rewards may be few compared with those the successful learner obtains' (p. 29).

On the other hand, maladjustment might be caused by factors outside school which then lead to inappropriate learning. Clark (1976), through her investigation of young fluent readers, has emphasized the importance of the adult–child interaction in the young child's school-related affective development and educational success. Wilson (1984) explains the importance of an affectionate relationship with caring adults and the relevance of the caring adult's attitude towards achievement and school success.

While attention had previously concentrated on the 2 per cent of the school population within special schools, studies increasingly began to consider a wider spectrum of all pupils with special educational needs in both special and ordinary schools. Swann (1985) identified an increase in children with learning difficulties and those termed maladjusted, and also detected a trend towards the segregation of these children in special schools and special classes in ordinary schools, especially in the younger primary age group.

Swann questions whether this is a result of a greater incidence of learning difficulties and behaviour problems, or a decline in the tolerance of ordinary schools towards learning difficulties and behaviour problems. It is interesting to note that the major reason for referral to a special school was underachievement in reading. Bayliss's (1987) report on Tizard's longitudinal studies of 250 pupils in thirty-three Inner London Education Authority primary schools concludes that, by the end of the top infant year, 39 per cent were identified by teachers as presenting behaviour problems such as aggression, disobedience and lack of concentration. Along similar lines Webb (1967) reports that of the 500 children who attended an infant school over a trial span of six years, eighty had shown behaviour and learning difficulties. There has been an obvious increase in the number of children with behaviour problems from the 1960s to the 1980s and this trend still continues in the 1990s.

This tendency also seems to exist in other European countries. In West Germany, where children must reach a chronological age of 10 years before being classed as 'behaviour disturbed', the maladjusted are (after pupils with learning difficulties) the largest group of children in special education (Bildung and Wissenschaft 1985).

Croll and Moses (1985) in their research into ten local authorities report a 'substantial growth in provision for the maladjusted, which is still continuing' (p. 98). In their enquiry teachers were asked to place pupils in the following three major categories: learning difficulties, behavioural difficulties and health problems. While 18.8 per cent of all pupils were classed as having special educational needs, within this set those deemed to have learning difficulties formed the largest group (81.9 per cent) and behaviour problems the second largest (41.1 per cent). There was also a considerable overlap between categories. 28.1 per cent of special educational needs pupils (and 5.3 per cent of all pupils) had learning *and* behaviour problems; two-thirds of pupils with behaviour and/or health problems had learning difficulties.

Although learning difficulties may be present without behaviour problems, and behaviour difficulties may appear alone, they often co-exist and there may be strong links, in particular, between reading difficulties and behaviour problems.

The association between learning difficulties and behaviour problems was an important element of the Isle of Wight study (Rutter *et al.* 1975) which established that 40 per cent of pupils with anti-social behaviour also had severe reading problems. Studies in the USA have also recognized the association of behaviour with learning success or failure. Lindsay's (1983) findings were that children with more behavioural problems also tended to be children who used less mature learning strategies, and Epstein (1985) revealed a strong pattern of behaviour difficulties amongst learning-disabled boys and girls aged 6–18. In January 1986 *The Journal of Learning Disabilities* published an analysis of parents' reports which stated that parents of pupils with learning problems observed more behaviour problems in their children than normative samples of parents. Similar results were reported by McConaughy (1986) in her work with parents and learning-disabled boys aged 12–16. Evidence from research clearly suggests that a considerable number of children suffer from *both* behaviour difficulties and an apparent inability to learn successfully. While it is not always clear whether the behaviour problem is a cause of, or a reaction to, the learning difficulties, findings consistently point to a strong relationship between the two variables.

THE NATURE OF THE INTERRELATIONSHIP – A QUESTION OF AETIOLOGY?

A study of the literature, although emphasizing the learning difficulty–behaviour difficulty association, also demonstrates its complexity. Some authors believe the learning difficulties to be the cause of behaviour problems, whilst others suggest emotional problems to be responsible for educational failure. Whichever is the cause or effect, once the vicious circle is started it can lead to more severe problems in both areas. The relationship is, in fact, often a reciprocal one. Although there is no consensus on the direction of the cause and effect, the nature and direction of the association are often important to educationalists making decisions about which intervention programme to use.

Where behavioural problems follow educational failure, a remedial skills' programme may be indicated, while when emotional problems are the primary cause, psychotherapy might be more appropriate. Occasions will also arise when *both* types of intervention will be needed. Recent reports concentrate on the effectiveness of a range of different intervention strategies. Most studies have been carried out in the area of difficulties in literacy achievement, this having been established as a major area of learning difficulty. Although a review of the literature presents conflicting findings, research has contributed to a greater understanding which offers a framework for shaping intervention strategies.

Emotional problems as a cause for learning difficulties

The existence of emotional problems as a primary cause of academic under-achievement seems obvious in Axline's (1964) moving description of the boy 'Dibs', who would neither talk nor play and, although a highly intelligent child, was judged to be mentally defective. Inside Dibs was a child 'very capable of intellectual achievement, whose abilities were dominated by his emotional disturbance' (p. 47), who found eventual help from psycho-therapeutic treatment.

The literature shows a large number of writers who hold the belief that problems in the affective domain precede difficulties in the cognitive area. This created a strong emphasis on therapeutic intervention, often to the detriment of academic programmes. The interpretations of the National Child Development Study (Davie *et al.* 1972) suggest that emotional problems frequently existed in young children well before school failure developed. In a similar vein both McMichael (1979) and Stott (1981) share the opinion that it is 'the initial maladjustment which produced the poor learning' (p. 163). Stott's results are based upon screening for behaviour problems of 1, 292 children. They were assessed for six characteristics (timidity, emotional distance, lethargy, hyperactivity, impulsiveness, hostility) on a four-point scale; 20 per cent of children were identified as suffering from faulty learning styles. The behaviour problems of the under-achievers were not greater after a three-year period of schooling than they were prior to such instruction. Pre-instructional behaviour problems were therefore found to be predictive of later under-achievement in reading. Lethargy and hyperactivity had the greatest association with poor reading performance.

The above research has implications for the early identification and resolution of inadequate learning styles in young children, since it demonstrates that early behaviour problems may interfere with cognitive processes required for successful learning. While early identification procedures have been criticized by some writers for their lack of predictive accuracy (Wedell and Lindsay 1980) with respect to future learning failure, Pasternicki (1983) draws attention to their predictive validity for pupils who are likely to have maladjustment and learning difficulties. On a small sample of boys from a community home he discusses how the use of a simple social disadvantage index could have been used to identify them earlier. As prevention is better than cure, the early identification of children at risk of later failure seems a commendable notion. However, as already implied, the predictive validity of many of the screening schedules which purport to do this leaves much to be desired.

Learning difficulties as a cause of emotional problems

While emotional problems might be responsible for school under-achievement in some pupils, it is a common observation that continuous academic failure can lead to behaviour problems. Pupils who lack success in learning often react to failure by non-involvement strategies. Their withdrawal of effort can show in various forms: total lack of motivation and retreat into dullness and laziness, avoidance strategies (such as distraction, fidgeting, day-dreaming) or resistance to the learning task expressed in actions such as antagonistic and aggressive behaviour. Stott (1978) explains these as 'specific anxieties arising from unfortunate learning experiences which block cognitive processes' (p. 148).

While some anxiety can be helpful and motivating in a learning situation, excessive levels can lead to dislike of the particular subject and lowered academic performance. Robinson (1972) contends that 'social maladjustment and even delinquency and crime have been listed as results of the failure to learn to read' (p. 114).

A number of researchers have found evidence to suggest behaviour problems result from educational failure. One of the conclusions of the Isle of Wight study (Rutter *et al.* 1970) was that educational under-achievement can lead to maladjustment. Herbert (1974), Leach and Raybould (1977) and Carlisle (1983) also stress that maladjusted behaviour is often precipitated by difficulties in learning. Ungerleider (1985) presents a detailed case-study of a pupil suffering from dyslexia and describes the growing feeling of contempt, increased school absence and growing behaviour problems. This negative affective outcome of learning failure often becomes the affective entry characteristic in a new learning situation, which makes the question of aetiology within the association difficult to answer.

The link between affective and cognitive development

There is a powerful connection between cognitive and emotional growth. One of the factors in affective development is the child's self-concept. This concept of self is fashioned by the individual's interpretation of feedback on his or her performances from significant others such as parents, peers and teachers. Feedback plays a crucial role for the child in defining his or her self-perception of ability. If the performance is satisfactory, future tasks are likely to be approached with confidence. Consequently the development of the self-concept begins with the feedback the very young child receives from parents during pre-school time and develops further from negative and positive school experiences.

It has been found that under-achievers tend to have a low self-concept, which often results in lack of motivation for cognitive learning. It is important, however, to note that school achievement is influenced by cognitive ability *and* the pupil's perception of those abilities.

Related to the self-concept are pupils' expectations regarding their future performance. Expectations reflect the ways in which pupils predict their own performance level. This in turn depends on previous experience. Self-expectation is therefore learned. It is influenced by parents, teachers and others, who signal their expectations through their interaction with individuals. Research has confirmed that patterns of interaction (e.g. Rosenthal and Jacobsen 1968) are shaped by adults' expectations of the child.

Children therefore develop a set of expectations regarding their future performance, predicting what they are likely, or unlikely, to be able to achieve. This attitude influences their actual performance. Chapman and Boersma (1980), in their study of 162 children, found that children with learning difficulties had developed a different set of affective characteristics in comparison with normally achieving pupils: they had a low self-concept and low expectations of themselves for future performance. They also showed a difference in their locus of control beliefs.

The locus of control concept, developed from Rotter's (1966) social learning theory, refers to the way individuals feel they can control the outcome of events. A person with an internal locus of control belief perceives success or failure as a consequence of his or her own action. In the case of an external locus of control, outcomes appear unrelated to the individual's action and beyond his or her control. Success or failure are attributed to, for example, luck, fate, chance, parents or the teacher. Locus of control beliefs are influential in determining pupils' levels of motivation and efforts. These beliefs have been found to be a useful predictor of achievement; under-achievers often being externally oriented and successful pupils internally oriented. If pupils believe that their own behaviour does not influence academic outcomes, but external factors do, they are likely to be unforthcoming (in terms of effort or persistence) to the point that their apparent laziness might be interpreted as dullness.

Locus of control beliefs are learned. While young children are externally oriented they usually develop towards internality with growing healthy experiences.

It has been shown that the self-concept, self-expectation and locus of control beliefs often determine pupils' responses to, and achievements in, the learning situation. The investigation of these factors has highlighted the close relationship between affective and cognitive performance.

Third-factor variables

Some writers suggest the concept of correlates, drawing attention to the fact that the initial cause of learning and behaviour problems may lie elsewhere outside the relationship.

One possible third factor is serious otitis media ('glue ear'), a middle ear condition which causes a conductive hearing loss and is said to affect 20 per cent of primary children. In 1974, Berman suggested that glue ear may be the cause of behaviour and learning difficulties in a significant number of children. Masters and Marsh (1978) report a relationship between learning disabilities and middle ear pathology. Developments in speech, language, cognitive and social skills depend on a child's ability to hear. For young children recurring otitis media, which is often associated with colds or allergies, can cause developmental delays in all these areas. In many cases it is also undiagnosed, since the child only suffers from the condition intermittently. A report in the *British Medical Journal* (Bax *et al.* 1983) points out the strong relationship between children with middle ear pathology and problems in speech, language and behaviour. Children with a history of otitis media are known to have lower attainments in reading and do less well on verbal IQ tests. Webster (1986), in a case report, argues that early temporary auditory deprivation results in the child's inability to tolerate competition, stress or frustration and thus has a negative effect upon later behaviour.

Other factors (see Chapter 2 for a more comprehensive list) possibly influencing behaviour and learning difficulties include problems in the home, such as lack of care, parents' illness, economic difficulties, divorce or separation of parents, death in the family, ethnic background, poor teaching and poor health.

During recent years, allergic conditions, and their effect upon children's behaviour, have attracted considerable attention in medical and educational circles. It has been suggested by some researchers, and it is a widely held belief now, that some common allergens such as dairy products, artificial flavours, colours and salicylates will cause hyperactivity in some children (Adamow 1982; Crook 1984) which shows in restlessness, inattentiveness, distractability, low frustration tolerance and aggressiveness, all of which may lead to school failure. Diets have proved effective with some children, but also highly structured learning situations with limited time periods for attention have reduced hyperactive behaviour.

Other factors identified as possible causes of behaviour and learning difficulties have been epilepsy (Dreisbach 1982) and diabetes (Sewell 1982). A television programme 'Q.E.D.', 'Your Child's Diet on Trial' (BBC, 20 January 1988), reported on two research projects where vitamin deficiency had been found to be responsible for learning and behaviour problems.

APPROPRIATE PROVISION

Current developments

Research during the past twenty years has steered away from the aetiological aspects and concentrated on intervention strategies for pupils with behaviour and learning difficulties. The focus is now more on educational needs and less on the causality. The findings of these investigations have much direct relevance for the classroom teacher.

Lawrence (1971, 1972, 1975, 1985) has shown how counselling can be used to improve children's reading attainment *and* personal adjustment. From interviews with poor readers he deduced that many of them had a poor self-image. They had unsatisfied emotional needs (not necessarily showing in overt symptoms of maladjustment) which prevented them from learning. To test this hypothesis, Lawrence set up four groups of twelve junior pupils with reading difficulties to examine the differential effects of three types of intervention upon their reading performance. Group 1 received traditional remedial help, group 2 individual counselling, group 3 a combination of remedial help and counselling and group 4 was a control group. After twenty weeks of intervention group 2 showed the greatest improvement in reading performance. While remedial teaching had concentrated on reading skills' development, counselling had paid attention to the child's emotional needs by working on an improved self-image. In his study Lawrence (1975) states:

> Counsellors were asked to establish sincere relationships with each child. The 'emphasis' was on valuing the child . . . changing the child's view of himself and was achieved by giving him self-respect . . . in the company of a person who understood him and enjoyed his company.
>
> (p. 14)

He repeated his experiment with non-professional counsellors (mothers) and achieved similar results. While the majority of pupils seemed to benefit from counselling, Lawrence (1975) warns against regarding this approach as a 'panacea for all ills', stressing that children with specific perceptual difficulties and those who are well adjusted are likely to need a different teaching approach.

In a later investigation Lawrence (1985) carried out therapeutic treatments (counselling and drama) with groups of children of different levels of self-esteem and found that the differences between treatment and results depended on the initial level of self-esteem. He emphasized the matching of treatment to each child's needs and therefore the necessity of assessing the child's self-esteem and warns that 'A therapeutic programme should be considered only after the skills approach has failed' (p. 198). One important finding, however, was that skills' teaching supported by therapeutic treatment produced greater improvement in reading than skills teaching in isolation.

Several studies have since used a counselling approach. Cant and Spackman (1985) describe group counselling carried out by a primary-school class teacher. Gains in measured self-esteem were matched by improvements in reading achievement. Counselling also resulted in a change towards pupils' increased internal locus of control beliefs, so that the pupils increasingly accepted responsibility for their success or failure. Charlton and Brown (1982) are of the opinion that the development of such internality should be an educational goal.

A number of other research enquiries have also demonstrated that counselling programmes which enhance pupils' internal locus of control beliefs can also produce gains in their reading performance.

Charlton (1986) found that of the two therapeutic interventions (operant conditioning and counselling) counselling produced greater increments in pupils' internal locus of control beliefs. In another project (Charlton and Terrell 1987), role play was used as a form of counselling. Pupils were presented with a failure setting and asked to identify and discuss behaviours which effected the failure outcomes, and then suggest – and role play – alternative behaviours which might lead to success outcomes. By encouraging pupils to practise strategies leading to success, internal beliefs were enhanced which then appeared to lead to improvements in reading achievement. Jeffreys (1986) describes how school drama improved the self-image, and motivation, of 15- and 16-year-old boys with learning difficulties and behaviour problems. Similarly, Blanton (1983) used role play and problem-solving exercises for the development of social skills and argues that social skills are essential for academic as well as social success. Research results seem to suggest that a breakdown of emotional resistance is a possible way into the vicious circle in the association between behaviour and learning difficulties and that a true remedial approach has to consider the 'whole child' and not just the development of cognitive skills in isolation (Charlton 1986). Two recent pieces of research have changed the emphasis towards an equal treatment of the affective and cognitive domain. James *et al.* (1991) found that a group of secondary pupils' spelling and reading performance improved through the use of peer counselling. They conclude that:

> pupils experiencing difficulties with their spelling/reading are likely to make greater performance gains where skills instruction is supplemented by counselling help designed to: a) enhance pupils' self-esteem levels and b) inculcate internal locus of control beliefs.

In response to the Elton Report's (DES 1989b) request to provide a whole-school behaviour policy Mosley (1991) recommends the 'Circle Approach' and demonstrates how teachers through this particular form of group discussion are able to 'help children reflect and take responsibility for their learning and behaviour'.

Implications for the teacher

For a long time the concurrent existence of learning difficulties and emotional problems in a substantial proportion of pupils has been ignored. Intervention programmes tended to be geared to one, or the other, of the two areas, usually the one which was most obvious, or disruptive, within a classroom setting for the teacher. Thus children with learning difficulties showing no overt symptoms of emotional maladjustment received remedial education, usually concentrating on skill development (for example phonics) in the area of reading. Pupils with more severe and disruptive behaviour problems would be given therapeutic treatments, often to the neglect of educational programmes.

Mary Wilson (1984) has criticized the lack of emphasis on cognitive growth in the education of maladjusted pupils and comments that 'we generally feel happier talking about aspects of care and treatment than about teaching' (p. 4). She warns that therapeutic treatment should not take precedence over academic work and stresses that 'Motivation and interest can both follow from planned success' (p. 9). Ramasut and Upton (1983) also emphasize that 'attempts to modify behaviour should not be given priority over "good teaching"' (p. 44). Conditions must be created under which successful learning takes place and success is experienced by the pupil. The focus is the teacher's ability and willingness to create a successful learning situation appropriate to the pupil's needs, and the emphasis is on a detailed and carefully structured programme based upon thorough identification and assessment of the learning difficulty. The initial diagnosis should be carried out for the purpose of teaching and therefore be mainly based upon criterion-referenced and curriculum-based assessment to determine the pupil's present level of performance in the identified area of difficulty. The teaching programme can then consist of sufficiently small steps for the pupil to experience success. A behavioural objectives approach (Ainscow and Tweddle 1979) has proved to be successful for some pupils with special educational needs. Continuous assessment is part of the teaching–learning programme, which is best represented in the precision teaching model (Muncey and Williams 1981).

DATAPAC (Daily Teaching and Assessments in Primary Age Children), developed by a group of psychologists at Birmingham University, offers teachers an example of finely sequenced behavioural objective programmes with built-in assessment in the areas of reading, handwriting, spelling and mathematics. Important for the implementation of such programmes are the choice of resources (e.g. the variety of books at pupils' reading interest level) and allocation of time for tasks (according to identified present attention span). Research projects such as 'Reading for pleasure' (1986) by the Educational Publishers Council give information of a general kind and have to be complemented by assessment of individual pupils' reading interest (e.g. Fry's reading interest inventory in Cohen 1978). Individual learning programmes for skill development, the manipulation of the classroom environment and the provision of appropriate materials are important considerations which help enhance motivation. Simmons (1987) argues for a focus on appropriate 'materials, resources and teaching methods, rather than on what is wrong with children' for pupils with learning difficulties and disruptive behaviour. She rejects a deficit approach and draws attention to the 'teacher who is failing'.

The need for a balanced approach, taking account of a range of factors, has become apparent. Jones and Charlton (1989) recommend a 'model for recognition' of special educational needs which encourages a consideration of the total learning context – affective and cognitive – and as a result allows the pupil access to a wider breadth of curriculum experience.

Access to a common curriculum

The introduction of the National Curriculum has made access to a common curriculum a legal requirement for all children. Certain aspects of the National Curriculum could, however, create disadvantages for children with special educational needs. Parker (1989), in an important reminder, identifies possible negative effects of the National Curriculum assessment procedures upon under-achieving pupils' academic self-concept. To avoid this requires sensitivity by teachers.

In the past several writers have drawn attention to the organization of special provision for children with learning difficulties and behaviour problems since this can deny access to a mainstream curriculum (Galloway 1985; Gipps et al. 1987). Remedial groups or classes can carry the stigma associated with extraction and segregation, and their use can be questionable especially where it leads to isolation and labelling. Simmons (1986) draws attention to a pupil's comment that 'I hate working in a small group because I feel small and stupid', and pleads for a shift towards the involvement of *all* teachers and support *within* the classroom. Gray and Noakes (1987) regard segregating pupils as 'taking the easy option'.

The practice of remedial groups and classes is certainly still widely used (Croll and Moses 1985; Gipps *et al.* 1987). A close investigation of an on-site unit for secondary pupils (Bailey and Dinham 1987) revealed a narrow concentration of work in English and mathematics and a lack of access to all eight areas of experience outlined by HMI (DES 1985) in *Curriculum 5–16*. Not only does the organization of such a limited and unbalanced curriculum hinder cognitive development, it may also create social stigma and lead to associated emotional difficulties. Policies and practices within the school are therefore important factors within the education of pupils with learning and behaviour problems. Numerous studies have demonstrated the strong and reciprocal relationship between behavioural and learning problems and no distinction should therefore be necessary in order to provide a separate form of provision.

The use of information technology, as discussed in a very useful article by Hopkins (1991), seems to fulfil these requirements by providing access to the mainstream curriculum and furthering children's academic skills, whilst at the same time proving valuable in enhancing children's self-image.

Pastoral care

Several writers have drawn attention to pastoral care structures within schools (see Chapter 7) and the importance of the pastoral role in the academic progress of children. Sceeny (1987) analyses the current academic–pastoral relationship in secondary schools and suggests the existence of a territorial divide. He pleads for an integration of the two roles and regrets that pastoral care is 'to be concerned with the control of pupils but not with their learning' (p. 67). The non-involvement of the pastoral care staff in the academic progress of pupils, which was regarded as entirely the domain of the academic team, is indicative of the situation in many schools and of approaches within classrooms. The academic staff, on the other hand, do not always accept responsibility in providing for emotional problems. A similar situation presents itself in primary schools where teachers, although aware of behavioural difficulties, do not feel they should, or are equipped to, make appropriate provision for these pupils. Croll and Moses (1985) see the reason for this neglect in the teachers' lack of knowledge of intervention techniques and the belief that problems are mainly rooted in the home.

While individual teaching and a good relationship with the special needs teacher often raises the pupil's self-concept, this approach is more incidental than intentional and systematic, and most teachers, in spite of the contrary evidence from research, believe in the sole development of cognitive skills. While special schools for maladjusted pupils have been criticized for their over-emphasis on therapeutic treatment, mainstream schools receive criticism for their continued concentration on the cognitive aspects. Elias and Maher (1983) use the notion of 'learning factories' and Askew and Thomas (1987) regard this as the reason for difficulties with the reintegration of children with emotional and behavioural difficulties into ordinary schools.

Implications for teacher education

One of the reasons for the unbalanced provision in ordinary schools seems to be that teachers feel their lack of expertise and support in providing appropriately for pupils with learning and behaviour problems (Croll and Moses 1985). In the study by Gipps *et al.* (1987) only 31 per cent of teachers had received any courses on teaching pupils with special educational needs in their initial training.

The EASI Teaching Programme, as discussed by Leo *et al.* (1991), aims to enhance teachers' understanding of self-image and schooling and is a response to the need in teacher training.

Balanced assessment

It has been shown that group counselling, for example, is an effective method, and a relatively easily acquired skill, for class teachers to use to enhance the self-esteem and internal locus of control beliefs which often seem to help to promote academic achievement. However, the assessment of the pupils' behaviour patterns is an essential prerequisite to any intervention, and should be part of a comprehensive diagnosis. Observations as suggested in Figure 4.1 can easily be collated and present useful data for the planning of appropriate provision. In addition, a wide range of inventories and checklists for the assessment of the child's emotional state are available, including:

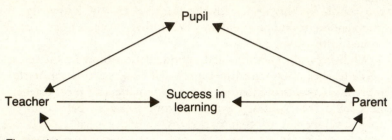

Figure 4.1

- children's behaviour questionnaires
- general self-concept scales
- academic self-concept scales
- anxiety scales
- behaviour problem checklists
- locus of control scales

Assessment lies at the very core of learning and has to consider *all* possible factors, emotional, cognitive and physical, to be embracing and meaningful. As Jones and Charlton (1989) comment: 'The spotlight in this approach shifts from a narrow focus on the child towards a wider beamed examination upon the *total learning context*.'

Usually assessment in school, however, is concerned with purely cognitive aspects; and then norm-referenced tests are most used to measure achievement, mainly in literacy and mathematics areas. Meaningful assessment cannot afford to concentrate on the child's deficiencies but has to evolve from a triangular information source based on the child, the parents and the teacher. On this information a programme can be based. Most important for the modification of self-concept is the pupil's classroom experience. His or her relationship with the teacher and peers forms a source of information about the 'self'. The 'feeding' of the pupil's self-concept with positive, neutral or negative reinforcement can enhance, or block, emotional growth and academic performance.

CONCLUSION

Considering the high incidence of literacy problems amongst learning difficulties and the recognized association between learning difficulties and behavioural problems, little support is given to teachers, with respect to pupils' emotional development, in the relevant literature. In the past very few books intending to give practical help to teachers have dealt with relevant affective variables, but have concentrated on such areas as perceptual problems, phonic skills and comprehension.

This separation of scholastic performance and emotional development is apparent not only in the content of the literature but also in books and journal titles (e.g. *Maladjustment & Therapeutic Education*). Despite the evidence from research the emphasis is mainly on one variable. This has inherent dangers. The division of the cognitive and affective domain is also reflected in the training of teachers. Programmes for initial and in-service training on courses for 'Children with learning difficulties' and others for 'Children with emotional and behaviour problems' often demonstrate this. It is not surprising that this reinforces inadequacies in current educational practice.

One of the few titles campaigning for an integration of the emotional and academic aspects in responding to the needs of children is *Supportive Education* (Bell and Best 1986). In this publication Bell and Best argue against 'the pastoral/academic split' and claim that 'The fact that schools can create divided systems of pastoral and academic (remedial) support is an indication of the degree to which such a division is entrenched in conventional thought and practice' (p. 24). They put forward solutions for an integrated support and concentration on assessment and emphasize the need for teacher awareness.

As has been noted herein some recent publications have suggested a modification in the approach to learning difficulties in order to meet the total range of pupils' needs. Zelan (1991), in an attempt to advise teachers on the diagnosis and treatment of learning problems, views the learning process as deliberate decision making by the child. In making a firm link between emotion and cognition and using Piaget's cognitive-developmental psychology Zelan decides that the non-learning child has either retreated from learning or actively fights it.

Concern for the 'whole child' does not permit compartmentalized thinking but lies in equal consideration of the affective and cognitive domain in both classroom practice and associated research and reference literature. Only by integrating therapy and cognitive skill development into one process of education can we hope to be effective in supporting children with learning and behaviour problems and indeed all pupils.

For the teacher: Question

1 Have you identified the pupil's exact level of performance in the diagnosed areas of difficulty by assessment on a series of finely graded objectives? (Examples in Ainscow and Tweddle 1979.)
2 Have you gained insight into the pupil's learning and problem-solving techniques by observing the pupil's strategies, as well as judging end products? For example, what are the strategies for solving a mathematical problem or dealing with the reading of unfamiliar words (refusal to attempt, ignoring, asking for help, making a wild guess, use of phonic knowledge, using context)?
3 Are you setting tasks at the appropriate level, so that success is achieved, or do you place the pupil under unnecessary pressure by setting tasks too high?
4 Do you give praise and credit for good achievements (even in small and easy tasks)?
5 Do you show a positive attitude in your comments to encourage the pupil?
6 Do you listen to the pupil and guide conversations so that the pupil has an opportunity to talk out any worries and difficulties?
7 Do you know of your pupil's interests and hobbies (choice of reading materials, topics for conversation)?

About the pupil: Observe

1 Does the pupil have a medical condition?
   (a) Has his or her vision/hearing been checked?
   (b) Has he or she any other physical illness/allergy?
   (c) Is he or she on medication?
2 What is the pupil's attitude to school?
3 What is the pupil's attitude to reading/maths/games etc.
   (a) at school?
   (b) outside school/at home?
4 Which reading materials is he or she
   (a) reluctant to read?
   (b) willing to read?
   (c) interested to read?
5 Is the pupil
   (a) lacking motivation?
   (b) often inattentive?
   (c) very quiet, withdrawn (with peers, with adults)?

(d) unsuccessful in most tasks set?
(e) very active, restless?
(f) attempting tasks without interest?
(g) often frustrated – disappointed about lack of success?
(h) wanting a lot of attention from the teacher?
(i) playing the class clown to draw attention?

Symptoms which indicate possible hearing difficulty

1 Frequent lack of response when addressed in a group (often interpreted as laziness or naughtiness).
2 Sudden changes in attention – times of good response interchange with times of no response; this recurs at frequent intervals. (Possible serious otitis media.)
3 Difficulty in following oral instructions.
4 Watching and following actions of other pupils.
5 Defects in speech.
6 Frequent asking for repetition of questions or instructions.
7 Head tilted at an angle.
8 Rushing of words together.

About the home: be aware

1 Are there any problems in the home, such as
  (a) death of parent or relation?
  (b) break up of family home?
  (c) financial difficulties?
  (d) illness?
2 Do parents take a positive and active interest in the pupil?
3 Do parents believe in the child's ability to succeed?
4 Are parental expectations
  (a) too low?
  (b) too high?
5 Are parents prepared to work with the school?

REFERENCES

Adamow, C.L. (1982) 'The nutrition/behaviour link: a review', *Learning Disabilities: an interdisciplinary Journal* 1 (7): 79–92.
Ainscow, M. and Tweddle, D.A. (1979) *Preventing Classroom Failure: An Objectives Approach*, London: Wiley.

Askew, H. and Thomas, D. (1987) 'But I wouldn't want to go back', *British Journal of Special Education* 14 (1): 6–9.

Axline, V. (1964) *Dibs – In Search of Self*, London: Penguin.

Bailey, T. and Dinham, H. (1987) 'Establishing an on-site unit for secondary pupils who are considered to be disruptive in schools', *Support for Learning* 2 (1): 41–7.

Bayliss, S. (1987) 'Black girls flying high in reading and writing', *The Times Educational Supplement*, 3 April, p. 14.

Bax, M., Hart, H. and Jenkins, S. (1983) 'The behaviour, development, and health of the young child: implications for care'. *British Medical Journal* 286 (4 June): 1793–6.

Bell, P. and Best, R. (1986) *Supportive Education – An Integrated Response to Pastoral Care and Special Needs*, Oxford: Blackwell.

Berman, B.A. (1974) 'Hearing loss and allergic management', *Hearing and Speech News* 72: 14–16.

Bildung and Wissenschaft (1985) *Das Sonderschulwesen in der Bundesrepublik Deutschland* Nr. 9–10, West Germany: Inter Nationes.

Blanton, G.H. (1983) 'Social and emotional development of learning disabled children', paper presented at the 20th Annual Convention of the Association for children and adults with learning disabilities, Washington, D.C., 16–19 February.

Bloom, B.S. (1976) *Human Characteristics and School Learning*, Maidenhead: McGraw-Hill.

Cant, R. and Spackman, P. (1985) 'Self-esteem, counselling and educational achievement', *Educational Research* 27 (1): 68–70.

Carlisle, J. (1983) 'Some relationships between behaviour and learning problems', *Links* 9 (1): 10–12.

Chapman, J.W. and Boersma, F.J. (1980) *Affective Correlates of Learning Disabilities*, Lisse Netherlands: Swets & Zeitlinger.

Charlton, T. (1986) 'Differential effects of counselling and operant conditioning interventions upon children's locus of control beliefs', *Psychological Reports* 59: 137–8.

Charlton, T. and Brown, B. (1982) 'Locus of control beliefs and children's academic behaviours; implications for the special class setting'. *Links* 7 (1): 11–15.

Charlton, T. and Terrell, C. (1987) 'Enhancing internal locus of control beliefs through group counselling', *Psychological Reports* 60: 928–30.

Clark, M.M. (1976) *Young Fluent Readers: What Can They Teach Us?* London: Heinemann Educational.

Cohen, L. (1978) *Educational Research in Classrooms and Schools: A Manual of Materials and Methods*, London: Harper & Row.

Croll, P. and Moses, D. (1985) *One in Five: The Assessment and Incidence of Special Educational Needs*, London: Routledge.

Crook, W.G. (1984) 'Yeast can affect behaviour and learning', *Academic Therapy* 19 (5): 517–26.

Davie, R., Butler, N. and Goldstein, H. (1972) *From Birth to Seven*, Harlow: Longman.

DES (1978) *Special Educational Needs* (The Warnock Report), London: HMSO.

—— (1981) *Education Act*, London, HMSO.

—— (1985) *Curriculum 5–16*, London: HMSO.

—— (1989a) *National Curriculum – From Policy to Practice*, London: HMSO.

—— (1989b) *Discipline in Schools* (Elton Report), London: HMSO.

Dreisbach, M. (1982) 'Educational intervention for children with epilepsy: a challenge for collaborative service delivery', *Journal of Special Education* 16 (1): 111–21.

Educational Publishers Council (1986) 'Reading for pleasure: the case for voluntary reading', *Books in the Curriculum*, London: Educational Publishers Council.

Elias, M.J. and Maher, C.A. (1983) 'Social and affective development of children: a programmatic perspective', *Exceptional Children* 49 (4): 339–46.

Epstein, M. (1985) 'Patterns of behaviour problems among the learning disabled', *Learning Disability Quarterly* 8 (2): 123–9.

Galloway, D. (1985) *Schools, Pupils and Special Educational Needs*, Beckenham: Croom Helm.

Gipps, C., Gross, H. and Goldstein, H. (1987) *Warnock's Eighteen Per Cent*, London: Falmer Press.

Gray, P. and Noakes, J. (1987) 'Time to stop taking the easy option', *The Times Educational Supplement*, 10 April, p. 21.

Gulliford, R. (1985) *Teaching Children with Learning Difficulties*, Windsor: NFER-Nelson.

Herbert, M. (1974) *Emotional Problems of Development in Children*, London: Academic Press.

Hopkins, M. (1991) 'The value of information technology for children with emotional and behavioural difficulties', *Maladjustment and Therapeutic Education* 9 (3): 143–51.

Hunter, M. (1982) 'Reading and learning difficulties: relationships and responsibilities', in Hendry, A. (ed.) *Teaching Reading – the Key Issues*, London: Heinemann Educational.

James, J., Charlton, T., Leo, E. and Indoe, D. (1991) 'Using peer counsellors to improve secondary pupils' spelling and reading performance', *Maladjustment and Therapeutic Education* 9 (1): 33–40.

Jeffreys, J. (1986) 'Lessons from the First World War', *British Journal of Special Education* 13 (2): 53–5.

Jones, K. and Charlton, T. (1989) 'Appropriate educational experiences?', *Support for Learning* 4 (1): 53–8.

Lawrence, D. (1971) 'The effects of counselling on retarded readers', *Educational Research* 13 (2): 119–24.

—— (1972) 'Counselling of retarded readers by non-professionals', *Educational Research* 15 (1): 48–54.

—— (1975) 'Remedial reading and counselling', *Reading* 9 (1): 12–17.

—— (1985) 'Improving self-esteem and reading', *Educational Research* 27 (3): 194–9.

Leach, D.J. and Raybould, E.C. (1977) *Learning and Behaviour Difficulties in School*, Wells: Open Books.

Leo, E.L., Charlton, T., James, J. and Indoe, D. (1991) 'Your "self" in school: self-image and academic behaviour', *Links* 17 (1): 18–23.

Lewis, A. (1991) *Primary Special Needs and the National Curriculum*, London: Routledge.

Lindsay, J.D. (1983) 'Paraprofessionals in learning disabilities', *Journal of Learning Disabilities* 16 (8): 473–7.

Masters, L. and Marsh, G.E. (1978) 'Middle ear pathology as a factor in learning disabilities', *Journal of Learning Disabilities* 11: 103–6.

McConaughy, S.H. (1986) 'Social competence and behavioural problems of learning disabled boys aged 12–16', *Journal of Learning Disabilities* 19 (2): 101–6.

McMichael, P. (1979) 'The hen or the egg? Which comes first – antisocial emotional disorders or reading disability?', *British Journal of Educational Psychology* 49: 226–38.

Mosley, J. (1991) 'A circular response to the Elton Report', *Maladjustment and Therapeutic Education* 9 (3): 136–42.

Muncey, J. and Williams, H. (1981) 'Daily evaluation in the classroom', *Special Education: Forward Trend* 8 (3): 31–4.

Parker, B. (1989) 'Self-concept and the National Curriculum: some early observations', *Maladjustment and Therapeutic Education* 7 (3): 189–91.

Pasternicki, J.G. (1983) 'A study of involving use of a social disadvantage index', *Remedial Education* 18 (3): 137–40.

Ramasut, A. and Upton, G. (1983) 'The attainments of maladjusted children', *Remedial Education* 18 (1): 41–4.

Robinson, H. (1972) 'Emotional and personality problems of severely retarded readers', in Reid, J.F. (ed.) *Reading: Problems and Practices*, London: Ward Lock Educational.

Rosenthal, R. and Jacobsen, L. (1968) *Pygmalion in the Classroom*, London: Holt, Rinehart & Winston.

Rotter, J. (1966) 'Generalised expectancies for internal versus external control of reinforcement', *Psychological Monograph* 80 (609).

Rutter, M. and Yule, W. (1972) 'Reading retardation and antisocial behaviour – the nature of the association', in Reid, J.F. (ed.) *Reading: Problems and Practices*, London: Ward Lock Educational.

Rutter, M., Tizard, J. and Whitmore, K. (1970) *Education, Health and Behaviour*, Harlow: Longman.

Rutter, M., Cox, A., Tupling, C., Berger, M. and Yule, W. (1975) 'Attainment and adjustment in two geographical areas', *British Journal of Psychiatry* 126: 493–509.

Sceeny, A. (1987) 'Towards the integration of the pastoral and the academic', *Pastoral Care*, February: 62–7.

Sewell, N.J. (1982) 'Project to explore the possibility of a connection between a family history of Diabetes Mellitus and school learning and/ or behaviour problems in students in Grades 1–8', *Educational Improvement Center – South*, New Jersey.

Simmons, K. (1986) 'Painful extractions', *The Times Educational Supplement*, 17 October, p. 19.

—— (1987) 'Withdrawal symptoms', *The Times Educational Supplement*, 3 April, p. 25.

Stott, D.H. (1978) *Helping Children with Learning Difficulties – A Diagnostic Teaching Approach*, London: Ward Lock Educational.

—— (1981) 'Behaviour disturbance and failure to learn: a study of cause and effect', *Educational Research* 23 (3): 163–72.

Swann, W. (1985) 'Is the integration of children with special needs happening?: an analysis of recent statistics of pupils in special schools', *Oxford Review of Education* 11 (1): 3–16.

Ungerleider, D. (1985) *Reading, Writing and Rage: The Terrible Price Paid by Victims of School Failure*, Rolling Hills Estates, Calif.: Jalmer Press.

Webb, L. (1967) *Children with Special Needs in the Infant School*, Gerrards Cross: Colin Smythe.

Webster, A. (1986) 'Facing the hazards of glue ear', *Special Children* 1: 22–3.

Wedell, K. (1988) 'The National Curriculum and special educational needs', in Lawton, D. and Chittly, C. (eds) *The National Curriculum*, Bedford Way Paper 33, London: Institute of Education.

Wedell, K. and Lindsay, G.A. (1980) 'Early identification procedures: what have we learned?', *Remedial Education* 15 (3): 130–5.

Wilson, M. (1984) 'Why don't they learn?: some thoughts on the relationship between maladjustment and learning difficulties', *Maladjustment and Therapeutic Education* 2 (2): 4–11.

Wragg, E.C., Bennett, S.N. and Carre, C.G. (1989) 'Primary teachers and the National Curriculum', *Research Papers in Education* 4 (3): 17–46.

Zelan, K. (1991) *The Risks of Knowing*, New York: Plenum.

Chapter 5

Understanding interaction
The dynamics of emotional and behavioural difficulties

Graham Upton

A SERIOUS INCIDENT OBSERVED

The following transcript of a brief series of interactions between a teacher and four pupils, and between the pupils themselves, is taken from the observation of a serious incident of disturbance and disruption in a special school for children with emotional and behaviour difficulties.

('P' refers to Pupil; P1 is also referred to as Carl; 'T' refers to Teacher.)

P1: (puts pen down emphatically) I'm not doing this, it's boring.

P4: Yeah, it's boring.

T: (calmly) If you are not on task you are going to lose points. You may get a nought.

(P4 pushing worksheet away, turns to P3 and they begin a conversation.)

P1: (pushing worksheet on floor, fiercely) I don't care. I'm not doing this boring shit work (gets out of seat and makes for the classroom door, which he opens).

T: If you go out of the room, you will get a nought on your contract.

(Teacher gives P1 a stern look, to which he responds with an impish grin, as he stands provocatively, holding the handle of the open door; looking as if he might step out of the room at any time.)

T: Sit down Carl and do your work.

(P1's grin fades to an aggressive scowl, as he moves away from the doorway and begins to roam the classroom with apparent aimlessness.)

T: Sit down Carl, or I'll have to give you a nought.

P1:   Balls!

T: If you're off task, I'll have to give you a nought; you know that.

P1:   Fuck off!

T: Carl, I want you to get on with your work.

P1:   Fuck off you bitch.

(P2 looks up from his work occasionally to see what is going on, but continues to work for the most part. P3 is by turns working and scuffling with P4, who has not resumed working. P3 and P4 stand up as if to fight.)

T: (to P3 and P4) Okay you two, you're off task; that's going to be nought, unless you get back to it.

(P3 and P4 exchange conspiratorial grins. They make as if to square up to one another. They sit down. P4 kicks a chair, sending it loudly spinning across the room. Meanwhile P1 has returned to the door; has opened it, and is hanging out of the doorway into the corridor.)

P1:   I'm fucking off.

T: I've told you, if you go out of the classroom, you're going to get nought on your contract.

P1:   So. If I want to go, I go. You can't stop me.

T: (to P1) If you don't do the work now, you'll have to do it later, at home. (Note that this is an established practice within the school.)

P1:   Fuck off.

(P1 starts to roam the room again. P4 picks up his worksheet, screws it up and throws it. The missile hits P1, who retrieves it and throws it. The teacher is in the line of fire, and is hit.)

P1:   (looking genuinely surprised and apologetic) Sorry Miss! (T gives P1 a stern look. P2, P3 and P4 snigger silently behind the T's back.) I didn't mean to hit you. (P2, P3 and P4 are now seated; apparently working.)

T: Right, that's a nought for you, Carl (writes on a piece of paper).

P1:   That's not fair!

T: What do you expect?

P1:   Fucking cow! Bitch!

(P1 sits down and angrily starts to write on a sheet of paper, which he then violently destroys.)

P1:   I'm not doing it. It's rubbish (scatters torn fragments over the floor).

T: You're just going to have to do it later.

P1:   Fuck off!

(P1 stands up and kicks his chair hard against the wall. He starts to walk around the room again. T deals with a query from P3 about the worksheet. P1 goes over to P4; they start to tussle; this time a little more seriously than before. T interposes herself between them.)

T: (firmly) Stop that!

P4:   (sits down) Give us another worksheet then.

(P1 is still standing in front of the teacher, in a confrontational stance. There is a sense of mockery in the stance, but only just. T walks away from P1. P1 follows, muttering barely audible swear words, the most audible of which is 'fuck'. T does not react. P1 bumps into teacher.)

P3:   Ooh! Carl's going to rape Miss!

(P2 and P4 laugh.)

P1:   (to P3) Fuck off, you cunt! Fuck off!

(There is a loud noise in the corridor. P1 goes to the door and opens it.)

T: (sharply) Don't go out there! I told you . . .

P1:   Fuck off! I'm not staying here! (He leaves the room and does not return.)

(Cooper and Upton 1990: 314–15)

There are many ways in which this incident could be analysed. For example, it could be viewed as a disciplinary problem in which context the pupils' behaviour might be seen as simply unacceptable and conclusions drawn about the need for the imposition of a more severe disciplinary regime. At another level questions could be asked about the relevance of the task which the pupils were being asked to undertake and the general adequacy of curriculum provision in the school; as a result the pupils' behaviour might be seen as being mitigated to some extent by the inappropriateness of the task to their present level of achievement and their educational needs. Equally, the teacher's inflexible use of behavioural management techniques could be criticized given her continued perseverance with the threat of no points for the lesson in the face of the failure of this threat to have any effect on the pupils' behaviour, and a solution to the problem seen in terms of helping her to develop more effective intervention strategies.

It is possible that any or all of the above analyses might prove helpful in creating a more effective learning environment in the classroom, but approaches like this are seen by some as superficial. In this chapter an attempt is made to consider the extent to which the understanding of interactions such as those which are described above (and those which are less severe) can be enhanced by a knowledge of the life histories of the participants and insight into the meaning of the interaction to those individuals. To do this we shall consider in turn the pupils and the teacher and attempt to understand the dynamics of conflictual situations from the viewpoint of the inner world of the individual participants and the interaction which takes place between them.

UNDERSTANDING PUPILS

The depth of feeling which is apparent even in this brief series of classroom interactions suggests that the situation may have arisen because issues within it have greater meaning to the pupils than a literal reading of the transcript would suggest. While the incident begins with Pupil 1 proclaiming that the work is boring it is highly unlikely that these pupils behave in the way they do and display such extreme aggression simply because they have been asked to do something which is boring. An alternative explanation is that the behaviour of these pupils reflects, in some measure, life experiences which have left them at the same time fragile and explosive, unable to tolerate normal levels of frustration and unable to exert the sort of control over their emotional reactions which is commensurate with their age.

Pupil 1, for example, is clearly an extremely unhappy young man whose life as a child may well have been disturbed and disturbing. The dominance of sexual expletives in his language and his extreme reaction to Pupil 3's suggestion that he might be about to rape the teacher could, for example, be indicative of a background of sexual abuse, highlight difficulties which he might be experiencing in establishing his own sexuality or reflect a pattern of physical violence and aggression towards women in his home background. This possibility has been highlighted recently by studies such as those of Conte and Berliner (1987) who found that approximately two-thirds of sexually abused children exhibit symptoms of moderate or severe behavioural and psychological disturbance. Equally, there could be many other factors in his life to date which could explain the pattern of aggressive and violent behaviour which led to his placement in a special school. Hall (1992), for example, draws attention to the potential effects on behaviour in school of parental neglect, chronic ill health, HIV and Aids, while Szur (1987) talks more generally of emotionally abused children who convey a confound sense of 'pain and distress' in their play and interactions with others and talks of teachers who have encountered such children having experienced the force of their pupils' 'humiliation, rage, despair and intensity of mental pain' (Szur 1987).

DYNAMIC PSYCHOTHERAPY

A theoretical basis for trying to understand behaviour in terms of its meaning for the individual and its historical antecedents has been provided by a range of theorists and clinicians whose general approach has been categorized as 'dynamic psychotherapy'. Such people have been concerned with the inner world of feelings and emotions and talk of behavioural difficulties in terms of inner conflict; conflict which may focus on 'dis-ease' or alienation about some aspect of self or dissatisfaction with some aspect of relationships with others. In this context, the behaviour of pupils such as those involved in the interaction above which has led to them being regarded as problems and placed in a special school is seen as a symptom of the distress produced by inner conflict. Such theorists generally also locate the origins of behaviour problems in the emotional experiences of the early years of life and the quality of early relationships. Winnicott (1965), for example, accounts for emotional disturbance and behaviour problems in children in terms of a failure in the infant's environment during the critical period of dependence (i.e. 0–3 years). Tony Charlton and John George explore this in Chapter 2.

To many teachers, dynamic psychotherapy has been seen as too specialized and esoteric to be of relevance to schools and in its pure form this is correct; psychoanalytic training, for example, involves formal training and personal analysis over many years, while psychoanalytic treatment involves daily sessions also normally over several years. The theory is highly sophisticated and its traditional techniques unsuited for classroom application. Nonetheless, some special residential schools (see, for example, Reeves 1983) have constructed therapeutic environments based on the principles of dynamic psychotherapy and it is also possible to utilize the basic principles of the approach in more rudimentary ways than are required in its purest application. Brown and Pedder (1979) provide a most readable summary of psychodynamic thinking and in the course of this discuss the possibility of therapy taking place at levels other than that of in-depth analysis. Within their framework the key to dynamic psychotherapy at whatever level is the quality of the relationship between the 'therapist' and the 'client'. To be effective therapy must focus on the resolution of the inner conflict as well as the internal symptoms expressed in behaviour, and for this to occur the client must feel accepted by the therapist and able to engage in honest and direct communication with him or her. In the context of a deepening relationship it is possible for the troubled individual to gain insight into the links between present events and previous experience. While this sort of relationship is easier to achieve in a carefully controlled clinical setting, Brown and Pedder argue that it can be achieved in a wide range of other contexts and even in quite informal situations; in this sense it is arguable that the principles of dynamic psychotherapy could have relevance to all teachers and all schools.

THE LIFE-SPACE INTERVIEW

A practical application of these ideas on a very basic level was popular in the 1960s under the title of 'life-space interviewing', and anyone interested in pursuing this line of thought will find much in a classic volume by Redl (1966) which has relevance to schools in the 1990s. Redl defined the life-space interview as being appropriate in 'those cases in which the adults find it necessary to surround a youngster's experience at a given time with some form of verbal communication that has the purpose of regulating the impact of this experience on the child' (p. 39). Chapter 10 also explores life-space interviews.

According to Redl, the life-space interview can be used for two main purposes; emotional first aid and the clinical exploitation of life events. Emotional first aid may be appropriate in any crisis situation where the aim is to help the pupil recover from an upsetting incident but where constraints of time or place may dictate that nothing more intensive is possible. Clinical exploitation is relevant when it seems that longer term gains may be made by the pupil from a more in-depth exploration of the issue. Clearly, not all situations in school lend themselves to such exploration and care has to be taken to ensure that the issue which is identified for a life-space interview is, in fact, appropriate – e.g. a potential disciplinary problem is unlikely to be suitable.

Detailed guidance for the conduct of a life-space interview have been provided by a number of authors. The following pointers for the way in which the interview should be conducted are taken from Morse (1969).

1 Make certain, in a non-judgemental and non-threatening way, that the perception of the pupil is clearly expressed and on his or her own terms, distorted though these may seem. Avoid trying to discover the legal truth or who did what first and so on.
2 Test for depth and spread of behaviour – is this an isolated incident or an instance of a recurring problem.
3 Try to discover how the pupil's value system relates to this problem – ask the question 'Well what do you think ought to be done about this?'
4 Highlight reality factors in the school situation which will have implications if the behaviour continues.
5 Explore the pupil's motivation for change – i.e. how might he or she be helped, and what role might the teacher have in supporting subsequent management of the behaviour in question.
6 Develop a follow through plan with the pupil – this must be realistic and relevant and based on an awareness of the school's resources, its willingness to act and its general ethos.

Such steps can provide a useful framework for a teacher to follow in trying to help extremely disturbed pupils, such as those involved in the incident outlined at the beginning of the chapter, but can also help to make even everyday interactions with pupils more therapeutic. More detailed suggestions for the development and use of psychotherapeutic interview skills with children and young people can be found in Copley and Forryan (1987).

Counselling is also an approach which owes much to the psycho-dynamic tradition (although it had its immediate origins in humanistic psychology) and which aims to help pupils cope more adequately with inner conflict. Based on the work of people like Carl Rogers, counselling came to be seen in the 1960s and 1970s as central to the ability of mainstream schools to cope with the diverse emotional problems presented by their pupils, but books such as that of Hamblin (1978) contain many excellent ideas which continue to have relevance in the 1990s. More recently, its principles have been incorporated into general thinking about pastoral care and personal and social education, and teachers interested in developing a greater degree of empathy and understanding with 'difficult' pupils will find much thought-provoking material in books such as those of Best *et al*. (1983) and Galloway (1990). Group work techniques derived from this theoretical background have also significantly influenced therapeutic practice in special schools (see Lennox 1982).

GAINING INSIGHT INTO THE ROLE OF THE TEACHER

It is unusual for any attempt to understand a behavioural incident in school to consider the significance of the life history of the teacher involved. Yet that can be vital. For in the same way as a pupil's behaviour in school may be influenced by other life experiences so too can that of the teacher. In considering teachers' involvement in problematic situations in school their behaviour must be influenced by their present emotional state, by their relationships both within and outside the school and by their personal and social history. In the situation outlined at the beginning of the chapter, why, for example, does the teacher continue to teach in what most might consider to be a most difficult and unrewarding situation? The answer to this question could be a very positive one and reflect a process of mature decision making but, equally, it is important not to deny the possibility of less than praiseworthy motives. There may be things in that teacher's relationships outside school or early life experiences which predispose her to engage in, or even provoke, violent and aggressive relationships; she may be deeply insecure and may be using the situation to satisfy her own emotional needs rather than those of the pupils; she may persevere in the use of a management technique that is clearly ineffective because at some level she does not want the pupils to improve.

To some teachers the suggestion that such consideration should be given to a teacher's personal life may seem offensive and professionally unacceptable. Unfortunately, recent cases of physical and sexual abuse in schools where teachers and other staff have been implicated suggest that such 'collegiality' may be misplaced. Consider, for a moment, how differently the above scenario may be interpreted if it had occurred in a school where, according to a recent newspaper report, a 14-year-old pupil alleged:

> Me and the three other boys used to have sex with one lady on the staff. She used to leave the duty room door open. . . . That meant it was first come, first served.
>
> (*The Observer*, 6 September 1992: 1)

If the teacher described in the above scenario had been the 'lady' referred to in the quotation and the four pupils were the four boys involved in the alleged sexual relationship, the lack of discipline in the class, the sexual innuendo and the bad language would have a very different explanation to any of those suggested above either in relation to the individual pupils or in relation to matters such as the relevance of the learning materials.

ATTITUDES AND VALUES

The role which teachers' attitudes and values may play in the identification and generation of behaviour problems can be equally significant. Teachers frequently differ markedly in their tolerance of behaviour difficulties and it is not uncommon for two teachers in the same school to have very different views about whether or not a pupil is a behaviour problem. This does not mean that one is right and the other is wrong; rather it reflects the different values and attitudes which the individuals hold and the different expectations they have for the behaviour of their pupils. The importance of this is highlighted by the disproportionate number of boys and pupils of ethnic minority origins who are identified as being behaviour problems and referred for special educational placement. Cooper *et al.* (1991), for example, in a survey of special schools and units for pupils with emotional and behavioural difficulties in England and Wales, found an imbalance in gender distribution in these facilities with the boys outnumbering the girls by a ratio of 6:1 and an over-representation of African–Caribbean pupils in relation to the proportion which they represent of the total population of the country by a factor of two. It is possible that these differences reflect 'real' differences in the behaviour of boys and African–Caribbean pupils. However, sociologists such as Hargreaves *et al.* (1975) argue that teachers can develop typologies of students and that even in the very early stages of a pupil's career in school a pupil can be labelled as a deviant. This labelling, they suggest, is often based on assumptions teachers make about pupils and derives less from knowledge of individual pupils than from the associations that particular characteristics of the pupil might have for the teachers. Evidence for this view has been found in a number of research studies. Driver (1981) and Wright (1986) have shown that white teachers often make judgements about African–Caribbean pupils, and boys in particular, which are based on misunderstanding the pupils' culture. Driver showed how teachers often misinterpreted the meaning of black students' body movements, posture and gesture, perceiving sometimes innocent behaviour as oppositional and in some cases mistaking a gesture of respect for one of disrespect. In relation to gender differences Davies (1984) argues that not only do the characteristics of the 'ideal' pupil fit more comfortably with the stereotypical female, but teachers often respond differently to male and female behaviour, tending to be more confrontational to boys than girls.

What is being suggested here is that teachers participate in the social construction of certain forms of deviance and may not be responsive in equal measure to the needs and interests of all pupils. Traditionally teachers work in professional isolation and the dangers of this are that idiosyncrasies and biases of the teacher are not necessarily noticed or monitored in terms of the effect which they have on pupil behaviour or the identification of difficult children. This offers no safeguard to the pupils, parents or colleagues and suggests the need for more careful consideration to be given to the process of how pupils come to be labelled as difficult than is usually the case. The intention here is not to criticize teachers or devalue the achievement of schools in working with difficult pupils but simply to stress the importance of recognizing the role which teachers may play, often unwittingly, in the identification of problem behaviour and the extent to which their interactions with pupils may be influenced by unconscious attitudes and values. Consider again for a moment how the above observational extract might be interpreted differently if the teacher involved was white and the four boys were black; even more so if the teacher was known to have racist tendencies. The aggressive behaviour of the pupils might then appear much more understandable.

SELF-AWARENESS AND STAFF SUPPORT

The practical implications of recognizing the role which teachers may play in the generation and identification of behaviour problems draws attention to the importance of teacher self-awareness but also points to the value of teachers, particularly those working in specialized settings, working within the context of staff support groups. Such groups facilitate the development of different perspectives on difficult situations and help ensure a meta perspective in which the role of the teacher is more easily recognized and monitored. The need for/importance of working in staff groups has been recognized by other professionals and in psychiatry, social work and family therapy, for example, the concept has been widely accepted (see Speed *et al.* 1982). Their potential in schools would appear equally great.

UNDERSTANDING INTERACTION

The introductory observational extract is made more comprehensible by insight into the life histories of the pupils and the teacher and the significance which the situation may have in relation to their values and attitudes as well as their present emotional state. However, it is important to recognize that the extract consists of a series of dynamic interactions which arise from the unique combination of what each of the key players brings to that situation.

The notion that behaviour is most fruitfully understood through the analysis of the interactions in which it occurs has gained considerable support in recent years. The interactive nature of behavioural patterns has been recognized by behavioural theorists (see, for example, Wheldall and Glynn 1989) and humanistically oriented psychotherapists such as Rogers (1951), but distinct 'systemic' theories have been advanced which seek to understand behaviour problems in terms of the interactions of the persons involved, either within the school situation or in related contexts such as the family of the pupil concerned, the staff group, etc.

The theoretical origins of systemic approaches can be traced back to systems theories in physics and biology. Bateson (1972), however, was one of the first to apply this ecological theory to problematic human behaviour, focusing on patterns of communication in families. Subsequently, however, such thinking came to be used as the rationale for the development of 'family therapy' which in recent years has achieved widespread use. There is a growing body of literature indicating the efficacy of family therapy approaches in the treatment of a wide range of emotional and behavioural difficulties (see Burnham (1986) for a general introduction to the theory and practice of family therapy) and recently some family therapists and educationalists have begun to look at behaviour problems in schools as symptomatic of dysfunctions in the family system, in the school system or in the family–school relationship system.

The application of these ideas in schools has been limited;

nonetheless, good examples of their potential do exist. Family therapists working with educationalists (see, for example, Dowling and Osborne 1985) have provided good case-study material to support the effectiveness of intervention based on systemic principles and this type of thinking has had a significant influence on the work of the educational psychologist (see, for example, Campion 1985). American workers (see, for example, Amatea 1989; Molnar and Lindquist 1989), in particular, have provided substantive evidence of their value in dealing with a wide range of school-based behaviour problems, but the ideas have recently come to be used in Britain too (Provis 1992).

THE ECOSYSTEMIC APPROACH

Cooper and Upton (1990) outline the principles of what they describe as the 'ecosystemic' approach to behaviour problems in schools. Within this framework problem behaviour is not seen as originating from within pupils but from within the interaction between pupils themselves and between pupils and their teachers. From the ecosystemic perspective, both pupils and teachers have a rational basis for behaving in the way they do but are often locked in a circular chain of increasingly negative interaction from which neither can readily escape. Thus, in the observational extract given earlier, the more the pupils misbehave, the more negative the teacher becomes, the more negative the teacher becomes, the more the pupils misbehave and so on until the situation becomes irretrievable.

The circular nature of interactional patterns of this kind mean that it is not appropriate to think of them in cause–effect terms; but each can be seen, and indeed is seen by the different parties, as the cause of the other. Whether we *blame* the pupils or their teachers depends on where we decide to *punctuate* the chain of events. Thus, in relation to the observational sequence presented at the beginning of this chapter, the behaviour of Pupil 1 in proclaiming the work to be boring and refusing to do it seems to precipitate the negative sequence of events which then occurred. However, it could be equally appropriate to see the teacher's negative response to that statement as the real cause of the subsequent deterioration of the situation. If the teacher had adopted a less confrontational stance and been more strategic in her response the situation may have been easily defused.

It follows from this that intervention can be effectively achieved at any point in the system. If the pattern of interactions is circular, the circle can be broken at any point and a change in the pupils' behaviour will necessitate change in their teacher's behaviour and vice versa. This, in turn, requires that the contribution made to the interactions surrounding a problem by all parties must be recognized and, in particular, requires teachers to analyse their own behaviour and its relation to the perceived problems. In this context, it would seem that teachers can optimally influence their students by eschewing confrontational approaches and entering into a cooperative relationship with them in which the 'problematic' behaviour is reconstructed in terms which are meaningful to both the pupil and the teacher. In constructing a picture of a problem situation it is necessary for the teacher to establish awareness of his or her interpretation of the situation and to set this against those of others involved. This involves the teacher in a degree of self-analysis in which evidence for the existence of the problem is amassed and scrutinized along with the teacher's behavioural expectations.

REFRAMING

There are many specific ways in which such an approach can be applied in schools but a technique described by Molnar and Lindquist (1989) as 'reframing' illustrates clearly how such principles can be put into practice. This technique is based on four propositions which, in combination, help us move towards a balanced understanding of difficult, yet common, classroom conflicts:

1 in a conflict situation we behave in accordance with our interpretation of that situation;
2 there are often many different but equally valid interpretations of any given situation;
3 if we change our interpretation we can change our behaviour;
4 change in our behaviour will influence the perceptions and behaviours of others, particularly if we break out of a pattern of behaviour which has become predictable.

To illustrate these ideas Molnar and Lindquist use the example of a pupil repeatedly calling out answers in class (pp. 45–6). The common reaction from teachers, according to Molnar and Lindquist, is to consider this behaviour as an inappropriate and unreasonable attempt to get attention. However, it is possible that the pupil may consider it necessary to call out because he or she believes that the teacher tends to ignore him or her. Such perceptions can lead to a vicious circle being perpetuated whereby the pupil and teacher are locked in a repetitive pattern of calling out and ignoring. Reframing in this situation would involve the teacher trying to see the situation differently and on the basis of this perception to change his or her behaviour accordingly and in so doing break the vicious circle that has developed. Thus, if the teacher could reinterpret the pupil's calling out positively as reflecting involvement and interest rather than the existing negative interpretation of attention seeking, then the teacher may see other ways of responding to the pupil than ignoring him or her. Far from being deliberately disruptive, the behaviour is now seen as a sign of keenness to participate and perhaps as even anxiety to please the teacher. Such a positive interpretation frees the teacher to initiate changes in the situation by behaving differently, a change which will, in due course, necessitate a change in the pupil's behaviour.

The approach will not, of course, produce instant results necessarily. Like any strategy, it needs to be considered and developed with full regard to the context in which it is to be applied. It will also need to be given time to work. The pupil will have to be convinced of the genuineness of the teacher's reframing, and be confident that this is not simply an example of teacher sarcasm. Achieving this may involve an act of faith by the teacher and a willingness to persevere beyond the initial trial of the method. When an intervention such as this is successful, however, there can be far-reaching consequences for the quality of the teacher–pupil relationship, which may evolve into a new found realm of co-operation with concomitantly positive effects on the quality of classroom relationships generally, which benefit from the removal of a source of tension.

CONCLUSION

It is the contention of the present author that control and management measures alone are likely to prove inadequate responses to the full range of behavioural problems encountered in schools. Such measures leave little room for consideration of the intra-psychic and dynamic aspects of the complex set of relationships and conflicts which are at work in situations such as those described in the observational sequence which was included at the beginning of the chapter. Hanko (1989) warns that 'unless behaviour management is based on a deeper understanding of anxiety generating disruption, it easily constitutes mere reaction to surface behaviour or turns into control by repression' (p. 140). Writers such as Schostak (1983) and Cronk (1987) have shown that, when we explore the perceptions held by disruptive pupils, we find that they often view their acts of disruption as rational and justifiable responses to the discriminatory and provocative behaviour of teachers. Similarly, research by Hargreaves (1967), Sharp and Green (1975) and Reynolds (1984) shows how teacher behaviour, which may be interpreted by pupils as provocation, is often highly rational when considered from the perspective of the particular assumptions held by teachers concerning their pupils. Such behaviour appears to be more fruitfully understood in terms of the situation in which it occurs and by recognizing that pupil behaviour is often inextricably related to teacher behaviour.

It is hoped that in this chapter the case has been established for teachers attempting to engage in dialogue with pupils who present behaviour difficulties with the aim of helping them gain greater insight into the nature of the difficulties and the reasons for their occurrence. In attempting this it has not been the intention to suggest that teachers should abandon all discipline and take on the role of psychotherapists or family therapists, nor that they should rush out to engage in in-depth exploration of all their pupils' emotional lives. Indeed, an understanding of dynamic processes should foster caution in entering into such relationships with troubled pupils. Rather it has been done with the aim of establishing that the principles of dynamic psychotherapy, family therapy and sociological enquiry can be translated into meaningful and realistic strategies which teachers can use to gain greater insight into their own behaviour and that of their pupils and use this to provide a more supportive and understanding environment for their pupils.

REFERENCES

Amatea, E.S. (1989) *Brief Strategic Intervention for School Behaviour Problems*, San Francisco, Calif.: Jossey-Bass.
Bateson, G. (1972) *Steps to an Ecology of Mind*, New York: Chandler.
Best, R., Ribbins, P., Jarvis, C. and Oddy, D. (1983) *Education and Care*, London: Heinemann.
Brown, D. and Pedder, J. (1979) *Introduction to Psychotherapy*, London: Tavistock.

Burnham, J.B. (1986) *Family Therapy: First Steps Towards a Systemic Approach*, London: Tavistock.

Campion, J. (1985) *The Child in Context: Family Systems Theory in Educational Psychology*, London: Methuen.

Conte, J. and Berliner, L. (1987) 'The impact of sexual abuse on children: clinical findings', in Walker, L. (ed.) *Handbook on Sexual Abuse of Children: Assessment and Treatment Issues*, New York: Springer.

Cooper, P. and Upton, G. (1990) 'An ecosystemic approach to emotional and behavioural difficulties in schools', *Educational Psychology* 10 (4): 301–21.

Cooper, P., Upton, G. and Smith, C. (1991) 'Ethnic minority and gender distribution among staff and pupils in facilities for pupils with emotional and behavioural difficulties in England and Wales', *British Journal of Sociology of Education* 12 (1): 77–94.

Copley, B. and Forryan, B. (1987) *Therapeutic Work with Children and Young People*, London: Robert Royce.

Cronk, K. (1987) *Teacher–Pupil Conflict in Secondary Schools*, London: Falmer.

Davies, L. (1984) *Pupil Power: Deviance and Gender in School*, London: Falmer.

Dowling, E. and Osborne, D. (1985) *The Family and the School: A Joint Systems Approach to Problems with Children*, London: Routledge.

Driver, G. (1981) 'Classroom stress and school achievement: West Indian adolescents and their teachers', in James, A. and Jeffcoate, R. (eds) *The School in the Multicultural Society*, London: Harper & Row.

Galloway, D. (1990) *Pupil Welfare and Counselling*, Harlow: Longman.

Hall, N. (1992) 'Psychological and health related problems', in Gulliford, R. and Upton, G. (eds) *Special Educational Needs*, London: Routledge.

Hamblin, D. (1978) *The Teacher and Counselling*, Oxford: Blackwell.

Hanko, G. (1989) 'After Elton – how to manage disruption', *British Journal of Special Education* 16 (4): 140–3.

Hargreaves, D. (1967) *Social Relations in a Secondary School*, London: Routledge.

Hargreaves, D., Hestor, S. and Mellor, F. (1975) *Deviance in Classrooms*, London: Routledge.

Lennox, D. (1982) *Residential Group Therapy for Children*, London: Tavistock.

Molnar, A. and Lindquist, B. (1989) *Changing Problem Behaviour in Schools*, New York: Jossey-Bass.

Morse, W.C. (1969) 'Training teachers in life space interviewing', in Dupont, H. (ed.) *Educating Emotionally Disturbed Children*, New York: Holt, Rinehart & Winston.

Provis, M. (1992) *Dealing with Difficulty*, London: Hodder & Stoughton.

Redl, F. (1966) *When We Deal With Children*, New York: Free Press.

Reeves, C. (1983) 'Maladjustment: psychodynamic theory and the role of therapeutic education in a residential setting', *Maladjustment and Therapeutic Education* 1 (2): 25–31.

Reynolds, D. (1984) 'The school for vandals: a sociological portrait of the disaffection prone school', in Frude, N. and Gault, H. (eds) *Disruptive Behaviour in Schools*, Chichester: Wiley.

Rogers, C. (1951) *Client Centred Therapy*, Boston, Mass.: Houghton Mifflin.

Sharp, R. and Green, A. (1975) *Education and Social Control*, London: Routledge.

Schostak, J. (1983) *Maladjusted Schooling*, London: Falmer.

Speed, B., Seligman, P., Kingston, P. and Cade, B. (1982) 'A team approach to therapy', *Journal of Family Therapy* 4 (3): 271–84.

Szur, R. (1987) 'Emotional abuse and neglect', in Maher, P. (ed.) *Child Abuse: The Educational Perspective*, Oxford: Blackwell.

Wheldall, K. and Glynn, T. (1989) *Effective Classroom Learning*, Oxford: Blackwell.

Winnicott, D.W. (1965) *The Maturational Process and the Facilitating Environment*, London: Hogarth Press.

Wright, C. (1986) 'School processes: an ethnographic study', in Eggleston, J., Dunn, D. and Anjali, M. (eds) *Education for Some: The Educational and Vocational Experience of 15–18 Year Old Members of Minority Ethnic Groups*, Stoke-on-Trent: Trentham Books.

Chapter 6

Behavioural approaches

John Presland

BEHAVIOURISTIC, HUMANISTIC, BEHAVIOURAL?

Behavioural approaches to problem behaviour can be thought of as arising from a combination of two broad theoretical standpoints – the behaviouristic and the humanistic. However, each of these terms stands for a family of approaches, and it is doubtful whether any living member of either family fully satisfies the criteria for either label. Intermediate positions are much more common.

THE BEHAVIOURISTIC STANDPOINT

The behaviouristic standpoint concentrates on specific observable behaviours, rather than on what is going on inside people's heads. These behaviours are seen as being determined largely by the person's environment. The approach to helping overcome problem behaviour would, accordingly, be:

1 to describe the problem behaviours as specifically and objectively as possible;
2 to draw up a plan to change the behaviours in directions felt to be more desirable;
3 to base this plan on knowledge and theories derived from scientific study of behaviour (mainly theories of learning) which are assumed to apply to people in general.

Reviews of early work of this kind carried out in education are provided by Altman and Linton (1971), Hanley (1970) and O'Leary and Drabman (1971). One of the early studies (Madsen *et al.* 1968) illustrates the kind of intervention with school pupils which came nearest to conforming to the label 'behaviouristic'.

	Action	Outcome
Week 1 Week 2	Observers recorded behaviour	Misbehaviour frequent
Week 3 Week 4	Teacher explained and reviewed rules	Misbehaviour still frequent
Week 5	Rules continued and misbehaviour ignored	Misbehaviour increased
Week 6 Week 7	Rules and ignoring continued and smiles or praise given for following rules	Misbehaviour decreased greatly – far less than in weeks 1–3
Week 8 Week 9	Rules, ignoring and praise discontinued	Misbehaviour increased again
Week 10 Week 11 Week 12	Rules, ignoring and praise and smiles reinstated	Misbehaviour decreased even more than in weeks 6–7

Figure 6.1

Madsen's study (whose main stages are illustrated in Figure 6.1) was with three young children in a mainstream school, one of whom was called Cliff, a boy of about 7 in a class of twenty-one children. Cliff would sit through entire work periods fiddling with objects in his desk, talking, doing nothing or misbehaving by bothering others and walking around the room. He had recently started hitting other children for no reason. His teacher said she was unable to motivate him into working on any task during the regular work periods, but that when kept in to do it at playtime, he would complete it quickly and accurately. The specially trained experimental observers who went into the classroom to record his behaviour for three twenty-minute periods each week confirmed the teacher's observation and described a whole range of silly behaviour apparently designed to draw attention to himself. The observers had instructions to record a number of very specifically defined inappropriate behaviours, such as getting out of his seat, standing up, tapping his pencil or other object, knocking his neighbours' books off the desk, kicking, talking when not permitted, whistling, turning round or ignoring a question from his teacher.

After six periods of the above observations, the teacher was asked to make a set of rules about behaviour very clear to the class, so that they knew exactly how she wanted them to behave, and to review them several times a day. Nearly two weeks later, the teacher was asked to continue this use of rules, but also systematically to ignore all misbehaviour (unless a child was being hurt). This was because commenting on misbehaviour, or even punishing it, is a form of attention and, as such, could encourage repetition of the behaviour. After a few days, the teacher was asked to continue with the rules and ignoring, but also to praise or smile at Cliff whenever he engaged in behaviour which followed the rules (such behaviour being made very specific for the teacher). The aim was to increase the frequency of this appropriate behaviour and, since it is difficult to behave and misbehave at the same time, also decrease the frequency of the inappropriate behaviour. After two to three weeks of this approach, there was a return to the handling before the intervention (no rules, ignoring or praise) for a week or so, and then about a month during which rules, ignoring and praise were again systematically used.

Careful measurements were kept of the rates of inappropriate behaviour during the various experimental manipulations. These indicated that:

1 the rules on their own had little effect;
2 ignoring the misbehaviour led to its increasing;
3 when these measures were accompanied by regular praise and attention for appropriate behaviour there was a striking decrease in the misbehaviour from the original (baseline) level;
4 when the baseline conditions were reintroduced, the rate went up again, but fell even more dramatically when the full programme was reintroduced.

Statistical tests indicated reasonable grounds for confidence that the differences were real, rather than due to 'chance'. It seemed fair to conclude that the systematic use of praise and attention as a consequence of appropriate behaviours increased the rate of these behaviours, so that they took the place of the inappropriate ones (which were ignored), which thus became less frequent.

THE HUMANISTIC STANDPOINT

The humanistic standpoint places emphasis on the individual person and the 'self'. Each person has to be understood as a whole – not split into specific behaviours or other elements – and is unique. Generalizations about human beings cannot be applied. The person is responsible for his or her behaviour – not the environment. Where there is problem behaviour, the resulting approach is:

1 to describe the problem, not as something in itself, but in terms of its meaning to the person;
2 to help the individual to come to a better understanding of 'self' and the overall direction of his or her life and potential for growth;
3 to help the individual realize this direction and potential by his or her own decisions and effort, rather than overcome specific behaviours or adapt to particular environments.

There has been little clear application of humanistic approaches within the classroom but the client-centred therapy of Carl Rogers (1951, 1974) is a humanistic approach which has been most influential from outside. Visser (1983) gives a brief account of it, along with a number of other humanistic approaches. Rogers stresses the self and its constant striving to improve or sustain itself by moving towards greater independence or self responsibility and away from control by external forces. A well-adjusted person has a view of himself or herself which relates satisfactorily to that person's view of the world. It follows that, to help somebody, it is necessary to try to see the world from that person's point of view. The therapist must try to develop:

1 *empathy* – sensitivity to the client's feelings and the ability to communicate these back to the client to show that they have been understood;
2 *warmth* – accepting the person and the person's experience as valuable, without imposing conditions or making judgements;
3 *genuineness* – responding to the client sincerely, in a way that is the therapist's real self, rather than a professional façade.

In describing specific techniques, Rogers makes much of listening techniques. The client is asked to talk rather than be bombarded with questions, such questions as are asked need to be open-ended so that yes or no answers are not possible, and the therapist has to demonstrate interest and understanding by 'interested noises' and paraphrasing what the client says to show that it is understood. The therapist may need to talk about his or her own feelings and experiences in a self-revealing way to provide an example for the client. Other specific techniques are described for exploring the client's revelations and resolving problems arising from them.

THE BEHAVIOURAL STANDPOINT

'Behavioural' is another broad label covering a family of approaches. British accounts include Cheesman and Watts (1985), Presland (1989) and Wheldall and Merrett (1984). Behavioural approaches, as recommended by leading authorities, follow the behaviourist line in their emphasis on specific observable behaviour and its objective description, in their strong emphasis on environmental determinants of behaviour and in their emphasis on scientific findings. The experimental rigour is, indeed, now commonly stepped up from a means of measuring the effects of the intervention to a part of the intervention itself. There are constant assertions that the behaviours being changed should be measured before, during and after intervention procedures, so that the effects of those procedures can be evaluated and further measures based upon the evaluation.

Behavioural approaches follow the humanistic line in a number of respects. First, there is considerable emphasis on studying each individual and the precise ways in which the individual and environment interact. Second, the specific behaviours involved can be verbal reports of thoughts and feelings, including descriptions of how the person views himself or herself and the world. Third, the individual is encouraged to participate in decisions about the direction of change and the methods to be used and to play an active part in the activities required. The person's views about his or her 'self' and how he or she would like it to change will clearly be relevant here.

In practice in schools, behavioural approaches tend to concentrate on changing observable behaviour. This is not inevitable. Such approaches have been used to change thoughts and feelings – but not to any extent in school situations. The bias towards behaviour stems from the nature of schools. The teacher is relating to a group of pupils rather than to individuals. Each member of the group is an individual with individual needs and wishes – and so is the teacher. While it is important to consider the needs of an individual who is behaving in unfortunate ways, it is also important to consider other pupils. The teacher also, as an individual human being, may find his or her own needs and wishes thwarted by the pupil's behaviour and consider that to be a sufficient reason for planning to change the behaviour.

In this complex situation, behavioural approaches may be 'humanistic' from a number of different perspectives.

1 The pupil may wish to change. Teacher and pupil may then plan together to decide which behaviours to change, how to go about it and how to evaluate results.
2 The behaviour may need to be changed for the sake of other pupils. There may then be negotiation between teacher and pupil, possibly involving other pupils too and an agreed plan may be formulated. If the negotiation fails, a teacher may feel the need to impose an intervention.
3 The behaviour may need to be changed for the sake of the teacher. Again, the intervention may be either negotiated or imposed.
4 A teacher may believe that the behaviour needs to be changed for the individual pupil's sake but the pupil may not agree. Negotiation might still be attempted, but if this fails, an intervention may be imposed.

THE BASIS OF A BEHAVIOURAL INTERVENTION

Despite the varied perspectives outlined, behavioural interventions have a number of common features, and the same systematic sequence can usually be followed for their implementation. For fuller accounts of the range of possibilities, the reader is referred to the British texts mentioned earlier.

The sequence to be described is based on the ABC analysis or behavioural analysis. This starts from the assumption that a behaviour occurs because of the circumstances and events occurring around the same time. Thus, if Sarah regularly hits Dawn in class, it is because of events that occur shortly before the hitting, shortly after it, or both. It may be that she hits Dawn when Dawn accidentally knocks her arm. It is also possible that whenever she hits Dawn other members of the class laugh and she likes this attention and so repeats the hitting either immediately or at another time. The third possibility is that the knocking precipitates the hitting *and* the laughing increases the likelihood of her responding to being poked in the same way in the future. These events are examples of three elements in what has become known as the ABC approach – *antecedents*, which make the behaviour more likely to occur, the *behaviour* itself and the *consequences* which make it more likely to occur again. The sequence is represented in Figure 6.2. If these events occur regularly, then hitting Dawn becomes an established habit which may persist even if Sarah is punished for doing it.

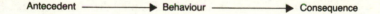

Antecedent ⟶ Behaviour ⟶ Consequence

(e.g. Dawn knocks Sarah)   (e.g. Sarah hits Dawn)   (e.g. other pupils laugh)

Figure 6.2

A behavioural approach assumes that, if a problem behaviour occurs because of particular antecedents and consequences, it can be made to occur less by changing those conditions. In Sarah's case, we might change the antecedent by removing Dawn to another part of the room, or we might change the consequence by persuading the class to ignore the hitting. Another approach would be to identify some behaviour that we wanted Sarah to engage in other than hitting, and to set up antecedents and consequences to make that habitual instead. We might, for instance, try to get Sarah to continue with her work when knocked, ignoring the knocking totally. We could remind her of this at intervals as an antecedent, and praise her whenever she ignores being knocked as a consequence. If this happens regularly, ignoring being knocked might become the new habit.

THE STAGES IN A BEHAVIOURAL INTERVENTION

A behavioural intervention can be divided into stages based on the concepts described above. The most common sequence is as follows.

Defining the problem

A written list is made of behaviours of a particular pupil which need decreasing because they are a problem. Then a further list is written of behaviours that need to be increased. This may be because their low frequency is a problem in itself, as with a child reluctant to speak to anyone. Alternatively, it may be that we wish a particular appropriate behaviour to replace a problem behaviour. When the lists are made, priorities for change need to be established, so that we choose one behaviour or a relatively small number of behaviours to work on first. Behaviours should normally be described very specifically (e.g. Sarah hits Dawn), rather than in generalized terms (e.g. Sarah is aggressive), so that it is clear exactly what the pupil does that is a problem. Wherever possible, the pupil should be involved in these identification and definition processes. He or she could be asked to suggest behaviours which need to increase or decrease and to contribute to the decision on which behaviours should be changed first.

Measuring the problem

It is usual to carry out some kind of observation and measuring procedure. First, this can confirm (or deny) that the problem is serious enough to justify the time and effort required to change it. Second, it provides a *baseline* with which similar measures after intervention can be compared to give an accurate, objective demonstration of how much change has occurred. It is most usual to count the number of instances of a behaviour, but other measures are also possible, for instance the amount of time a behaviour takes up. There is much to be said for having pupils measure their own behaviour, and this has been shown to be feasible.

Determining existing antecedents and consequences for a problem behaviour

The above two steps have concentrated on identifying the *behaviour* element in the ABC analysis of problem behaviours. It is now necessary to carry out observations to identify the circumstances or events that occur immediately before and immediately after this behaviour. Those that occur regularly could well be antecedents and consequences promoting the behaviour and therefore in need of changing. Pupils could themselves contribute to identifying these influences.

Deciding what changes to make in antecedents and consequences

If antecedents and consequences promoting a problem behaviour have been identified it could be helpful to remove or minimize them, as suggested earlier for Sarah hitting Dawn. Sometimes, in addition or instead, new antecedents and consequences are used to decrease the behaviour – a warning of some sanction could be an antecedent and the sanction itself would be a consequence.

A more common practice is to work on the appropriate behaviour that has been identified for increasing. Antecedents and consequences need to be identified that will make that behaviour more likely to occur – as suggested for Sarah getting on with her work instead of hitting Dawn.

How, though, are these new antecedents and consequences identified? Here, it must be said that the use of antecedents in behavioural approaches is in its infancy. It is rarely described in published studies and there are no established methods for identifying those most likely to succeed. However, some antecedents are clearly likely to be helpful. Instructions as to how to behave, and regular reminders, are obvious examples. Giving the pupil work that brings success, or which is enjoyable, is also likely to promote appropriate behaviour. The teacher's knowledge of an individual pupil will obviously help, and the pupil could also make suggestions.

The most common device is the use of consequences which make appropriate behaviour more likely to occur. This process is known as *reinforcement*. The consequence which has this effect is called a *reinforcer* and the behaviour which increases is said to be *reinforced*. Problem behaviour can be reinforced, as Sarah's hitting was by the laughter of other pupils. For a behavioural programme, however, we need to identify reinforcers that will increase appropriate behaviour. There are many possibilities. Most children's appropriate behaviour is reinforced by the approval and attention of adults – or, indeed, by their own success at work or in relating to others. Some children, however, are not easily motivated in these ways and, at first, will respond only to more primitive measures. Some may be influenced most by material rewards, such as sweets, toys, trinkets or money. Others may react best to being allowed to participate in certain actions, such as a favourite lesson or kind of work, 'free activity', popular group activities or classroom jobs. Pupils of secondary age are most likely to be influenced by prizes, free time and other privileges, good marks (which might be given for behaviour as well as for work), favourable reports and letters home and success for a team or house. Praise also means more at this stage than is commonly supposed, though it can misfire if used with some pupils in front of peers.

Perhaps the most obvious way of discovering effective reinforcers is to ask the pupil what he or she likes. If this is not particularly revealing, parents, friends and other teachers might be asked to make suggestions. Watching the pupil can be helpful – any activity carried out at all frequently when a pupil is left to his or her own devices might be effective as a reinforcer.

When enough possibilities have been collected, they could be discussed with the pupil and an agreement reached on which could be used as 'rewards' for the behaviour required.

Planning and implementing a programme

From the information gathered so far, an intervention programme can be planned, preferably negotiated with the pupil. Basically, it should be designed to present systematically to the pupil a pattern of antecedents and consequences that will make problem behaviours occur less and appropriate behaviours occur more. To achieve this, it should specify:

- the behaviours to be worked on
- the antecedents and consequences selected
- the precise ways in which the antecedents and consequences are to be used
- when and where the programme will be carried out

- how the programme is to be introduced to the pupil
- how the pupil is to be involved in its execution

Identifying the behaviour and selecting antecedents and consequences have already been described. How should the antecedents and consequences be used? At first, it is probably wise to use the planned antecedent whenever a particular appropriate behaviour is required or a particular problem behaviour anticipated. Similarly, an appropriate behaviour should be reinforced either every time it occurs or every time it has occurred for a pre-determined period of time (say one minute). An alternative is to reinforce the pupil every time he or she has *not* engaged in a problem behaviour for a pre-determined period – one is, as it were, reinforcing any kind of behaviour *other than* the defined problem behaviour. Sarah, for instance, could be reinforced whenever she lasts five minutes without hitting Dawn.

A commonly used device for delivering reinforcers is through a *token system*. Here, points, gummed paper stars or other 'tokens' can be the immediate reinforcers. When a pre-determined number of tokens has been won, they can be exchanged for a more meaningful reinforcer, such as being allowed to choose an activity.

Programmes do not necessarily need to be planned to operate full-time. Often, they are used for a short period each day to begin with and extended to other times later if necessary.

It is usual to write down the programme planned. Sometimes, this is in the form of a contract signed by teacher and pupil – examples are provided by Fletcher and Presland (1990) and Harlatt (1989). Whatever the format, the programme should then be implemented exactly as written down. Consistency is most important – even if there is no obvious change in behaviour, the programme should usually be adhered to for two or three weeks before considering changes in design.

Throughout the period of implementation, the measuring procedures carried out before the intervention programme was introduced should continue in exactly the same form, so that valid 'before and after' comparisons can be made.

Further action

The measuring procedures, combined with the teacher's and pupil's own impressions, will allow a judgement to be made on how successful the programme has been. If the behaviour has improved, the programme may well be phased out. This is best done gradually, since abandoning it suddenly is more likely to lead to the return of the problem behaviour. Antecedents and consequences are therefore usually faded out gradually, until eventually only those that can be seen as a part of normal existence are left – for instance, occasional praise and privileges.

An alternative, particularly where the behaviour tackled by the programme has been the first step towards a larger change or a series of changes, is to transfer the programme to a new behaviour. This, too, can be faded out gradually when improvement has been obtained.

If the programme does not change behaviour sufficiently, then replanning is needed. Each element of the programme needs to be examined in turn and changes made which are thought likely to lead to greater effectiveness. Different antecedents or consequences may be needed, or changes may be required in the precise ways they are used, in the times of day the programme is implemented, and so on.

As with other stages, discussion and negotiation with the pupil are needed, in the hope of reaching agreed decisions.

Throughout the above stages, the pupil's involvement in planning and implementation has been constantly stressed. It is important that this is more than lip-service. Serious attempts must be made to discover what the pupil really thinks and wants. This may be difficult if the pupil is reticent or feels a need to deceive the teacher. The various skills involved in counselling, briefly introduced earlier, should be helpful in establishing the kind of relationship and forms of communication necessary to achieve these objectives. They are more fully described by Munro *et al.* (1983, 1989).

To show how the stages of implementation can operate in practice, two examples will now be described, one from a primary school and one from a secondary school. Both were carried out by teachers as a result of attending a workshop organized by the author. Teachers were asked to plan and report back on a behavioural programme as part of the workshop activities.

TERRY – A PRIMARY-SCHOOL PUPIL

Terry was a 9 year old in a primary-school class. His teacher, Miss M., reported that he was 'naughty' in so many ways that it was 'a full-time job' to write down all his misdeeds. When asked to list

very specifically the behaviours she wanted to decrease, she identified the following: irritating other children by physical interference
with them, talking to them and name-calling; moving around the
classroom at times when he is supposed to be working at a desk;
fidgeting and playing with things in the classroom; crossing out
large amounts of work and throwing away work; sulking when
asked to do things he did not want to do; and grinning insolently
if reprimanded. The appropriate behaviours which Miss M. wanted
to increase were: actively working on the task given; accepting
correction without fuss; remaining quiet while the teacher is
addressing the class; and sitting in one place for a reasonable period
of time. The behaviours selected from these as priorities to work
on were interfering with other children and its more appropriate
alternative of remaining in his seat and working.

Miss M. opted to measure Terry's behaviour during a half-hour
period each morning when the class was working at Maths or
English. She noted each incident of interfering with other children
and then collated the records to find the number of such incidents
per period.

No antecedents for the problem behaviour were identified, but
it did appear as though consequences maintaining it included
attention from other pupils – particularly their telling Miss M.
about his problem behaviour and retaliating when he interfered
with them.

Miss M. now began to think about what changes in antecedents
and consequences would be helpful. First, it could be helpful to
reduce the consequences thought to be reinforcing the problem
behaviour. The rest of the class could, for instance, be asked to
ignore the behaviour rather than reporting it to Miss M. or
retaliating. Second, new antecedents and consequences could be
introduced to make appropriate behaviour more likely to occur. As
an antecedent, Terry could be given explanations of the kinds of
behaviour required of him. In determining consequences, Miss M.
first listed possible reinforcers. These were: praise from Miss M.;
showing the headteacher good work; tokens; playing a specific
video game; playing scrabble; money; and having something from
a 'bootie bag'. In drawing up this list, both Terry and his parents
were consulted. Terry, for instance, mentioned the video game,
scrabble and the bootie bag, and it was discovered that money was
frequently used as a reward at home. Terry also asked if he could
have extra Maths or Science or be allowed to read as a reward, but

Miss M. was doubtful about how effective this would be. From these possibilities, Miss M. selected playing the video game, but decided to implement it through the use of tokens.

In working out the programme, Miss M. consulted both Terry and the rest of the class, and their comments contributed to its design. This was appropriate because Terry's difficult behaviour was a problem for the class as a whole, rather than just for him. Furthermore, Miss M. wanted to ensure that the rest of the class understood and were involved in the programme and were keen to help with it. The final form was based on dividing the day into four sessions. During each session, Terry was to be reinforced for every ten-minute period he remained in his seat working without interfering with other children. If he was able to do this, he was to stick a star on a chart. If he gained four stars during a session, he could complete that session by playing with his video TV game with another member of the class. The other pupils were asked, as far as possible, not to retaliate if he did interfere with them, and not to tell Miss M. about his behaviour until the end of the ten-minute period. When that period ended, there was a discussion with the class to establish if he had earned the star.

During the operation of the programme, there was further consultation with the class and, even though it was working well, modifications were made in response to their views. They felt that too much was expected of Terry because he was required to behave better than other members of the class. For instance, if one of the other children 'pinched' a friend's pencil for a joke they would not necessarily be punished, but if Terry did it during the programme he probably would not get his star, which they thought was a punishment. They were therefore involved in making a more democratic decision about whether he had earned the star or not. This change was introduced after about a week. Another change at this time was to cut down the programme to only the first three of the four daily sessions.

Measuring continued during the programme, but was implemented throughout the whole period of the programme. Strictly speaking, it should have been for half an hour per day as during the baseline period, but fortunately the change did not prevent the results being helpful in evaluation. During the eight baseline measuring sessions, the number of incidents of interfering with other children per daily half-hour period ranged from two to six, with an average of 4.1. During the programme, the incidence occurrence was measured per one-hour session, but, despite this longer period of opportunity to misbehave, the incidents per hour over fifteen days ranged from zero to three, with an average of fractionally less than one. Miss M. concluded that Terry's behaviour had improved and was somewhat better even at times when the programme was not in operation. She decided to discontinue the programme to see if the improved behaviour was maintained without it. When she did this, she felt that his behaviour did deteriorate slightly but was still better than before the programme was implemented. She felt that her relationship with Terry had improved as a result of what had happened and that the rest of the class were more understanding towards his problem.

MIKE – A SECONDARY-SCHOOL PUPIL

Mike was a 13-year-old boy in the second year of a comprehensive school. He was in the 'remedial' band and was generally regarded as a 'pain to everybody'. Miss T. taught him French for four half-hour periods per week. She identified the following behaviours to reduce: shouting out comments persistently without raising his hand when the class was working or the teacher was talking; asking silly questions to get attention; moving from his seat without permission; doing minimum work; leaving the classroom when the bell went before being dismissed; and delaying the start of lessons by engaging the teacher in conversation usually designed to shock her. Behaviours Miss T. wanted to increase were: putting up his hand before talking and waiting for the teacher to ask for his contribution; asking questions relevant to the lessons; staying in his seat until given permission to leave the room or borrow something from a friend; getting on with his work without delay; producing work to the best of his ability; and going straight to his seat when he arrived at the lesson.

Misbehaviour in the class was not restricted to Mike, and it looked as though the behaviour of class members generally might provide antecedents which helped set off problem behaviour in others, including Mike. If one pupil talked to or threw something at another when they were supposed to be working, this could result in similar behaviour from the recipient. It also seemed very likely that the attention of other pupils to each individual's misbehaviour provided consequences which reinforced it. Possibly, Miss T.'s attending to the behaviours was also reinforcing.

Miss T. began by thinking in terms of an individual programme for Mike, and she measured some of his behaviours and discussed with him the kinds of reinforcers which might be used. However, she eventually concluded that it would be better to institute a programme for the class as a whole. This was done in discussion with the class. In this discussion, they made it clear that they preferred to be rewarded for good behaviour and work rather than punished for unsatisfactory work or behaviour. A system was therefore worked out by Miss T. in consultation with the class.

The system needed to be related in a number of ways to the likely antecedents and consequences maintaining problem behaviour. Means had to be found whereby pupils did not provoke misbehaviour in each other and did not reinforce each other's misbehaviour. It was also important that Miss T. did not reinforce problem behaviour with her attention. Ideally, pupils should influence each other to, and reinforce each other for, appropriate behaviours, which also needed to be reinforced by Miss T.'s attention.

To these ends, the class was divided into two teams subjectively matched for bad and good behaviour and academic performance, trying to keep friends together but splitting 'nuisances' who might otherwise encourage one another in their misbehaviour. For the whole of all four periods, the pupils could win points for their team as follows:

- answering questions correctly during a five-minute quiz time at the end of each period gets one team point for each correct answer
- getting eight out of ten or better for work gets one team point; full marks gets two team points

Team points could also be lost for 'bad' behaviour such as talking without putting a hand up, moving from a seat without permission, distracting others, throwing things across the room and putting feet on chairs and tables. One team point was deducted for each instance. Each team started with twenty points at the beginning of the week. At the end of the week the team with most points was deemed to have won, unless their total was under fifteen points in which case nobody had won. Each member of the winning team was given a sweet at the end of the week. Any pupil who lost three points for the team during a lesson was excluded from the game for that lesson and sent outside the room into the corridor. This device, agreed by the class as a whole, meant that the pupil was deprived of any reinforcement available within the classroom for the misbehaviour.

To relate the above programme more specifically to changes in antecedents and consequences, the system was explained as a game which would make the pupils work harder, behave better and get recognition by Miss T. and the rest of the class. Miss T. tried, also, to ignore bad behaviour and simply take a team point off with the minimum of telling off.

Unfortunately, there were no measuring procedures that were particularly helpful for the evaluation of this programme. Measurement of Mike's behaviour was discontinued when the programme began. During the programme, Miss T. kept records of the points won by each team during the first two weeks, but these were not particularly revealing. In the first week team 1 won 74½ points and team 2 won 83½. In the second week, team 1 won 100 points and team 2 won 60. It looked as though team 1 improved greatly. However, team 2 gave up towards the end of the second week as they saw their chance of winning disappearing, so it is hard to say, on the basis of these records alone, whether they were improving or not. Miss T.'s own views, after these first two weeks of the programme, were that the class had been better behaved generally. The most marked change had been in the standard of work, which had improved greatly. Mike, in particular, had taken to the game and had been perfectly behaved and produced pleasing work. The class generally settled more quickly and was more willing to work. Oral lessons were still difficult because of interruptions, but there had been an improvement.

The programme continued for several more weeks, until the end of term came and Miss T. left the school. The improved behaviour and higher standard of work was maintained during this period. The pupils modified one another's behaviour as they did not want to lose points.

RANGE AND SCOPE OF BEHAVIOURAL APPROACHES

Behavioural approaches have been used helpfully in a wide variety of educational settings. The present author has documented successful applications in primary schools (Presland 1978a), secondary schools (1980) and schools for pupils with adjustment problems (1977), moderate learning difficulties (1978b) and severe learning difficulties (1981, 1989). Merrett (1981) and Merrett and Houghton (1989) have provided more comprehensive reviews of the range of applications within the British education system. Access to the much more extensive literature in the USA is provided by Pikoff (1980).

Not only have behavioural approaches been found to be helpful in virtually every kind of educational situation, they are also applicable to almost any kind of problem – learning problems, behaviour problems and problems of personal adjustment and happiness have all been tackled by such approaches. Similar techniques have even been used to influence how pupils think and feel. For our purposes here, it is safe to conclude that virtually any behaviour problem in school can be interpreted in behavioural terms and tackled by behavioural methods with a good chance of success.

Behavioural approaches are normally offered as 'packages' consisting of a number of intervention activities. The most common package for behaviour problems in schools is some variety of the scheme outlined earlier – identification of specific behaviours, measurement, identification of antecedents and consequences and implementation of a programme based on changes in these applied systematically. It is wisest to use these packages in their entirety, since these are the forms in which they have been validated. There is little evidence, however, to show that deviations lead to disaster. Even in the experimental literature, it is hard to find intervention procedures which do not leave out, or do not deal satisfactorily with, some aspect of the relevant standard package. It will be noted that the practical illustrations provided in this chapter omit certain parts of the package described – for instance, no antecedents for problem behaviour were identified for Terry and there was no satisfactory measuring for Mike or the class to which he belonged. Despite this, both teachers felt something had been achieved. Falconer-Hall (1982) describes how behavioural principles can be used extensively and apparently successfully within the special needs department of a comprehensive school without devising rigorous individual programmes or measuring systematically. Even detaching individual elements from packages can have its value. For instance, the teacher who, as a policy, replaces constant nagging for misbehaviour with seeking out and praising appropriate behaviour is likely to gain much from it.

There are, of course, many more packages than those described here and the reader should refer to the standard works quoted earlier for relevant information.

LEARNING TO USE BEHAVIOURAL TECHNIQUES

It should not be assumed that teachers can read an account such as is given earlier in this chapter and immediately apply behavioural methods in the classroom. As Merrett and Wheldall (1982) have demonstrated, learning *about* behavioural approaches does not necessarily lead to changes in classroom performance, though it is likely to improve attitudes towards such approaches. Reviews of the literature on training teachers in this area (Merrett and Wheldall 1984; Clayton 1985) suggest that performance is most likely to improve when teachers actually apply the techniques under some kind of supervision.

What kind of guidance and monitoring, then, do teachers need? First, we must be aware of over-generalization – some teachers do *read* how to do it and then apply at least *some* of the principles with apparent success. For the majority needing more than this, there are two main sources of guidance – individual and workshop based.

Individual guidance is most likely to be available from an educational psychologist visiting the school regularly, though there are other possibilities such as a tutor at an institute of higher education running in-service courses for teachers. Recently, schemes have been increasing in which support teachers based in, or visiting, schools advise teachers in those schools on implementing behavioural programmes (Coulby and Harper 1985; Long 1988; Presland 1990). The most helpful approach is likely to be some initial reading to absorb the main principles and techniques, then guided observation of a pupil in the classroom along the lines followed earlier in this chapter, and then working out a programme with the help of the adviser, implementing the programme and reporting back regularly. It is also likely to be helpful for the adviser to visit the classroom, observe the teacher in practice and provide supportive and corrective feedback – though his or her presence can make the behaviour of both teacher and pupils different from normal, and this needs to be taken into account.

In a workshop, participants would normally engage in some reading and go through the various stages described earlier, implementing each in turn and reporting back to the workshop tutor. In the Wiltshire workshops (more fully described by Clayton 1985), for instance, there were six main sessions, one on each of the following topics: identification of problem behaviours; observation, measurement and recording of behaviours; selection of reinforcers; construction of programmes; implementation of programmes; and evaluation. Each participant was asked to select a pupil to work on and then implement the activities introduced at each session and report back at the following session. There was also a follow-up meeting arranged some weeks after the final main session, when long-term evaluation and future planning were possible. As with the individual supervision approach, classroom visits by the tutor are an additional possibility.

Other workshop models do, however, exist. The work with Mike and Terry, for instance, emanated from a single 1½ day workshop. Participants were sent, in advance, literature on behavioural approaches and briefing documents for identifying behaviours, measuring behaviours and selecting reinforcers. At the workshop, queries about the approaches were discussed, the data were examined and individual programmes were planned. Further reporting back and guidance were arranged at a later date – by post and through a third party. This 'light supervision' approach was thought possible because the participants all had degrees in psychology and were teaching prior to training as educational psychologists.

Yet another model, developed at Birmingham University, is that represented by BATPACK, BATSAC and the Positive Teaching Packages (Wheldall and Merrett 1988). This is concerned with applying behavioural principles to classroom management generally, rather than to individual problems. Classroom supervision of teachers is an integral part of the approach.

Other models could include training in a course for a wider purpose. For instance, in Wiltshire, a full-time three-week course was organized for teachers appointed to work in a support role in dealing with adjustment problems. The course covered many topics, but included a two-day workshop on applying behavioural techniques to individual problems, and this included practice in such skills as observation and programme planning. A self-study version of the course has been published (Wiltshire Education Department Psychological and Advisory Services 1989) and also a supplement which extends the training for those in post (Wiltshire

Education Department Psychological, Advisory and Support Services 1992).

BEHAVIOURAL APPROACHES AND CLASSROOM MANAGEMENT

The main emphasis in this chapter has been on dealing with behaviour problems. Techniques which are successful with specific problems of behaviour, however, may well have implications for classroom management in general. These, in turn, may make it possible to prevent behaviour problems from occurring in the first place.

Application of behavioural methods has often moved towards this more general field. The case of Mike described earlier involved their use for influencing behaviour of a whole class, a phenomenon quite common in the behavioural literature. Behavioural psychologists, moreover, also sometimes apply their techniques to classroom management generally – as in the BATPACK scheme already referred to, and in a set of proposals for structuring the classroom to prevent problem behaviours, provided by Bradley and McNamara (1981) for teachers in schools for pupils with emotional and behavioural difficulties. However, the evolution of overall classroom management schemes has not yet become a major aspect of research into and practice of behavioural techniques.

The research literature on classroom management has not, for the most part, been carried out within a specifically behavioural framework. However, its findings (Emmer 1987) suggest that many of the elements of behavioural approaches could be extremely relevant. The following are particularly notable.

1 Behavioural approaches define and specifically describe the problem behaviour and the alternative behaviours which should replace it. Thus classroom management research finds that the effective teacher makes clear to pupils from the start what behaviour is expected from them. Procedures and routines are established for all classroom activities and there are clear rules of conduct.

2 Behavioural approaches attempt to use antecedents and consequences systematically to influence behaviours. The effective teacher makes sure the room is arranged to allow movement without disruption and to give clear lines of sight for teacher and

pupil. Learning tasks are carefully analysed and presented in an appropriate sequence, communication is clear and skills are demonstrated. Behaviours that interrupt, slow down or deflect the progress of the lesson are avoided. Pupils' problems are anticipated. The consequences of behaviour are also clear. Pupils are given feedback on their work and the work itself is rewarding, as is the teacher's reaction to good work and behaviour. Inappropriate behaviours are noticed, and the teacher either ignores them where this is safe, reminds the pupil of the rules or gives a warning in a way that does not interfere with the lesson. Punishment is reserved for major misbehaviour and is used in a consistent and relevant way.

3 Behavioural approaches measure the occurrence of specific behaviours to assess the effectiveness of intervention. Though effective teachers have not been shown to do this, they do monitor behaviour carefully, moving round the classroom to see what is happening and ensuring that requirements and deadlines for work assignments are adhered to.

Behavioural approaches do, therefore, recommend a number of ways of behaving which have much in common with what effective teachers do. They therefore offer a framework within which knowledge in this area can be conceptualized, investigated and extended.

WHERE NEXT?

Behavioural approaches lead to many questions being asked and issues raised, practical, philosophical and ethical. They are too numerous to be dealt with in what is basically an introductory account. The basic texts already recommended should resolve some of them and, hopefully, others will be dealt with in some training context. It is hoped that the account of these techniques given here will stimulate readers to seek such further experiences.

REFERENCES

Altman, K.I. and Linton, T.E. (1971) 'Operant conditioning in the classroom setting: a review of the research', *Journal of Educational Research* 6: 277–86.

Bradley, G. and McNamara, E. (1981) 'The structured treatment of problem behaviour: prevention is better than cure', *Behavioural Approaches with Children* 5: 4–12.

Cheesman, P.L. and Watts, P.E. (1985) *Positive Behaviour Management*, London: Croom Helm.

Clayton, T. (1985) 'The workshop approach to training behavioural skills', *Educational and Child Psychology* 2 (1): 69–83.

Coulby, D. and Harper, T. (1985) *Preventing Classroom Disruption: Practice and Evaluation in Urban Schools*, London: Croom Helm.

Emmer, E.T. (1987) 'Classroom management', in Dunkin, M.J. (ed.) *The International Encyclopaedia of Teaching and Teacher Education*, Oxford: Pergamon, pp. 437–46.

Falconer-Hall, E. (1982) 'Behaviour modification in the special studies department of a comprehensive school', *Remedial Education* 17 (3): 99–101.

Fletcher, P. and Presland, J. (1990) 'Contracting to overcome adjustment problems', *Support for Learning* 5 (3): 153–8.

Hanley, E.M. (1970) 'Review of research involving applied behavior analysis in the classroom', *Review of Educational Research* 40 (5): 597–625.

Harlatt, L. (1989) 'Behavioural contracts and self-management techniques', in Wiltshire Education Department Psychological and Advisory Services *WASP: (Wiltshire Adjustment Support Preparation)*, Cheltenham: College of St Paul and St Mary, pp. 116–22.

Long, M. (1988) 'Goodbye behaviour units, hello support services: home-school support for pupils with behaviour difficulties in mainstream schools', *Educational Psychology in Practice* 4 (1): 17–23.

Madsen, C.H., Becker, W.C. and Thomas, D.R. (1968) 'Rules, praise and ignoring elements of elementary classroom control', *Journal of Applied Behavior Analysis* 1 (2): 139–50.

Merrett, F.E. (1981) 'Studies in behaviour modification in British educational settings', *Educational Psychology* 1 (1): 13–28.

Merrett, F. and Houghton, S. (1989) 'Does it work with the older ones? A review of behavioural studies carried out in British secondary schools since 1981', *Educational Psychology* 9 (4): 287–309.

Merrett, F.E. and Wheldall, K. (1982) 'Does teaching teachers about behaviour modification techniques improve their performance in the classroom?', *Journal of Education for Teaching* 8: 67–75.

—— and —— (1984) 'Training teachers to use the behavioural approach to classroom management: a review', *Educational Psychology* 4 (3): 213–31.

Munro, E., Manthei, R.J. and Small, J.J. (1983) *Counselling: A Skills Approach*, 2nd edn, Auckland: Methuen.

——, —— and —— (1989) *Counselling: The Skills of Problem Solving*, London: Routledge.

O'Leary, K.D. and Drabman, R. (1971) 'Token reinforcement programmes in the classroom: a review', *Psychological Bulletin* 75 (6): 379–98.

Pikoff, H. (1980) 'Behavior modification with children: an index of reviews', *Journal of Behavior Therapy and Experimental Psychiatry* 11 (3): 195–201.

Presland, J.L. (1977) 'Behaviour modification in two schools for maladjusted children', *Therapeutic Education* 5 (1): 26–30.

—— (1978a) 'Behaviour modification – theory and practice', *Education 3–13* 6 (1): 43–6.

—— (1978b) 'Behaviour modification in Day ESN (M) Schools', *AEP Journal* 4 (5): 33–7.

—— (1980) 'Behaviour modification and secondary schools', in Upton, G. and Gobell, A. (eds) *Behaviour Problems in the Comprehensive School*, Faculty of Education, University College, Cardiff, pp. 54–64.

—— (1981) 'Behaviour modification in ESN (S) Schools', *British Psychological Society Division of Educational and Child Psychology Occasional Papers* 5 (2): 25–32.

—— (1989) *Overcoming Difficult Behaviour: A Guide and Sourcebook for Helping People with Severe Mental Handicaps*, Kidderminster: BIMH Publications.

—— (1990) 'Behavioural approaches for support teachers', *Positive Teaching* 1 (1): 3–17.

Rogers, C. (1951) *Client Centred Therapy*, Boston, Mass.: Constable.

—— (1974) *On Becoming a Person*, Boston, Mass.: Constable.

Visser, J. (1983) 'The humanistic approach', in Upton, G. (ed.) *Educating Children with Behaviour Problems*, Cardiff: University of Cardiff Press, pp. 103–11.

Wheldall, K. and Merrett, F. (1984) *Positive Teaching*, London: Unwin.

—— and —— (1988) 'Packages for training teachers in classroom behaviour management: BATPACK, BATSAC and the Positive Teaching Packages', *Support for Learning* 3: 86–92.

Wiltshire Education Department Psychological and Advisory Services (1989) *WASP (Wiltshire Adjustment Support Preparation)*, Cheltenham: College of St Paul and St Mary.

Wiltshire Education Department Psychological, Advisory and Support Services (1992) *Supplement to WASP (Wiltshire Adjustment Support Preparation)*, Cheltenham: Cheltenham & Gloucester College of Higher Education.

Part III

Classroom and school practices

Kenneth David considers pastoral care in schools in Chapter 7. He offers a critical review of the weaknesses in pastoral care systems and considers how the quality of the work can be assessed. He then considers teachers' relationships with children, and the needs of children. The 1988 Education Reform Act and the National Curriculum are reviewed, with particular reference to personal and social education, and the measures which make a school effective are discussed.

Chapter 8, by Kevin Jones and Mick Lock, discusses how teachers, parents and other professionals have moved to more positive procedures whereby they share responsibilities in order to respond in more appropriate ways to problem behaviours. This mutual act of informing, advising and providing is illustrated by recent work with pupils and their parents.

Chapter 9, by Kenneth David, considers agencies working with schools and reviews the support which professional and voluntary agencies can offer to schools, particularly where children's problems require time and expertise beyond that which teachers can reasonably make available.

Tony Charlton and Kenneth David, in Chapter 10, consider many of the issues raised in earlier chapters, and offer a checklist of guidelines for good classroom and school management practices for teachers and students to consider. A summary of recent legislation and reports affecting education is given in the Appendix.

Chapter 7

Pastoral care in schools

Kenneth David

INTRODUCTION

Children inhabit private and family worlds, hardly known for
quietness and security in our society. Schools can therefore be
places of refuge and stability in the lives of many children: teachers'
responsibilities for enabling their pupils effectively to learn must
therefore include their pupils' emotional as well as intellectual
backgrounds. A teacher has in a class of twenty to thirty children
an immense range of differing private and family worlds, and the
way children were brought up, and their varying personalities,
moods and emotions, must affect their ability to learn. This is the
rationale for pastoral care.

Children lead complicated lives, often filled with adult and
sophisticated happenings. When we begin to add together the
materialistic and fractured family life that many children experience,
the assaults on children of a strident media world and the pressures
on teachers at the present time, we can see that teaching is a very
demanding profession. Teachers' professionalism is strengthened by
knowledge of and skills in pastoral care.

Pastoral care is not new, for teaching has traditionally had a
pastoral implication. Comprehensive schools, which presently
contain 90 per cent of our secondary age pupils, have in recent years
seen major developments in blending the academic and pastoral
roles of teachers.

By pastoral care we mean the primary- and secondary-school
systems planned to care for the personal development and individual and group support of pupils. In secondary schools this has
included the appointment of specialist staff, sometimes including
school counsellors. Pastoral care can include welfare, administrative

work and pupils' records, assessment and evaluation of studies, coordinated personal and social education schemes and curricula, tutorial work, individual and group counselling, liaison with parents and with agencies concerned with pupils and their families, disciplinary matters and leisure and extra-curricular activities.

CRITICAL ATTITUDES

In weighing up the value of pastoral care systems it is not difficult to be cynical: 'I'm paid to teach my subject, not to be a social worker' has been heard, to which the response might be, 'To teach well you surely have to care about those you teach?'. The fact that teachers' careers are widened, and their school lives become more enjoyable, with a pastoral and social dimension in their work has to be constantly reiterated. With reduced public esteem and modest professional status, good teachers are to be admired for continuing to work as hard as they do in a demanding and questioning community.

One fault of pastoral care practice is that it is still blandly seen in some schools as being concerned only with control and mundane welfare, rather than as a developmental system in its own right, a system and an attitude which is concerned with the all-round education of a child. More than twenty years of comprehensive education and of pastoral care developments, extensive in-service education and a mass of appropriate literature should have clarified this point, but there are still failures of understanding. Such failures can be caused by cynical and unimaginative leadership in schools, and also by a well-intentioned but foolish view of pastoral care as 'doing some good'. Hamblin (1981) writes of hard working but ineffective teachers providing 'emotional first aid . . . as the equivalent of a social worker or welfare officer' (p. 3).

To be of real value pastoral care should be demanding, practical and positive. It requires objectives, clear forward planning, rigorous evaluation and the best teachers; academic achievement and better standards can then be built on the right foundations. Hamblin (1983) comments, 'Guidance . . . becomes self defeating or ineffective unless we scan continuously and monitor the implications of what is offered' (p. 4), and 'poor pastoral care reflects a malaise in other aspects of teaching' (p. 3). The need for in-service education in these matters seems obvious, with priority on the relationship between pastoral and academic aims.

Pastoral care can sometimes be condescending and can under-estimate pupils' potential for sensitivity and maturity. Although childishness is common, children can be wise beyond their years: teachers need to be aware of the continuum from innocence to knowingness, from naivety to sophistication and from thoughtless-ness to wisdom and maturity among their pupils. Peter Lange (1983) discusses pupils' comments on pastoral care procedures and says, 'Some pupils possessed a very high level of understanding, in some cases as good or maybe better than that of many teachers' (p. 167). Pupils can have very accurate perceptions of life and of their abilities and failings, and can resent being 'talked down to'.

In classroom teaching and in pastoral arrangements we can sometimes underestimate pupils' potential for cooperation. Planned and thoughtful informal teaching methods can change the motiva-tion of pupils and reduce the proportion of disinterested and difficult children – they can be involved in our aims. An element of insecurity, nervousness and occasionally even fear can underlie teachers' attitudes to their more difficult youngsters, who may be labelled as immature, unresponsive and difficult, to conceal teachers' fear of being challenged. (I sometimes think that a major survival skill for teachers is the ability to reply briskly, aptly and with humour to adversarial challenges from pupils – the quietening retort.) Teaching can be about risk taking in our methods, and once pupils glimpse relaxed sincerity and humour in their teachers, as well as authority, hopefully, then ill-discipline lessens. Headteachers will continue to puzzle over how best to manage the work of weaker teachers.

Changes resulting from the 1988 Education Reform Act can result in school governors having to be persuaded of the meaning and value of pastoral attitudes in facilitating learning and easing the work of teachers. Local management of schools is likely to reduce the advisory and supportive roles of local education authorities, of which an increasingly centralized government is so sadly dismissive and apparently ill-informed. With in-service work being financed from school budgets there may be less support for teachers' development in pastoral as well as academic work. One hopes also that special educational needs, closely associated with some pastoral systems, will continue to receive the support they require, and that examination results will not have total priority. The education of less motivated and perhaps difficult children will also require immense patience and the investment of experienced teachers' time as well as school financial support, and one wonders if this will apply in grant-aided 'opt-out' schools and schools too devoted to their competitive status.

ASSESSING PASTORAL CARE

In assessing the value of pastoral care systems we can gather a variety of intuitive opinions from experienced staff, from pupils who often have perceptive opinions, from parents and others in the neighbourhood and from advisers, youth workers and other agency workers. Such evaluation may well be relevant and useful, for measured academic evaluation of pastoral work is exceedingly difficult. What can we measure? Accumulated knowledge and skills gained in discussion type work can be seen as improving. Study skills can be observed and assessed. Habits can change and be measured – in health matters, perhaps. Changes in attitudes cannot easily be measured, though they can sometimes be glimpsed – views on racial matters, for example. Perhaps changes in attitude, in tolerance and responsibility and in care and sensitivity, should be measured by parents, though experienced class teachers can observe and have views. Whether a child is better motivated and is progressing better in class work can be measured though, and the link with what is offered in a pastoral system can then be made.

In reviewing the pastoral arrangements in schools we can use a checklist of questions such as the following, some of which are appropriate for secondary schools, some for primary schools. Readers will add others.

- What are the pupil (and perhaps staff) attendance records like?
- What exclusions of pupils have been made?
- Have the governors discussed the school's pastoral arrangements?
- Do the governors and parents understand the National Curriculum, cross-curricular plans for health education, sex education and personal and social education, and are they being implemented?
- Is there in-service provision for teachers in pastoral care matters?
- What are the school's plans for involving apathetic or disinterested parents and pupils? Is the school valued in the neighbourhood?
- What pastoral appointments or responsibilities have been made and are they successful? How is this proved?

- Is there staff expertise in each secondary-school pastoral team or primary-school staff in counselling, in discussion and group work, in health education, in study skills, in pupil record keeping and administrative tasks and in personal and social education?
- Is there effective liaison with other agencies?
- Is there a good communication system in the school to keep staff and pupils well informed of what is going on, and does the system include ancillary staff as well as parents and governors?
- Is misbehaviour of pupils studied and discussed or just reacted to? Is there a continuing review of discipline matters?
- Does the timetable and curriculum illustrate pastoral and social as well as academic attitudes?
- What school rituals are useful, and which might be without value?
- Are there obviously good relationships between staff, between staff and pupils and between staff and parents? Is the school evidently valued in the neighbourhood?

Pastoral care is, of course, an attitude rather than a list of duties. It can carry over into class teaching, with successful motivation evolving from pastoral activities and methods. Pastoral care therefore permeates all that a school does, and is intended to bring order, increased learning, good diagnosis of problem behaviour and reduction of tensions; and it is continuous and preventive in intent.

While pastoral care is aimed at all children in a school, certain arrangements are specifically aimed at reducing problem behaviour. Staff should plan a set of long-term goals and short-term objectives for problem pupils, should meet regularly to review these and should have developed the diagnostic skills to review under-achievement and to analyse problem behaviour as reviewed in this book. The morning tutorial time, or whatever term may be used for 'settling in' time in primary schools, should be planned to illustrate a positive start to the day with whatever personal and social education work may be done then. All pastoral care systems are aiming to show that every child must be well known by at the very least one member of staff.

So much in the end depends on the quality of the staff and the leadership of the school – that is the fundamental question in viewing the effectiveness of any school's pastoral care system.

LEADERSHIP AND THE QUALITY OF TEACHERS

The majority of teachers are reasonable people, often anxiously committed to their work. Many can be pedestrian in their aims and imagination, and have the normal failings of lack of patience and fear of being seen to fail; everyday life will also produce some who are under pressure, distracted, perhaps cynical and militant. A percentage of these, as with lawyers and plumbers, are of low quality and may be too safeguarded; every headteacher and adviser knows teachers who should not be teaching, and who produce bored and difficult pupils. Nevertheless most are responsible, reasonably competent and often puzzled as to why they do not have public esteem, and professional quality is outstanding amongst a large minority of teachers, often senior in position. A graduate profession has evolved, and teacher training standards have lengthened and deepened, with weaknesses sometimes in classroom practice and also in such themes as group work, informal discussion work, counselling and other pastoral care skills. Headteachers' and deputies' leadership skills are being emphasized and improved through training and better selection procedures. Leadership skills are increasingly important in a restive profession; and length of service may not incidentally develop these skills, while professional senior management training often can. Leadership is not only a personality matter, it can also be studied and learned.

Teaching and the leadership of teachers is a demanding job, for families are producing pupils who are lively, less disciplined and more difficult to motivate. Half an hour observing in a busy supermarket or shopping centre in the school holidays may illustrate some difficult future and present clients of ours.

The effect of school leadership of high quality cannot be over-emphasized; good headteachers eventually produce good schools, and the converse is all too clear as well. Headteachers can be isolated and vulnerable, have heavy responsibilities and sometimes serve too long – might fixed contracts help, one wonders – but when they are of strong personality, good intellect and with confident patience and humour, then commitment in teaching, rigour in achievement and contentment in human relationships tend to increase in their schools.

All professionals need periodic retraining, and in-service work is an essential part of school life; this is how the quality of teachers and the calibre of leadership is enhanced and monitored. In-service work not only revises facts and updates methods, it also gives time to think and debate the everyday work teachers are doing. Having unhurried and unharried time to listen to colleagues, being required to articulate opinions and beliefs and having attitudes and methods challenged by others is a very useful part of pastoral and academic professional (and personal) development. It will be seen that in-service training, to my mind, is not a question of sitting in sleepy rows listening to too many lectures: it is a matter of lively debate and discussion.

RELATIONSHIPS AND DISCIPLINE

New kinds of relationships are necessary in the world of young people today, as they test their teachers' authority and ability. Respect for authority in the last few decades has changed, in public life as well as in schools. Confrontation, however, does not always succeed, which is not understood by the public, who think that avoidance is weakness and do not note that skilled teachers may seek to avoid scenes with difficult pupils in favour of other methods.

Hargreaves (1975) writes of teachers as lion tamers and entertainers. Woods (1978) suggests that pupils from a 'working class' background value relationships more than the intrinsic value of work, and the traditional skills of teaching lie partly in making work more interesting and partly in improving our methods and skills in facilitating teacher–pupil relationships. These skills are the foundation of good pastoral care practice, implying not 'softness' but attempts to win trust and friendship with children, to make learning more attractive.

We want children to want their schooling, and we can do this partly by good humoured, committed and interesting teaching and partly by a planned and progressive programme of personal and social education for the form tutor or class teacher. Disruptive behaviour can be reduced through good pastoral care planning, with more discussing and less shouting.

Young people are within a society which has had fifty years of confused decline, have different family traditions and memories and belong totally to their demanding present and their strengthened peer groups. They see a traditional and ageing society around them, and know only a welfare state and a less disciplined society which still clings to historical rather than modern views of life. To educate them for their future we need to change many educational approaches. 'Human capital is the most important resource of post-industrial societies', Stonier (1983) insists, and 'A massively expanded education system to provide not only training and information on how to make a living, but also on how to live' points to the way many schools are working with programmes in personal and social education.

Disruptive pupils exist in schools and appear to have increased in number. Galloway (1982) points out that there can be a question as to whether more suspensions are occurring, though recent evidence from schools and local education authorities seem now to point clearly to an increase. Not all schools are affected: *Aspects of Secondary Education in England* (HMI 1979) states that: 'The majority of schools reported they had no disruptive pupils . . . 37 per cent said they had some' (11.3.7), with, HMI continue, 'poor behaviour and discourtesy being more frequently associated with schools serving inner city areas.' (9.3.26)

Disruption can, of course, be caused by poor teaching, ugly settings and urban pressures. A report on a survey of science teaching in London schools (*The Times*, 21 March 1987) notes that inspectors reported that 15 per cent of 200 lessons were good, 30 per cent satisfactory, 40 per cent unsatisfactory and the rest unrelievedly bad. This makes disruption almost reasonable.

In desperation some schools turn to suspension and expulsion, but these are ineffective signs of disapproval rather than a cure for disruptive behaviour. Other schools use withdrawal units. Putting pupils aside admits failure by class teachers who are claiming that they cannot interest, motivate or control their pupils, but such units can be necessary and helpful, providing a respite and pause for consideration by teachers and pupils, far better than impatient suspensions at times. With the best teachers in charge (one of the best withdrawal units I have ever seen was run by a very patient, very large and very senior teacher), such units provide good 'cooling off' periods, often facilitating the pupils' return to normal class teaching later.

It would be good if such units, imaginatively staffed, could be part of a 'development unit': a variety of special educational needs teaching could be carried out, counselling and group work developed, coaching given to pupils returning after absences, difficult pupils given a changed setting for a while and extra coaching given to particularly gifted pupils. Attendance problems might also be dealt with in such a unit, with sanctions or counselling as required.

We need to make pastoral arrangements 'user friendly', and should teach pupils how to use the school's systems, explaining exactly what the school's tutorial or pastoral arrangements are supposed to do and discussing the school's successes and failures in class or group discussions. We do not need to distance ourselves so much from pupils' opinions and potential cooperation. As part of preparation for adult life we need also to teach about rights and responsibilities in the welfare state.

Ill-discipline has always existed and can best be controlled by in-school methods, providing there is adequate and efficient staffing, appropriate liaison and support from other agencies, and from parents, and occasional exclusion for a very limited number of violent, perhaps emotionally and mentally distressed, pupils – most psychopath criminals have, after all, gone through the schooling system one presumes. There is a case also for occasional early leaving, before the statutory leaving age for a few pupils, with obvious safeguards and the right for education or training to be resumed later.

With the strong probability that exclusions are increasing considerably in some areas and some schools, we must be watchful that such actions are rare and essential. This must be monitored carefully by governors and local education authorities. It can be easier to be rid of troublemakers instead of undertaking a deeper diagnosis of their actions and problems, and making various attempts to limit their impact on the school. Trouble can come from unrecognized and untreated special educational needs (SENs), and difficult SEN pupils can be tempting targets for transfer or exclusion if their education is expensive.

CHILDREN'S NEEDS

Although we cannot explore children's minds and know their deeper needs, we can attempt to meet their presumed or expressed personal needs through individual or group counselling, and in class or tutorial group discussion work.

In primary schools we should be concerned with a child's understanding of physical growth and development, with family life and individual emotional development, with the expansion of relationships and friendship and with the growth of intellect and the problems of learning. These and other needs will underlie some of our planning in pastoral care, particularly in planning a syllabus of work in personal and social education. There can be many worries and pressures on young children, occasionally crippling in their effect, which schools must attempt to discern and lessen, partly by school means and partly by good liaison systems with outside helping agencies, as discussed in Chapter 9.

Secondary-school pupils have similar and additional needs, which can affect learning and make teaching a burden if pastoral concern does not bring observation, support and counselling of individuals and groups. Many personal worries and concerns of individual pupils are, of course, solved silently by the individual as he or she listens to teaching or discussion of their particular anxiety, which emphasizes the importance of a range of discussion topics being planned and presented by teachers.

One list of suggested normal adolescent problems is as follows:

- puberty and adolescent status
- emotions, moods and self control
- sexuality
- intelligence level and study skills
- physical development, clumsiness and body image
- self-consciousness
- family relationships, independence and feelings of security
- social competence and peer group pressures
- friendship
- relationships with authority
- money, jobs and employment

Primary- and secondary-school pupils' more personal needs may include:

- good health habits and attitudes
- security and affection
- being respected as a person, and seeing themselves both as an individual and as a member of a group
- having skills of listening and of easy conversation, so that they can speak of their feelings and say what they think
- learning how best to relate to different adults of all ages

It is interesting to compare the needs and problems of early teenage years with those of the 16–19 age group. Hamblin (1983) writes of this group, 'What is essential . . . is the process of negotiation . . . and their involvement in the selection and construction of (guidance) materials' (p. 164). The same thought can with varying emphasis apply to younger pupils. There is so much in pastoral care, discipline and the personal and intellectual development of pupils that can be discussed and negotiated instead of being imposed.

In considering the particular needs of SEN pupils, has integration into mainstream schools worked in practice and have resources and staff actually been made available? Are schools successfully dealing with the needs of these pupils, some of whom may not have employment prospects for the future, and what part can pastoral care take with these boys and girls? It could be argued that the pastoral care practice of a school, especially the counselling and discussion work aspects, provide a vital part of their education. Does pastoral care simply patch and support, or does it permeate a school's approach to these pupils? How far does curriculum planning and assessment take account of the changed concept and expectations of work (and perhaps of differing patterns of family life) in the future of these children?

In considering the needs of pupils of any age we constantly have to consider the results of the weakening of family structures in our society. Teachers, whether they wish it or not, face this major social and family dimension in their pupils' ability to learn, which reinforces the need for well-planned personal and social education programmes, with their impact on pupils' future lives through discussion and teaching on the problems of modern living and changing relationships. Family life sets most of a child's perceptions of life and of their attitudes to personal, family and group relationships, to work and to imagination and feelings, but teachers can be a more than marginal influence on their pupils' gathering of knowledge and attitudes which point towards a satisfying adult life. Some teachers are the sole reliable reference point in some children's lives. We cannot solve all family and society problems (though some of us long to be a dictator for a while!), but we can in schools clarify and discuss them with children, individually or in class or tutorial work.

Schools have the capacity to help their pupils in at least six ways, according to the now dated but sensible publication, *The Practical Curriculum* (Schools Council 1981: 15). They still provide good pointers for a pupil's pastoral as well as academic aims:

1 to acquire knowledge, skills and practical abilities, and the will to use them;

2 to develop qualities of mind, body, spirit, feeling and imagination;
3 to appreciate human achievements in art, music, science, technology and literature;
4 to acquire understanding of the social, economic and political order, and a reasoned set of attitudes, values and beliefs;
5 to prepare for their adult lives at home, at work, at leisure and at large, as consumers and citizens;
6 to develop a sense of self-respect, the capacity to live as independent, self-motivated adults and the ability to function as contributing members of cooperative groups.

Later the same paper suggests that the teaching and learning process should lead pupils towards 'an ability to be sensitive to the needs of others in order to develop satisfactory personal relationships' (p. 16).

Osman (1973) reminds us that 'educators must remember that their goal is to produce well-adjusted, rational people who can relate and feel, not just non-linear calculating computers'.

These are idealistic aims, and it could be said that we are talking of education in general rather than of pastoral care. Both are closely intermingled, but it is reasonable to say that organized and planned pastoral systems are sharpening those aims which are looking to the future lives and personal development of pupils, within the general term 'all-round' education.

In considering pupils' future lives, what then will their needs be that we are attempting to forecast? This is when cynics may deplore raising teachers' eyes from the everyday ground to the hills beyond. The revolution in computing indicates the speed of economic change and presumes very different concepts of work and career in the future. There is an explosion of new knowledge, manufacturing industry and commerce are being turned on their traditional heads, family life and marriage are changing and comparative material comfort and sophisticated entertainment fill the leisure of most people. Inflation and materialism may change established ideas of family expectations in financial thinking and in ideas of probity and actual need. Such changes in our society, and the differing views of the future that they develop, are well illustrated by, among others, Hopson and Scally (1979), Whitfield (1983) and Stonier (1983). Teachers have to attempt to interpret these forecasts to suggest the advice, curriculum, discussion topics and training that may best prepare youngsters for times ahead.

THE 1988 EDUCATION REFORM ACT

This act has given the school world a useful jolt and considerable work, too much in too short a time in some cases. A broad and balanced National Curriculum is to be provided which:

1 promotes the spiritual, moral, cultural, mental and physical development of pupils at the school and of society; and
2 prepares pupils for the opportunities, responsibilities and experiences of adult life.

Three basic core subjects and seven foundation subjects are at the present date compulsory, and pupils are required to be tested at ages 7, 11, 14 and 16, making our pupils one of the most tested groups of pupils in the world it appears. The ten compulsory subjects will be augmented by:

- religious education
- additional subjects beyond the ten subjects of the National Curriculum
- an accepted range of cross-curricular elements
- extra-curricular activities

Although these aims appear to fit with the ideas advanced in this chapter, there will be great pressure on schools to work for test and examination results, rather than for anything more idealistic; one suspects that, 'Eyes on the basic subjects test results, and not too many frills' will be heard in some places. Sadly, personal and social education and preparation for future personal and family life may be a 'frill' in some eyes. There is hope, however, in enlightened use of the suggested National Curriculum cross-curricular elements. These are divided into three aspects.

1 *Dimensions*, 'such as commitment to providing equal opportunities for all pupils and a recognition that preparation for life in a multicultural society is relevant for all pupils and should permeate every aspect of the curriculum', and 'Teachers have a major role in preparing young people for adult life . . . in which the roles of men and women are changing and both sexes are likely to have dual responsibilities for home and work'.
2 *Skills*, including communication, problem solving and personal and social skills.
3 *Themes*, including health education, education for citizenship and economic and industrial understanding.

There is therefore opportunity in the National Curriculum for any primary or secondary school to coordinate and put into practice a personal and social education (PSE) curriculum as part of their pastoral care aims.

The Health Education cross-curricular theme is described in Guidance 5 of the National Curriculum Council, and is an alternative title for much work in PSE. There are PSE links also with key stages in the Science, Technology, English and Mathematics programmes of the National Curriculum. Guidance 8 of the National Curriculum Council deals with Education for Citizenship, which contains other elements of a pastoral curriculum and 'promotes concern for the values by which a civilised society is identified'.

PERSONAL AND SOCIAL EDUCATION

PSE in one form or another has to be part of all pastoral care systems. It is the teaching and discussion work element, carried out by class teachers in the primary school and subject teachers and form tutors in secondary schools, and sometimes has other titles such as education for personal relationships, personal education, tutorial work or the pastoral curriculum. This assembly of topics, many listed in a previous section of this chapter, will have been planned by the staff to suit their particular pupils, and will operate with all children in a progressive programme year by year with different age groups.

PSE may be presented in the following ways:

1 as a coordinated programme integrated into the normal academic curriculum with all the staff taking part in their various class or subject departments, with a senior member of staff acting as coordinator;
2 as a programme of topics for use by class teachers in the daily tutorial or class assembly time;
3 as material for residential or in-school special conferences;
4 as a weekly period in the normal timetable, specifically used for PSE work.

The National Curriculum Council in *The Whole Curriculum* (1990a) describes PSE – 'The whole curriculum . . . contributes to the personal and social education of all pupils' – and goes on to emphasize the importance of the work:

The education system is charged with preparing young people to take their place in a wide range of roles in adult life. It also has a duty to educate the individuals to be able to think and act for themselves, with an acceptable set of personal qualities and values which also meet the wider social demands of adult life. In short the personal and social development of pupils is a major aim of education; personal and social education being the means by which this aim is achieved.

The necessity of PSE is given a National Curriculum imprimatur; now it remains to see whether schools have the will (they certainly have the ability) to carry out this work while dealing with the pressures of assessment and examinations.

An alternative description of PSE composed by a national committee is as follows:

> PSE includes the teaching and informal activities which are planned to enhance the development of knowledge, understanding, attitudes, and behaviour, concerned with: oneself and others; social institutions, structures and organisation; and social and moral issues.

> (David 1982)

It is a balance to the media presentations of today's society and to the tawdry attractions and lowered values that may press on some pupils. It can help also in illustrating to children disenchanted by school, perhaps demonstrated by difficult behaviour, that school relevance in their personal lives is possible.

In primary schools there is now a less intuitive and more planned approach to the curriculum as a result of the National Curriculum. There is still a need for training and support to give more shape and purpose to pastoral care structures and liaison, to better coordination with secondary schools and to the concept of a coordinated and cross-curricular PSE programme. Primary-school children are capable of working positively in groups and can contribute to thoughtful discussion, and useful programmes of PSE have been implemented in many schools. There have been excellent pastoral developments in such approaches as arranging extended 'interviews' of a range of different visitors to primary classrooms, learning of other people's views, values and attitudes. More can be done, as the importance of the primary school as the beginning of pupil's understanding in relationships and as the start of good health habits and of positive attitudes which contribute to satisfying living is obvious. Pastoral care in the primary school is dealt with in some detail by David and Charlton (1987).

In secondary schools there have been considerable improvements in PSE tutorial work in recent years. Baldwin and Wells (1979–83), Button (1981), Hamblin (1986) and others have put the case well, and much in-service work has been done in well-led schools. Brilliant, difficult and backward pupils are passably well known to secondary teachers; good tutorial work ensures that the more anonymous middle group are better known as persons. Improved tutorial periods have many advantages: planned programmes of PSE, health education, study skills, reviews of classwork and discussion on school incidents or group worries are dealt with; and the start of the day is more purposeful. Teachers report that they have developed better 'survival' tactics for their own enjoyment of teaching through the discovery of informal discussion methods, and in gaining better cooperation from poorly motivated and difficult pupils.

When a school is considering the need for a better planned PSE programme, Curriculum Matters 14 (DES 1989) is helpful with objectives. Many questions will arise, the answers depending on the school and its setting and on the staff's views and skills. Such questions might include the following.

- Is it sufficient just to answer children's questions on life as they arise, individually or incidentally in class work?
- How will the topics for PSE be chosen, and what part will parents and pupils play?
- On what do we base such a selection of topics: local needs, future needs, children's worries and confusions, media topics, crises as they arise?
- What support is needed from outside the school, and could parents contribute?
- What preparation is needed for teachers, and are most topics capable of being dealt with at the children's age level by an educated adult?
- What topics involve adults' prejudices, and how are these topics dealt with, or are they avoided?
- What degree of confidentiality is required?
- What limits are to be put on searching questions by children?
- How far do the National Curriculum cross-curricular suggestions meet the needs of a planned PSE programme?

- How best can children's questions about controversial themes that arose in late night TV or in the home newspaper be dealt with?
- To what extent can there be a negotiated 'contract' between teachers, parents and pupils in this area of work?

Knowledge of the dynamics of groups and of counselling skills are useful to all teachers, particularly in PSE, but are seldom introduced adequately in initial training. Regular school-based in-service work in these areas is valuable and helps to enliven classroom teaching, increasing teachers' awareness and observation of children and making more likely the care and attention of pupils with special personal, behavioural or educational needs. Teachers' sensitivity can be strengthened with effective training.

In PSE then we are attempting, like parents, to offer and develop knowledge, habits and attitudes leading to a mature personality, at stages appropriate to a child's age. Total success is a fantasy, an attempt is a duty.

EFFECTIVE SCHOOLS

An HMI (1979) report stated that secondary schools were evidently concerned that the pastoral care should:

- attempt to coordinate consideration of the pupils' personal, social and academic development
- facilitate the development of good relationships between teachers and pupils
- try to ensure that each pupil knows and is known by a particular adult
- make available relevant information through the development of effective communication and record systems
- involve parents and outside agencies in the work of the school, where appropriate
- enable someone to respond quickly and appropriately to pupils' problems or indeed to anticipate a problem which might arise
- by these means improve the learning of pupils

Now much later, in 1993, these still remain good, concise and up-to-date aims, and can apply in primary schools as well. They are clearly aimed at producing effective schools, and link pastoral care with learning as well as with pupils' more personal problems and needs.

Another report attempted to identify the key factors which make a school effective (Mortimore *et al.* 1988), and commented that the performance of children was significantly affected by the effectiveness of their school, and that disadvantaged children at a good school could have higher achievements than more advantaged children at less effective schools, with the ages 7–11 being highlighted as particularly important. We could, I suggest, speak of difficult and even disruptive children in this connection, for the effective school manages their misbehaviour better.

And when we talk of effective schools we are inevitably talking of effective pastoral care – a pastoral attitude – as an integral part of educational practice and theory.

In reflecting on the key factors of effectiveness in schools the level of staff professionalism is important. It is always fascinating to see the range of differing personalities on a staff, and to ponder on the effect on children of a wide range of staff attitudes to life and work, of their differing styles of living, of dress, of speech and of teaching methods. This variety among a familiar and educated group of adults is an important part of a child's education in relationships. Teachers' professionalism includes being a model to youngsters, whether teachers enjoy that fact or not. Pupils are shrewd and generous, however, and do not expect perfection!

Hamblin (1981), by the way, reminds us that 'Schools are not only for pupils: they are for teachers who have the right to satisfaction in an arduous task' (p. 20). Problems and pastoral care are not limited to pupils. Stress affects teachers also; an article by Freeman (1987) suggests that the group of teachers found to be most stressed was the secondary-school pastoral year heads. Breakdown among teachers is familiar to most headteachers and advisers, and pastoral care should include arrangements for counselling for teachers as well as advice on their career and personal development. This may be of increasing importance in future, and some authorities have encouraged the appointment of staff tutor/counsellors in schools.

CONCLUSION

Improvements in pastoral care in recent years are both idealistic and pragmatic. Idealism lies in a belief that education can be improved, and is not only about knowledge and qualifications; it is about pupils being valued as individuals, being educated for a future in which personal competencies will be essential and having their schooling made more personal and meaningful. Pragmatism requires better support and less stress for teachers, with more motivated pupils, more effective control, more humanizing of large institutions and more gaining of the cooperation of the disenchanted.

This chapter has attempted a personal and critical reflection on the purpose of pastoral care and on a few of its failings and values, with attention also on the problem of dealing with pupils' misbehaviour. Carl Rogers (1969) wrote, 'It is the perception, not the reality which is crucial in determining behaviour.' Introducing children to knowledge is a traditional teaching reality, but now we need increasingly to help them clarify their perceptions of what life today is, and what it could be in the future.

REFERENCES

Adams, F. (1986) *Special Education*, Harlow: Longman, Council and Education Press.

Adams, S. (1989) *A Guide to Creative Tutoring*, London: Kegan Paul.

Argyle, M. and Trower P. (1979) *Person to Person*, London: Harper & Row.

Baldwin, J. and Wells, H. (eds) (1979–83) *Active Tutorial Work*, Oxford: Blackwell.

Blackburn, K. (1975) *The Tutor*, London: Heinemann.

Charlton, T. and David, K. (eds) (1990) *Supportive Schools*, Basingstoke: Macmillan.

Button, L. (1981) *Group Tutoring for the Form Tutor*, London: Hodder & Stoughton.

David, K. (1982) *Personal and Social Education in Secondary Schools*, London: Longman.

—— (1992) 'A classroom plan for personal and social education in the primary school', in Jones, K. and Charlton, T. (eds) *Learning Difficulties in Primary Classrooms, Delivering the Whole Curriculum*, London: Routledge.

David, K. and Charlton, T. (eds) (1987) *The Caring Role of the Primary School*, Basingstoke: Macmillan.

David, K. and Williams, T. (eds) (1987) *Health Education in Schools*, 2nd edn, London: Harper & Row.

DES (1989) *Personal and Social Education from 5 to 16*, Curriculum Matters 14, London: HMSO.

Elton, Lord (Chairman) (1989) *Discipline in Schools*, London: HMSO.

Freeman, A. (1987) 'Pastoral care and teacher stress', *Pastoral Care in Education* 5 (1): 22–8.

Galloway, D. (1982) *Schools and Disruptive Pupils*, New York: Longman.

Galloway, D. and Goodwin, C. (1987) *The Education of Disturbing Children*, London: Longman.

Hamblin, D. (1981) *Problems and Practice in Pastoral Care*, Oxford: Blackwell.

—— (1983) *Guidance 16–19*, Oxford: Blackwell.

—— (1986) *A Pastoral Programme*, Oxford: Blackwell.

—— (1991) *Staff Development for Pastoral Care*, Oxford: Blackwell.

Handy, C.B. (1981) *Understanding Organisations*, Harmondsworth: Penguin.

Hargreaves, D. (1975) *Interpersonal Relationships and Education*, London: Routledge.

HMI (1979) *Aspects of Secondary Education in England*, London: HMSO.

Hopson, B. and Scally, M. (1979) *Life Skills Teaching Programmes*, Leeds: Life Skills Associates.

Jones, N. (1989) *School Management and Pupil Behaviour*, London: Falmer Press.

Lang, P. (1983) 'How pupils see it', *Pastoral Care in Education* 1 (3): 164–75.

—— (1988) *Thinking about Personal and Social Education in the Primary School*, Oxford: Blackwell.

McGuiness, J. (1982) *Planned Pastoral Care*, London: McGraw-Hill.

—— (1989) *A Whole-School Approach to Pastoral Care*, London: Kogan Page.

Mortimore, P., Sammons, P., Ecob, R. and Stoll, L. (1988) *School Matters: the Junior Years*, Wells: Open Books.

National Curriculum Council (1990a) *Curriculum Guidance 3. The Whole Curriculum*, York: NCC.

—— (1990b) *Curriculum Guidance 5. Health Education*, York: NCC.

—— (1990c) *Curriculum Guidance 8. Education for Citizenship*, York: NCC.

Osman, J. (1973) 'A rationale for using value clarification in health education', *Journal of School Health* XLIII (10).

Pringle, K. (1974) *The Needs of Children*, London: Hutchinson.

Rogers, C.R. (1969) *Freedom to Learn*, New York: Merrill.

Schools Council (1981) *The Practical Curriculum*, London: Methuen Educational.

Stonier, T. (1983) *The Wealth of Information – A Profile of the Post-Industrial Society*, London: Methuen.

Steed, D. and Lawrence, J. (1988) *Disruptive Behaviour in the Primary School*, London: Goldsmiths College.

Tattum, D. (ed.) (1986) *Management of Disruptive Behaviour in Schools*, Chichester: Wiley.

Thomas, G. and Feiler, A. (eds) (1988) *Planning for Special Needs – A Whole School Approach*, Oxford: Blackwell.

Watkins, C. and Wagner, P. (1987) *School Discipline: a Whole-School Approach*, Oxford: Blackwell.

Whitfield, R. (1983) 'Family structures, lifestyles and the care of children', *Aston Educational Monograph* 9.

Woods, P. (1978) 'Relating to schoolwork: some pupils' perceptions', *Educational Review* 30 (2): 167–75.

Chapter 8

Working with parents

Kevin Jones and Mick Lock

Despite considerable advances in the development of effective working relationships between parents and professionals, particularly within the area of reading (Wolfendale 1986; Topping 1991), there have been comparatively few reported accounts of successful liaison which focuses upon behaviour problems (McConkey 1985). Jowett and Baginsky (1991) refer to 'missed opportunities for productive collaboration'. Research suggests that practice is, indeed, often counterproductive, in that when confronted with behaviour problems some teachers and parents have been ready to 'blame the other side' (Galloway 1985: 60). Croll and Moses (1985: 47) show, for example, that teachers see behaviour problems as 'in the main deriving from the home and parental circumstances of the child'.

It is our intention, within this chapter, to illustrate how teachers, parents and other professionals *have* moved towards more positive procedures whereby they share responsibilities in order to respond in more appropriate ways to problem behaviours.

The benefits of such an educational partnership are discussed, together with examples of particular approaches which show how the sharing of information, advice and practical support can be of benefit to the pupil concerned.

The chapter also considers the practical steps which need to be taken in the development of effective working relationships and examines factors which appear to affect the degree to which behaviour problems can be ameliorated in this way.

THE CONCEPT OF SHARED EDUCATIONAL RESPONSIBILITIES

There is now a considerable body of advice which suggests that teachers and parents can usefully work together in active partnership (Warnock Report, DES 1978: Paragraph 4.29; Fish Report, ILEA 1985: Chapter 14). This advice is based upon the belief that through the sharing of information, advice and practical support, the resultant assessment of, and subsequent provision for, special educational needs will reach a level which neither the teacher nor the parent would have been able to achieve on their own.

In response to the above statement, we propose that the development of a shared educational responsibility towards behaviour problems will allow for a deeper understanding of the whole range of factors which are relevant to a particular behaviour and subsequent responses to it. This will require a positive form of joint action which seeks to accurately describe the behaviour, the factors which contribute towards it and the consequences which follow.

The results of various parent–professional initiatives, described throughout the text, present evidence to support the above view that joint responses can, and often do, lead to more effective responses to behaviour problems.

The potential value of joint action is clearly illustrated in the following description of how a mother, working with an educational psychologist, was able to assess and respond appropriately to the behaviour problems which were being exhibited by her daughter.

HEATHER

Heather's mother describes the background to the problem.

> Heather has been a very difficult child to cope with for some years now. She suddenly has very bad outbursts of temper tantrums, usually over some minor incident; having a bath, or being told to get dressed, brush her hair, her teeth, or being told to come into the house after she has been out playing. Over the years the tantrums have gradually decreased but she still has occasional outbursts. If she got really bad and was badly behaved for a few days, I would talk with her headmaster at school and he would have a word with Heather. After this she would calm down again for a few months.
>
> When Heather reached the age of 11 years, she obviously had to change schools. I expected a certain amount of trouble over this, as Heather shows great resistance to change, and since she was going to a special school she not only had to accept the

change of school and teachers, she also had to make new friends, as all her other friends were going to the local comprehensive school.

At first, all went surprisingly well, for the first couple of weeks she was quite happy and seemed to have settled in her new surroundings very well. Then suddenly the tantrums started again. Usually they were about coming in at night when she was told, but eventually things got so bad that life seemed to be one constant argument with Heather. At this time I decided to have a word with her headmaster, as I felt that I had completely lost control over her. No matter what I asked Heather to do the answer was always no. When I insisted that she did as she was told she would start to swear, kick, scream and throw things and I really felt that I was at the end of my tether, and that if things went on as they were, I would be in danger of cracking up under the strain. I have an older daughter, who is 21 and at work all day, and she also felt that things could not go on as they were. I would like to say, at this point, that my friends and family were very helpful, in that they would fetch her for an hour or so until she had calmed down. I would also like to point out that Heather only behaved in this way with me or her sisters and with no-one else. When the tantrum was over she would behave as if nothing had happened.

The response which the parent makes in this situation suggests that there are a very limited number of ways in which she can respond to the problem behaviour. Seeking to get over this commonly held illusion, the psychologist tried to help Heather's mother to solve the problem for herself.

In this case Heather's mother was asked to cassette record a typical argument with her child. Such a request forces the parent consciously to consider the factors which appear to lead up to and support the problem behaviour. This procedure is often, within itself, a successful form of intervention.

When the parent and psychologist listened to the tape recording together, it soon became apparent to Heather's mother that, through the very solutions she was using to solve the problem behaviour, she was helping to maintain it. She explains the insights she obtained in the following way:

After discussing the matter at some length it became apparent that on the occasions that I had not argued back with Heather, or by switching off and ignoring her, she calmed down much more quickly. Heather does not like to be ignored, and we decided that what she was doing, and in fact succeeding, was getting my *total* attention. When I was arguing with her, I was not reading, watching television, or talking to anyone else. She had my total attention, to the exclusion of everything else.

We decided that what I had to do was to be completely consistent in my approach to Heather. From now on I would not argue with her at all. I would ask her to do something and, if she refused, then I would say 'then I am not going to speak to you for five minutes'. During the five minutes that I was not going to speak to her, I did not have to react in any way at all, to show that she was getting to me, no matter what she said or did.

The resultant action, which was jointly planned by the psychologist and parent, was based very heavily upon a change in the mother's behaviour. This required her to adopt a consistent approach, through sometimes difficult circumstances. The following account demonstrates, quite clearly, the resources which parents can, themselves, offer, in dealing with problem behaviours.

The first time I tried this out on Heather, she was stunned. Although I had ignored her before, I had never stated that I was doing it and never set a time limit on it, so she obviously thought that if she was outrageous enough I would react, but this time I had to be careful not to react at all. The first time I did it she calmed down, almost immediately, but as days went by she got gradually worse. At the end of the first week I was ignoring her about five times a night. At this stage I saw the psychologist again; after discussing it with him I realized that she was getting really desperate to get my attention. She had always succeeded before by throwing a tantrum and she could not understand why she was failing now. Anyway, we decided to carry on. By the end of the fourth week things were almost unbearable. I was hardly speaking to Heather at all. I must stress, at this point, how extremely difficult it is not to react when a child is screaming and swearing at you. I never realized how difficult it would be until I actually tried it. Sometimes I had to walk out of the room, because I felt that if I stayed there another minute I would have to smack her. I usually consoled myself by thinking that I had stood it for four weeks and that if I reacted now I would have undone all the good I had done. If I had broken down just once, Heather would have kept on and on until I did it again.

By the time the fourth week was over Heather was really getting desperate to get my attention and she was trying every way she knew to get me to react. She decided to change her tactic, shouting and swearing was not working so she decided to start pushing me. Again I must point out how difficult it was not to start arguing with her. When she started to punch and smack I thought, this is the end, I can't stand any more, but carried on.

I found that when the pushing started I had to go out of the room, and she followed me from room to room, trying desperately to get me to speak or react in some way. In the end I had to lock myself in the bathroom because I really felt that I couldn't stand it any longer. I didn't want to break down, but I felt that if I didn't get away from her, I would. On the final day, I spent almost the whole day locked in the bathroom, out of her way, and again I must stress that it was very difficult not to just give in to my feelings to smack her.

After this really bad day, Heather seemed finally to realize that there was no way, no matter how badly she behaved, that I was going to argue with her and she simply gave up. For the next nineteen days we did not have one day when I had to ignore her. The difference was absolutely unbelievable. When I asked her to do something, although she had a little moan and groan about not wanting to do it, while she was complaining she was doing as I asked and never refusing to do anything. I must also say that Heather was much happier in herself and much more cheerful than she had been before. I also felt much better. I felt for the first time that I was in control and that I didn't have to turn to other people all the time for help.

Occasionally, Heather will still test me out and try and argue, but when she does, it is only occasionally, and as soon as I say I am not going to speak to her, she is the one who walks away. She just goes to her bedroom for a while and when she comes down again, she is quite calm, and although there are minor disagreements occasionally, as there are with all children, there have been no more major upsets or arguments as I refuse to argue.

I must also say that it is very important that when Heather is being good I go to great pains not just to ignore her, but to talk to her all the time, so that she realizes that to gain my attention she has got to be good and not naughty.

Twelve months later Heather's mother confirmed that she is still able to respond to the behavioural needs appropriately.

We are left with very little doubt, in the above example, that parents and professionals, when working together, can, even under difficult circumstances, assess and make appropriate responses to problem behaviours.

The success of the above case did, however, depend upon the high level of *cooperation* which was achieved between parent and professional. The mother's eventual response was clearly dependent upon the guidance of the psychologist, who in turn relied heavily upon the responses of the mother. We can also appreciate the high level of *trust* which was needed when the mother was required to examine, in detail, the effects which her own responses had upon Heather's behaviour. This process would have been very difficult if suitable levels of cooperation and respect had not been built up.

When behaviour problems occur in school the probing of the circumstances leading up to and sustaining the behaviour will need to be based on a similar level of respect and trust between teacher and parent, both of whom will need to examine the effects which they are having upon the behaviour. This level of cooperative activity will demand a very open and frank exchange, which will be very difficult to achieve if parents and teachers are intent upon blaming each other for the problem behaviour. Thomas (1991: 186) states that 'good team work is notoriously difficult to achieve' and discusses some of the issues which need to be considered if partnerships are to work effectively.

The first task, then, in developing positive joint responses to behaviour problems in school, must be to create conditions whereby suitably cooperative relationships can emerge. This issue is now examined, in some detail, in the following section, where it is suggested that this might best be achieved through four stages.

STAGES IN THE DEVELOPMENT OF A SHARED EDUCATIONAL RESPONSIBILITY

Misunderstanding between teachers and parents, and the apportioning of 'blame' for certain behaviours, may come about because of

1 a lack of understanding of the role and intentions of each other;
2 a failure to appreciate the constraints under which the other person is working;
3 an insufficient awareness that certain behaviours may be specific to particular situations, occurring, for example, in school but not in the home, and vice versa (Rutter *et al.* 1971; Hanko 1985: 96).

If the above misconceptions are to be avoided and parents are to become 'active collaborators in their own children's learning and development' (Jowett and Baginsky 1991: 201), it would appear to be necessary, as Smith (1980: 176) suggests, to establish a procedure whereby parents and teachers, in the course of their own duties towards a pupil, are given the time and opportunities to develop an understanding of, and appreciation for, each other's role and how they might usefully complement each other. This change in perception is least likely to occur if teachers and parents only liaise when something appears to be 'going wrong'. It is more likely to develop if they can meet, initially, under positive conditions, which are part of a normal and integral part of the education of all pupils.

Experience suggests that a useful way to avoid potential conflict and to build up the above levels of understanding and shared responsibility towards behaviour problems is through four stages of parent–teacher involvement, which we have called:

1 the introductory stage
2 the informative stage
3 the joint provision stage
4 the shared responsibilities stage

Throughout each of the stages, which are described in more detail below, schools will signal the extent to which a sharing of educational responsibilities is supported.

If the school wishes to promote an active partnership with parents this message will need to be made clear from the earliest stages, since this is likely to influence not only the extent to which parents feel welcome in the school, but also future patterns of working. The clearest message will be carried by the extent to which the school values contributions from parents, compared with teachers. If both sets of contributions are considered to be equally valuable, this is likely to be interpreted as a positive sign for joint involvement.

When schools present teachers as 'experts' to guide parents this is likely to be seen as a suggestion that their contribution is not as valuable as the teacher's and that they, therefore, should adopt a more 'passive' role. The result of this process, as will become clear in later sections of this chapter, is likely to have a marked effect upon the eventual pattern of working which is adopted in response to problem behaviours, with consequent effects upon the degree to which the difficulties are ameliorated.

Cunningham and Davis (1985) describe three ways of working, each of which is likely to give parents a good indication of the degree to which a school wishes to incorporate them into the educational process. The first model presents the teacher as the expert and is very similar to the example given above. A more active form of participation is implied in the transplant model, within which certain aspects of the teacher's expertise is transferred (transplanted) to parents, who might then be able to utilize them to effect certain changes in their own and the pupil's behaviour. This model, whilst involving parents in certain ways, retains a high level of dependence upon the teacher and does not recognize that parents may be able to participate in a reciprocal pattern of working, whereby they can offer useful guidance and support to the teacher. The acceptance of this 'equivalent expertise' is more evident in the consumer model, where parents, as consumers of a service, are considered to have important contributions to make regarding the educational provision which is given.

Schools will need, therefore, throughout the various stages of parent–teacher involvement, to be wary of the messages they transmit. If an active partnership, which is potentially more valuable to pupils experiencing behaviour problems, is to be achieved, this will require clear indications, throughout the four stages, that both participants have equally relevant parts to play. Those stages are now described in more detail, with practical illustrations to demonstrate how a sharing of educational responsibility has been achieved.

Before proceeding to discuss each of the four stages two issues must be raised. The first concerns the use of the term 'parent'. Under the terms of the Children Act (1989: Section 3(1)) the term 'parent' includes anyone who has *parental responsibility* for the child (e.g. this could be a grandparent or a guardian). Thus the actual 'partnership' which is developed must be with this particular person or persons. Second, whilst the vast majority of partnerships can, and should, be built out of mutual trust the authors realize that in exceptional circumstances some 'partnerships' will arise out of more formal circumstances (e.g. as a result of an 'education supervision order' (Children Act 1989)). Whilst the following stages might still be of relevance in such cases it is likely that differences will occur. A useful introduction to the above mentioned issues is given by Hodgson and Whalley (1992).

1 The introductory stage

In the beginning stages of any new working relationship neither parents nor teachers may be aware of the expectations which are being made of them, or of the benefits which may accrue if they develop certain methods of working together. Their own views about liaison might well be out of date. Parents' impressions of the degree to which they should get involved with the school might, for example, reflect views which existed during their own school days, during which their parents might not have been welcomed 'across the threshold'. Likewise, teachers new to particular schools, or experiencing a change in school policy, might also need to change their attitudes towards parental involvement to accommodate new ways of working. It is important, therefore, that adequate opportunities are provided within an introductory stage, during which new levels of understanding can emerge.

Activities, at this stage, if they are to enhance educational provision, should seek to introduce parents and teachers to each other in such a way that they can feel comfortable together, to develop a mutual understanding and respect for each other's intentions towards a particular pupil and to begin to realize the benefits of working together more closely. The relevance of this process will not be limited to the early years of schooling and should, therefore, be a recurrent feature which takes place at any significant time in a pupil's education (e.g. change in class, curriculum etc.).

There are many ways in which schools can introduce parents and teachers to positive ways of working together. Educationally and/ or socially biased activities can be designed to allow teachers and parents to meet in non-threatening situations. Helpful examples of activities which fulfil this introductory function have been described by Bailey et al. (1982) and include invitations to assemblies, displays and concerts, coffee mornings, introductory talks about selected aspects of the curriculum and discussions about ways in which teachers and parents can join together in the sharing of educational interests. If a school wishes to demonstrate that it places a high value on a sharing of responsibility, it may convey this message quite clearly to 'new' parents by involving 'experienced' parents in the planning and running of some of these introductory functions.

The school will also put forward its views on the value of partnership by certain hidden messages. These include various hints and may suggest, for example, whether all parents are equally welcome, whether success in pupils is only ascribed via academic excellence and whether pupils experiencing behaviour problems are considered to be a 'nuisance' or to have needs which are seen to be proportionate to any other educational need (e.g. reading needs). The way in which the school, unwittingly, broadcasts these messages is likely to have an effect upon the eventual success of joint ventures which aim to respond in the most relevant and effective way to problem behaviours.

The introductory stage, as described so far, has focused attention on the development of working relationships *within* the school. Not all parents, however, become involved in this way, often leading teachers to complain that certain parents, whom they would most like to see, never turn up. Some parents, due to various constraints (e.g. shyness, transport problems, single-parent households), have genuine reasons for not being able to attend the introductory sessions, whilst others will need their interest aroused. Successful schemes have overcome this problem by arranging for teachers to work through the home base, rather than attempting to bring all parents into the school. This change of venue often helps to erode barriers and introduce parents to useful ways of working with teachers.

At the culmination of this stage, parents and teachers will have received certain messages, either consciously or unwittingly transmitted, about the degree to which they are encouraged to work together. If these messages have sought to welcome their joint involvement this may have a considerable effect upon their readiness to work together, rather than against each other, if behaviour problems occur. The next stage of activity is designed to build upon these introductory activities by involving teachers and parents in the process of information sharing.

2 The informative stage

Having started to build suitable relationships through the above activities, the informative stage offers opportunities for consolidation and the beginnings of a more active involvement between teachers and parents which focuses more directly upon the development, needs and interests of a particular child in whom they have a mutual interest. Activities within this stage are directed towards the practice of giving and receiving information.

By keeping each other informed about educational progress, needs and interests, parents and teachers may be able to adjust particular aspects of educational provision at school, or within the home, to match those general needs. Parents may, for example, highlight a specific feature of the curriculum which their child has shown particular interest in, or conversely may bring to the attention of the teacher the pupil's negative reaction to certain experiences within the school which may, if they are not given suitable attention, lead to the occurrence of certain undesirable behaviours.

Teachers, in a similar way, can also use the informative process to relate progress to parents, who may in cases of strengths (e.g. desirable behaviours) consolidate success by appropriate forms of praise (e.g. verbal praise, special treats). Where difficulties occur information should still be passed on, but should not stop short at merely conveying that something is amiss. This could, as will be discussed later, lead to inappropriate responses being made in a retaliatory manner. The most appropriate response in this situation would be to stress the importance of working together through the following two stages, which emphasize the need to respond to the behaviour in a carefully considered way which is based upon an adequate analysis of the difficulties which are being experienced. Without this move towards carefully considered action, information giving will be an empty and, at worst, dangerous process.

Informative liaison most often occurs through consultation evenings. A typical pattern is for parents to have a specified ten-minute 'slot' with the class or subject teacher. Despite the time limitations which are imposed at these events, a useful, confidential, exchange of information, as suggested above, can still occur. Some schools, because of the time constraints, choose to supplement this activity by developing home–school diary systems. These can be used in a number of ways to allow parents and teachers to inform each other about daily progress in selected areas of interest (e.g. reading development, specified behaviours). Enhanced opportunities for discussion might also be afforded through involvement in the next stage (joint provision), where parents and teachers work closely together within the school or on a joint scheme of provision for a particular child.

3 The joint provision stage

A transition to the joint provision stage should occur fairly naturally from the previous stage of information sharing, which, as discussed above, will be somewhat of an empty process unless it is seen to lead to the planning and implementation of suitable provision.

Joint provision can be made at two levels:

1 for whole classes/groups/individuals within the school; and
2 for a particular child in whom both teacher and parents have a mutual interest.

At the level of general help within the school, parents may be involved in activities such as workshop sessions (e.g. redesigning and building a resource area), classroom support (e.g. helping pupils on individually structured programmes) or working with particular groups within a particular area of their own interest (e.g. a hobby). Through these activities parents and teachers can begin to develop much closer working links which will help them to understand and appreciate each other's role and the constraints acting upon them.

Joint provision for particular pupils may take a number of forms. There are now well-documented accounts of the various benefits which accrue from the joint involvement in the teaching of reading (e.g. Webb et al. 1985). At a more individualized level parents, class/subject teachers and special educational needs support teachers might be involved in providing, in a coordinated way, for specific pupil needs. An account of this method of involvement has been given by Jones and Charlton (1992).

The advantages of joint provision through these structured forms of involvement can be measured in terms of the provision of additional support to the school and individual children, and in affording opportunities for teachers and parents to work alongside each other and consequently have opportunities to understand and appreciate each others' roles. The next stage moves beyond this level of 'guided' involvement towards a situation where both participants accept a greater sharing of responsibility.

4 The sharing of responsibilities stage

The aim throughout the above three stages has been to develop a working relationship based upon mutual respect and trust which will promote a sharing of responsibilities. By the time the fourth stage is reached various forms of joint action at the informative and sharing of provision stages will already have given indications of ways in which educational responsibilities can be shared.

The sharing of responsibilities stage attempts to utilize and build upon the success of previous forms of collaboration in order to merge roles even further. This is particularly important when behaviour problems are encountered since, as will be argued later, an adequate assessment of, and provision for, behavioural needs is dependent upon the contributions of both teachers and parents.

Before considering the actual form which those contributions should take, let us first consider a scheme which clearly demonstrates how the behavioural needs of pupils in secondary schools have been met by a sharing of responsibility between parents, teachers and other professionals. For convenience, we have entitled the scheme 'The Wiltshire Project' (see Fletcher and Presland 1990).

The Wiltshire Project

A support teacher for adjustment problems was appointed to each of four comprehensive schools in one area of the county. The aim was that the support teacher should work as a member of an in-house *team* which would examine problem behaviours 'in context' and attempt to find effective ways of responding to those problem behaviours.

Some support teachers adopted behavioural approaches which were based upon the development of a 'contract'. The procedure for setting up contracts involving the school, the pupil and the parents is outlined by Fletcher and Presland (1990: 157):

1 decide on the priority behaviour targets;
2 partly draw up the contract prior to interviewing the parents;
3 interview the parents and establish rewards and sanctions;
4 get all parties to sign the contract;

Mark agrees to:
1 Bring the necessary equipment to each lesson.
2 Not to move from his seat without permission.
3 To be quiet when the teacher is giving instructions.
4 To hand the contract to the teacher at the beginning of each lesson and to show the contract to his parents daily.

The school agrees to:
1 Sign Mark's contract at the end of each lesson.
2 Write positive comments when appropriate, and indicate other aspects of behaviour that Mark may need to improve.
3 To communicate with home on a weekly basis, or more frequently if necessary.
4 To review the contract in one month's time, or earlier if necessary.

The parents agree to:
1 'Gate' Mark on Tuesday and/or Saturday nights if he breaks his contract more than twice in one week.
2 Remove all Mark's pocket money and pay him 15p for each successful lesson plus an extra 50p per week if the contract has not been broken.
3 Remove his computer/TV for a day each time Mark breaks his contract.

Signed

. . . . Pupil
. . . . Parents
. . . . School

Date . . . .

Figure 8.1

5 agree a review date for the contract (e.g. about one month hence);
6 agree a method of monitoring the contract and a method of feedback to the parents so that rewards and sanctions can be applied as soon as possible after the event;
7 inform teachers about the contract;
8 if the contract does not work, troubleshoot, but do not expect 100 per cent improvement;
9 collect information for possible revision of the contract at a later date;
10 praise, praise, praise (in private).

An example of a behaviour contract which was developed via this approach is given by Fletcher and Presland (1990: 155) and is reproduced in Figure 8.1. The contract shown in the figure had a simple recording format (called the contract progress report) on the reverse of which teachers wrote positive comments and also recorded instances of unfavourable behaviour that were not covered by the terms of the contract.

The use of such contracts in the Wiltshire Project led to the reduction of problem behaviours. The success of this approach has meant that 'contracting' has now been more widely adopted in many of the schools which participated in the project.

A similar approach was used by Melton and Long (1986) to attempt to modify the behaviour of secondary-aged pupils by linking their performance in school to specific consequences in the home. This form of joint action, to provide for pupils' behavioural needs within the mainstream school, reduced the need for transfer to off-site units.

The above initiatives demonstrate the degree to which problem behaviours can be responded to more effectively when parents, teachers and other professionals enter into a sharing of responsibility.

We do not, however, wish to suggest that *all* forms of shared activity would necessarily result in the above level of success. There appear, as suggested earlier, to be certain factors which determine the outcome of these initiatives. One variable, which has already been discussed, concerns the degree of cooperation which can be achieved. The following section of this chapter examines other factors.

FACTORS AFFECTING THE SUCCESSFUL OUTCOME OF EDUCATIONAL PARTNERSHIPS

An analysis of cases where parents and professionals have jointly and successfully responded to behavioural needs leads us to suggest that the outcome of various forms of involvement will be dependent upon the quality of shared:

- information
- advice
- practical support

Various ways in which teachers and parents could work together on each of these criteria will now be examined in order to assess their relative worth in meeting behavioural needs.

Information sharing

Information sharing will only be of maximum use if it helps to determine relevant responses to problem behaviours. Two kinds of activity can be distinguished, the first of 'keeping each other informed' is potentially less influential than the process of 'shared information gathering'.

Keeping each other informed

We have already seen, at the informative stage, that the sharing of information about particular needs, interests and levels of motivation might be useful in helping to match the curriculum to general needs. It was also suggested that this action might help to prevent the occurrence of problem behaviours. We now go on to consider the usefulness of this procedure once difficulties have been encountered.

Parents and teachers, through a sense of commitment or legal duty towards each other, may wish to 'keep each other informed' about a certain problem behaviour, passing on impressions or facts about which the other person may or may not be aware. The very act of 'passing on' information in this way suggests that both parents and professionals are intent on taking their own forms of action upon the basis of the information which they are given. When action becomes separated in this way it is possible for parents and professionals to make quite different responses to a behaviour which, due to the resultant inconsistency and confusion to the pupil concerned, may have only a limited impact.

Information which is 'passed on' in this way also runs the risk of being too shallow to guide relevant action. Vague descriptions such as:

> Jill doesn't pay much attention, she is always gazing out of the window, or chatting to others,

and:

> Paul drives us mad in the evenings, always arguing with us and never doing what he is told,

tell us very little about the behaviour itself or what is *needed* in a particular situation. Indeed, armed with information which at worst may be impressionistic, some parents and teachers might take action which, because it is not founded on an adequate analysis of needs, could lead to a worsening of the situation. If, for example, parents were to punish their child for undesirable behaviour at school, this could, feasibly, lead to a worsening of the situation, resulting, for example, in school refusal.

There is also the danger that certain levels of anxiety might interfere with the process. The need to 'tell' another person about certain behaviour problems is often accompanied by the desire to 'offer an explanation'. This process, at worst, could lead to the 'naming' of a particular behaviour, a process which, we suggest, is often entered into to make the listener more comfortable about the occurrence of the difficulties, almost as if it is acceptable because other people have 'got it'. Labelling a particular behaviour in this way will not, however, clarify exactly what the *needs of the situation* are, and will not 'lead to a plan of action about how to change it' (Westmacott and Cameron 1981: 9).

The process of 'keeping each other informed' about problem behaviours, if it is limited to the above levels of activity, is not then sufficient to lead to the planning of appropriate provision. If, however, the procedure goes further in an attempt to guide some form of consistent, joint activity, it could result in a much more positive outcome whereby parents and teachers are able to develop joint plans of shared action. If information sharing reaches this level, however, we would suggest that something more than 'keeping each other informed' is taking place, and that participants are now entering into the process of shared information gathering.

Shared information gathering

The process of shared information gathering is a much more positive procedure, whereby teachers and parents accept a joint responsibility for getting adequately informed.

It is all too easy, as we have intimated previously, to describe problem behaviours in vague or general terms which are not based on a sufficient account of the difficulties which are being experienced. Describing a pupil as disruptive, lazy, withdrawn or maladjusted is a labelling process which suggests that the 'problem' lies entirely within the child. Information which is couched in these generalized terms cannot help parents and teachers to plan appropriate joint responses because it fails to give any indication of precisely what is required. Attempting to plan action from these vague descriptions can only lead to hazardous guesses about the responses that should be made, which might, at worst, include reactions such as 'she needs a good spanking' or 'he'll grow out of it'.

If information sharing is to lead beyond uncalculated or negative reactions to problem behaviours, it will need to move towards a much more precise gathering of information which describes, precisely, the difficulties which are being encountered. This implies a process which goes beyond the lighting up of problems within the child to a wider-beamed search which comprises an analysis of *all* the factors which promote a particular behaviour.

Within the process of shared information gathering teachers and parents will therefore need to collect adequate and appropriate data which will allow them to act in a much more positive way. To do this effectively they will need, first, to arrive at a precise description of:

- the behaviour itself
- factors leading up to and surrounding the behaviour
- the consequences which follow the behaviour
- expectations about future behaviour

The rationale behind this detailed form of analysis is discussed by Presland (Chapter 5), who also describes a relevant procedure which can be followed to arrive at an adequate understanding of behavioural needs. When this kind of procedure has been followed (e.g. as in the case of Heather), this has often led to appropriate pointers for action which, because they have led to a consistent approach, have often resulted in success.

If parents and professionals enter into the above process *together*, the resultant outcome is likely to lead to a gathering of information which neither party would have been likely to achieve on their own. This enhanced level of needs analysis is likely to occur because of the high level of objectivity which is implied in the above process. In attempting to assess in a carefully calculated way *all* of the factors which contribute to and sustain a particular behaviour, parents and professionals, by working together, may:

1 highlight significant aspects about a behaviour which might otherwise have been overlooked, perhaps because either party 'didn't want to see them' (McConkey 1985: 97); and

2 promote a more accurate account of the behaviour which is not distorted by the 'strong emotional attachment between the child and the parent' (Cunningham and Davis 1985).

When an adequate assessment of needs has been achieved through the above form of joint action, it is then possible, through the next stage of advice giving, to begin to plan action to meet those needs.

Advice sharing

The outcome of this form of joint activity can be evaluated in a similar way to that of information sharing. Two different kinds of sharing of advice are suggested, the first of 'advising another person' is considered to be potentially less influential than the practice of 'advising each other' about the most relevant form of action to take.

Advising another person

At the most basic level, a person could seek to give 'advice' to someone else by adopting the role of expert, which was described earlier. This level of activity, whilst suggesting various ways in which it might be advisable to respond to a particular behavioural need, may have only limited success, due to the fact that it is often only based upon a general recipe for action which seems to work 'in most cases'. This level of advice may or may not work, depending upon how closely the particular case fits the general pattern.

The second level of advice giving adheres to the transplant model, whereby various skills are transferred to the parent who then attempts to assess needs and modify a particular behaviour through his or her own resources. This process could again be based upon very generalized responses to behaviours, which might not, necessarily, lead to successful intervention. If, however, the model involves the parent heavily in the process of needs identification (as in the case of Heather) this can have a considerable effect upon the behaviour.

In cases where both parents and professionals are directly involved with the behaviour, as in the case of problem behaviours in school, there is a need to enter into another level of advice sharing, whereby they attempt to 'advise each other' about the most relevant form of action to take, with the ultimate aim of agreeing upon a response which they can both make with some consistency.

Advising each other

When parents and professionals advise each other about the most relevant response to a problem behaviour (e.g. changing the consequences or promoting a different behaviour) they may be able to guide each other about specific factors, relevant to the plan of action, with which the other person might not be familiar.

It has been suggested, for example, that parents have a particular knowledge of their children, 'their needs and strengths and how they feel those needs might best be met' (Hanko 1986). This aspect of a parent's knowledge was used to guide the action which was taken in the Wiltshire Project, described earlier. In that particular case the parents' knowledge of particular rewards and sanctions which their children valued was used to modify that pupil's behaviour in school.

Professionals, themselves, may be in possession of another form of knowledge, which we might term 'technical knowledge', which could be useful in guiding both participants through tried and tested procedures which help to determine behavioural needs and provision. This form of guidance was brought into operation in the case of Heather, which was described in an early part of this chapter.

Advising each other about particular forms of intervention which may work in particular situations is also vital to their successful outcome. Teachers may, for example, be able to offer general advice about what forms of action might 'work' within the home, but it is the parents' own intimate knowledge of that situation which is required in fine tuning the plan to ensure success.

When an agreed form of action has been agreed, it is then possible to consider what action might take place in the final stage of practical support sharing.

Practical support sharing

A sharing of responsibility, through the final stage of practical support, can, if it takes advantage of the resources which each of the partners have to offer, lead to a change in behaviour which might otherwise have been difficult to achieve.

At school, some teachers may be at a loss for rewards and sanctions which are as powerful as those which are available to parents in the home. Where parents can become involved in the control of the various treats which a child enjoys, these can, as we have already seen, lead to a modification of a pupil's behaviour.

CONCLUSION

Various parent–professional initiatives, which have been outlined in this chapter, lead us to suggest that a sharing of educational responsibility towards behaviour problems can result in a change in the total environment in which the child finds him or herself, thereby leading to more desirable behaviours.

Joint responses towards problem behaviours rely, however, on a high level of cooperation between parents and professionals, which is not likely to occur if they seek to blame each other for the behaviour. We have recommended, therefore, that four stages of collaboration are necessary if appropriate relationships and understandings are to be developed.

Where good relationships have been built up through the above stages, the effectiveness of the resultant joint activity appears to be dependent upon the quality of the shared information gathering, advice giving and practical support which takes place. Various factors which appear to affect the quality of these three factors have been discussed.

REFERENCES

Bailey, G., Bull, T., Feeley, G. and Wilson, I. (1982) *Parents in the Classroom*, Coventry: LEA Community Education Development Centre.

Children Act (1989) *The Children Act*, London: HMSO.

Croll, P. and Moses, D. (1985) *One in Five*, London: Routledge.

Cunningham, C. and Davis, H. (1985) *Working with Parents; Frameworks for Collaboration*, Milton Keynes: Open University Press.

DES (1978) *Special Educational Needs* (The Warnock Report), London: HMSO.

Fletcher, P. and Presland, J. (1990) 'Contracting to overcome adjustment problems', *Support for Learning* 5 (3): 153–8.

Galloway, D. (1985) *Schools, Pupils and Special Educational Needs*, London: Croom Helm.

Hanko, G. (1985) *Special Needs in Ordinary Classrooms*, Oxford: Blackwell.

Hodgson, K. and Whalley, G. (1992) 'Spotlight on children', *Education*, January: 72–3.

ILEA (1985) *Educational Opportunities for All* (The Fish Report), London: ILEA.

Jones, K. and Charlton, T. (eds) (1992) *Learning Difficulties in Primary Classrooms. Delivering the Whole Curriculum*, London: Routledge.

Jowett, S. and Baginsky, M. (1991) 'Parents and education – issues, options and strategies', *Educational Research* 33 (3): 199–204.

McConkey, R. (1985) *Working with Parents. A Practical Guide for Teachers and Therapists*, London: Croom Helm.

Melton, K. and Long, M. (1986) 'Alias Smith and Jones', *Times Educational Supplement*, 11 April.

Rutter, M., Tizard, J. and Whitmore, K. (1971) *Education, Health and Behaviour*, London: Longman.

Smith, T. (1980) *Parents and Preschools*, London: Grant McIntyre.

Thomas, G. (1991) 'Defining role in the new classroom teams', *Educational Research* 33 (3): 186–98.

Topping, K. (1991) 'Achieving more with less; raising reading standards via parental involvement and peer tutoring', *Support for Learning* 6 (3): 112–15.

Webb, M., Webb, T. and Eccles, G. (1985) 'Parental participation in the teaching of reading', *Remedial Education* 20 (2): 86–92.

Westmacott, E.V.S. and Cameron, R.J. (1981) *Behaviour can Change*, London: Macmillan.

Wolfendale, S. (1986) 'Involving parents in behavioural management, a whole-school approach', *Support for Learning* 1 (4): 32–8.

Chapter 9

Agencies working with schools

Kenneth David

PASTORAL TEAMS

Our welfare state makes a considerable effort to supply varied support to help families in need, whether they are deviant, improvident, aggressive, inadequate or unfortunate. Yet there can be difficulties for the teacher who may be seeking support or advice in dealing with the problems of a pupil: not only may there be a local absence or inadequacy of particular support, but there can also be difficulty in managing liaison with, and understanding the characteristics of, various aid agencies who do not necessarily work well together, and who may even give the appearance of cordially disliking each other at times. Many headteachers seek a more standardized and efficient liaison system with the agencies with which they seek to deal. The school appears to be the institution at the centre of the web of aid which is best suited to manage liaison about children with the various professional and voluntary workers, but there may be professional jealousies, differing qualities of staff, differing standards of training, contrasting values, greatly differing work loads and sometimes a distrust of a teacher or school to bedevil coordination.

The fundamental goodwill and caring nature of most professional agency workers does produce sometimes harrassed support for teachers, pupils and families, but it could be better. The occasional well-publicized cases of children who come to harm through failures of the school and welfare services illustrate this. A team leader needs to be clearly identified in all care groups of statutory agencies linked with a school. Sometimes a senior teacher can be the leader for such referral and liaison teams; often it will be someone from educational psychology, health or social services.

Experience and seniority count most, rather than professional status ranking. Such teams have been used in child abuse and drug education matters, and local 'committees of concern' and 'pastoral liaison groups' do exist and function usefully. Early liaison over troubled families and pupils can later save time and cost for our society.

Wetton (1982) writes of the school having a central position in inter-service attachments and multi-professional in-service training. Too much inter-agency cooperation is developed accidentally and incrementally, sometimes with a political background, instead of an emphasis on children's needs rather than the safeguarding of the system itself.

A more structured approach to such liaison requires agreed regular meetings and secretarial and communication arrangements, producing more positive and concerted action with pupils and families. Debate continues at times on the level of state, community and school intervention into the affairs of families and their children, with the implication that schools should concentrate on teaching those who want to learn, worrying less about the troubled and improvident who sometimes take so much time and attention. Such harsher views ignore the investment of earlier rather than later pastoral (or perhaps custodial) care, apart from humane values.

Recent changes in education brought about by the Education Reform Act of 1988 have brought fresh challenges to school pastoral care. A greater dependence on governors under the local management of schools is bringing changes, particularly in finance. As always, much will depend on the personality and educational values of the headteacher. Governors will have to be persuaded of the value of pastoral care appointments, of the need for experienced staff to deal with pastoral as well as academic work, of the continuing need for staff in-service training and of the need for the school to support pupils with special educational needs, who may not add much to academic assessment successes. On the positive side governors can be a strength in their knowledge of the school's locality and people, perhaps supporting children of known families at risk, perhaps refusing to exclude children for whom the school could best provide care and protection, perhaps at times viewing poor attendance figures with understanding rather than with a crusading desire for normality when compared with other schools.

SECONDARY SCHOOLS

Secondary schools have usually developed strong pastoral systems which may attempt to deal with the following objectives:

- involving all staff in pastoral as well as academic work
- advising on special educational needs
- dealing with learning difficulties and study skills
- supporting the various welfare needs of pupils
- watching for and attempting to cope with physical, emotional and behavioural problems
- assessing and recording achievement
- liaising with parents and outside agencies
- ensuring order and enforcing discipline
- managing a coordinated programme of tutorial work and personal and social education
- organizing and dealing with the administrative tasks of the school
- concern with sports, leisure and community affairs

Larger secondary schools have a teenage population which inevitably will have normal adolescent problems, and there are normally pupils with behavioural problems, and the usual and increasing numbers of family problems. Secondary schools have the advantage of more senior staff members concerned with managing such problems, often with great experience and skills and often with a useful network of contacts in outside agencies. With such staff initiating a good liaison with other agencies, and with efficient tutorial systems and pastoral care teamwork, a school should provide a reasonable screening of pupil problems, though no school ever avoids its share of failures. The strength of the National Association of Pastoral Care in Education illustrates the growth of pastoral care professionalism in recent years.

Some schools have 'extra care' lists for staff, noting particularly vulnerable children – families involved in divorce or separation, bereavement or recent unemployment, for example. Other schools have regular 'concern groups' of staff who meet at intervals to review the development of all the children in a year group. All pastoral care developments must inevitably include cooperation with others outside the small world of the school. Closer links with parents and the community are obviously essential in the complicated task of motivating children for successful schoolwork, for the personal worlds of children affect their ability to study and learn and the academic tasks of teachers depend in turn on what pastoral care systems make of those personal worlds. As part of that process easier communication between professional workers and better combined knowledge of pupils are priorities.

PRIMARY SCHOOLS

In primary schools there may be a greater depth of knowledge of children and a better contact with their families than in a secondary school, but there is:

- less specialization of staff
- less time available for managing pastoral matters and contact with other agencies
- great reliance on the education welfare officer (EWO) and his abilities
- less inclination by outside agencies to liaise with small educational units

Sometimes primary schools can group themselves to arrange larger gatherings of primary-school teachers with their agency colleagues, for mutual increase of trust and exchange of information. Sometimes, but still too seldom, a secondary school works closely with its feeder schools in pastoral and agencies liaison.

Schools will in future depend more than ever on the quality and concern of the governors in developing such liaison work, in developing in-service work for teachers in pastoral matters and in developing personal and social education. Further consideration of personal and social education is given in Chapter 7.

FAMILIES AND SCHOOLS

Every teacher knows that a considerable proportion of the families with which they deal have human failings which prevent them functioning well with their children: irrespective of social standing and respectability family life can be stressful and can affect children. Some families are inadequate and harmful for their children. Because we can never see inside any family other than on a superficial level, we have to be sensitive in judgement, but evidence of immaturity, selfishness and violence is common. Much problem behaviour in pupils is the fault of schools themselves, but clearly poor family life creates children who are more vulnerable to problem behaviour. We have a duty to the children of such families, as well as the normal pastoral care for all children, whose families may or may not be well known to us.

We act on behalf of parents, and pastoral care and close cooperation with the other caring professions is part of our task, however much we attempt at times to retract into the purveying of knowledge as our sole task.

It is wrong to be too idealistic. We cannot change society only through education, and we cannot cure ills and problems which are rooted in politics and economics, but we can do better than we are doing at present. With prison populations rising, mental illness and stress so common and materialistic and selfish attitudes commonplace, we have a social role in schools. The diagnosis of and action on child abuse is one example; schools can sometimes provide the opportunity to break the circle of abuse which can repeat itself in families.

Teachers resist the gibe of 'amateur psychiatrists' for their main role is to ensure learning opportunities for their pupils. To manage learning, however, demands a dual academic/pastoral role for the teacher (a traditional schoolteacher's role incidentally) – they cannot teach effectively without it, for society and its pressures permeate every classroom.

Care is an inter-professional matter, and in the following sections we provide a brief reminder of the agencies with which schools have to liaise at times, for there are limits to teachers' time and expertise in dealing with more serious behavioural and family problems.

THE EDUCATIONAL PSYCHOLOGY SERVICE

Teachers with qualifications in psychology and further post graduate training provide schools with advisory support as educational psychologists. A principal educational psychologist coordinates the service, and each educational psychologist normally serves a group of schools. They are concerned with the educational development of all children, and work in schools, in the community with pre-school children and their parents and with medical and social service colleagues. In schools they may work with individual children or with their teachers, making an assessment of intellectual, psychological and emotional development and behaviour problems, providing recommendations for transfer of children to special schooling and mutually negotiating with teachers on a wide variety of other educational advice.

When working with a local child guidance service in dealing with individual children's problems and with home situations the educational psychologist and parents may consult clinical psychologists, psychiatric social workers, child psychotherapists, perhaps special needs support teachers and consultant child psychiatrists.

Where local authority economies have closed child guidance clinics, educational psychologists are increasingly coming under pressure from referrals through general practitioners and their hospital connections and from local social service departments (which are facing many changes and different challenges under the Children Act of 1989).

Chapters in this book illustrate the wide variety of helpful liaison which can develop between schools and their educational psychologists, who are increasingly seen as valued members of school care teams and as supporters and advisers to individual teachers.

THE EDUCATION WELFARE SERVICE

The education welfare service employs EWOs who have statutory duties relating to compulsory education, the general welfare of children at school and children's part-time employment. The basic duty of the service is to provide a social work service within the schools, ensuring that every child receives and benefits from the opportunity of a suitable education. Experienced EWOs often have a deep knowledge of their communities and of the families of school children, and can help in establishing close links between teachers and parents. They deal regularly with problems of school lateness, truancy and non-accidental injury, and help with cases of badly clothed, uncared-for and under-nourished children. They deal with free school meals, travel and clothing grants, and employment permits. They can be a major contact with health and social services departments, police, probation and the NSPCC, as well as with WRVS and other voluntary bodies.

EWOs are facing new challenges following the 1991 enactment of the 1989 Children Act. Parents can still be taken to magistrates' courts for their children's non-attendance at school, but former care orders are more difficult to obtain and the EWO will now probably have an educational supervision order (initially for one year, but this may be extended on more than one occasion for up to three years at a time) from a Family Proceedings Court, not always seen as important to the EWO's more difficult clients. The purpose of the Act is to increase parental authority and to keep children out of care and within their family, but this worthy aim reduces the EWO's ability to cope with very difficult cases; persuasion is replacing potential authority and the parent is presumed to know best unless clearly proven otherwise.

Exclusions from schools are increasing massively in some areas where increasing violence and the breakdown of authority are reported, and with the reduction in the powers, funds and authority of the local education authority we may see fewer exchanges of pupils between schools and more excluded children on the streets. This will especially be the case if grant-aided or 'opt out' schools increase, for competition between schools is not likely to add to the wish to cooperate in accepting difficult pupils.

THE SCHOOL HEALTH SERVICE

The National Health Service is responsible for school health services, with a consultant community paediatrician or a senior clinical medical officer having a clinical responsibility for the service. Clinical medical officers work in all types of schools and are concerned with emotional as well as physical problems. With the help of the school nurse they will examine children in school and offer routine immunizations. The school nurse will also do routine hygiene inspections and will be involved in health education programmes.

In some areas school nurses offer health interviews to pupils in secondary schools. Health visitors are experienced in the normal development of children and can give valuable advice. Their duties are to visit all young children to promote their welfare and proper development and to advise and assist parents in this. Health visitors are particularly helpful in their links with local medical practitioners (with whose practices they are often closely linked) and they also contribute to teaching and advising in health education.

Doctors in general practice have a considerable knowledge of patients and their families, in addition to a knowledge of their medical history and current ailments. Together with their attached health visitors they are in a good position in many instances to diagnose situations of risk for children. Doctors place a high value on confidentiality as part of medical ethics, and this can cause conflict in some situations when liaising with other professionals.

Paediatricians are specialists in the medical care and treatment of children, based in hospitals or clinics. They can arrange careful examinations of a child when abuse is suspected, and can give expert advice concerning the significance of injuries.

Psychiatrists in hospitals or clinics are specialists in mental disorders. Dental officers deal with school dental inspections. Audiologists and speech therapists deal with hearing and speech problems. Nurses and midwives may know children and their families and help in certain circumstances in school problems.

Teachers normally deal with their school nurse or health visitor and their school medical officers who should have a considerable knowledge of local homes and families. It should be noted that no one has the legal power of entry to visit a child, and no power to examine a child, without parental consent.

SOCIAL SERVICES

Social workers employed by local social services departments have a statutory duty to investigate all complaints relating to the neglect or ill-treatment of a child, and have a general duty to promote or safeguard the welfare of children for whom the department of social services has a responsibility. Most previous legislation is now repealed and the Children Act of 1989 now forms the basis of their work with children.

Professional social workers are employed in hospitals, voluntary agencies, clinics, residential establishments, nurseries, day centres and some schools. Social workers are trained in group work, counselling and community casework, and an important part of their work is attempting to form professional relationships with their clients. Their role places them in a good position to recognize the signs of family and personal problems as potential risks to a child. Good relationships cannot be achieved without trust, involving confidentiality and resulting sometimes in inter-professional conflicts.

Social services register and supervise child minders, foster parents, private nurseries, play groups and adoption arrangements and provide intermediate treatment facilities for young offenders.

The Children Act of 1989 has brought many changes for social workers dealing with children. The Act aims to develop a new model of parenthood, to have the child's welfare as the paramount feature, to have more consistent decision-making principles and to strengthen parental authority. The local authority still has a duty to provide day care for vaguely defined 'children in need', but it is far more difficult to remove children from their families. Every authority must have a written plan for every child involved with the social services, and parents can see these plans and discuss changes.

This new requirement for openness and partnership with parents means that social workers are required to share information with parents and children, sometimes causing difficulties with other professions.

Social workers can still intervene in families and seek a care or supervision order in court if children suffer 'significant harm', which is not defined as it is different for each child. The child may have a voice in court, and custody cases have fallen. Considerable evidence is now required before the case goes to court at all. Emergency protection orders may be given in extreme cases.

A child can therefore be taken away from a family and into care, but it is a far more difficult process than in the past, and a child of 'an age and understanding' cannot be forced to have a medical or psychiatric examination in abuse cases.

Social workers have in many cases been withdrawn from child guidance clinics to deal with mainstream social service work. This and other changes may make liaison between education and social services more limited, and schools may have to be faced with more in-school pastoral and counselling care of pupils with problems of misbehaviour, poor attendance and perhaps violence.

School attendance problems are no longer the responsibility of social workers; this is now an educational concern and 'care and supervision' is no longer a remedy.

OTHER HELPING AGENCIES

Police officers have powers, subject to assessment of the evidence by the Crown Prosecution Service, to institute criminal proceedings against an adult alleged to have committed a criminal offence against a child, including cruelty. They can institute civil proceedings in respect of a child thought to be likely to suffer significant harm. Senior officers have discretion as to whether or not to institute proceedings of either sort. A police officer can remove a child to police protection on his own initiative. Whilst there is provision under the Children Act 1989 for the police to apply to the magistrate for an emergency protection order, the onus would normally fall on the local authority social services department. There is a clear obligation on the police to advise and liaise with the local authority in these cases. It is interesting to note that it is only the police who have authority under the Act to remove children without a court order.

Officers often have information which might suggest a situation of risk, either directly through a complaint about a child or indirectly perhaps by being called to a domestic disturbance or a neighbours' quarrel. Investigation of an alleged offence is not necessarily followed by a criminal prosecution, and the matter may begin and end at a case conference.

The Act gives parents more responsibility, and police or social workers can no longer remove children from a family 'just in case', and with police responsible for their own actions there may continue to be a natural reluctance to intervene in family situations unless it is very clear that a child has been ill-treated or abused. While anyone can claim that significant harm is being done to a child, it is the magistrates who decide if it is so, with the parents' voice clearly heard.

Police community relations officers can be useful allies of teachers and Schools liaison officers are appointed in some areas to work closely with schools.

Probation officers have the task of advising, assisting and be-friending probationers and reporting breaches of probation orders to magistrates. They are usually experienced in counselling skills, including marital counselling, and can be helpful with individual problem children from families known to them. They would normally expect to take on supervisory orders made in the juvenile court on offenders of over 14 years of age.

The NSPCC offers a range of services to children and their families. The NSPCC Child Protection Helpline (0800 800 500) is a national free twenty-four-hour telephone service receiving referrals and offering counselling and advice on child protection matters. The helpline will pass information requiring further action or investigations to NSPCC teams and projects, social services or police. The society has a network of over seventy child protection teams and projects which undertake a range of activities including investigations, assessment and therapeutic work, family care, training, a consultation service to other child care professionals and specialist work.

The society offers an information service on all aspects of child abuse. A national training programme of short courses is offered, run mainly from the NSPCC Training Centre in Leicester. The society's library contains a comprehensive collection of books and materials on child abuse and protection and also handles the sale of NSPCC publications.

The Samaritans, Relate (Marriage Guidance Councils), The Catholic Marriage Advisory Service and the Citizens' Advice Bureau are increasingly being used by young people for help with their problems, and close liaison by schools can be useful. The Citizens' Advice Bureaux are a treasure house of information on our welfare society, and are increasingly helping families with debt counselling as well as other advice.

Youth workers often have considerable knowledge of young people of a locality, frequently having a very different view of pupils in informal and out-of-school settings. They are trained in groupwork and counselling, and form good members of liaison teams.

Local clergy and The Salvation Army can be helpful with their knowledge of the community and local families. Some are experienced in counselling skills, making them helpful in referral work when this is acceptable to them. Some churches have organized youth counselling schemes.

Local authority housing officers know local community affairs well, and usually have a deep knowledge of disadvantaged and problem families.

School ancillary staff are local people who know pupils and their families. They can sometimes be the trusted confidants of children. Some schools have co-opted ancillary staff to their pastoral care team meetings, when they are known to be particularly popular with pupils.

Local people such as shopkeepers and neighbours of a school can be helpful in advising on potential or actual behaviour problems of pupils, and also in commending good behaviour.

Parents are the prime carers for their children. We must always involve them in all decisions about their children, constantly attempting to act in parallel with them, even when they appear disaffected or disinterested. Parent governors can be very helpful in reporting on parental worries and concerns.

Specialized national support services exist in great numbers and can be contacted through social and health workers, through EWOs and advisory and teachers' centre staffs and through public reference library facilities.

Examples of agencies concerned with various aspects of family life and pupil problem behaviour could include the following:

- Advisory Centre for Education (parents and child-centred education)
- Alcoholics Anonymous (families)
- Child Poverty Action Group
- Children's Legal Centre (children and the law)
- Church of England Children's Society
- Commission for Racial Equality
- Contact a Family
- Council for Children's Welfare (pre-school children)
- Cruse (widowed parents and their families)
- Dr Barnardo's (children in need, fostering and adoption)
- Depression Anonymous
- Family Conciliation Councils, in some areas
- Family Rights Group (advisory and publications)
- Family Welfare Association (families in need)
- Friends of the Children's Society (needy and deprived children)
- Gingerbread (single parents and their families)
- Independent Panel for Special Education Advice (free advice for children with special educational needs)
- Institute for the Study of Drug Dependence (help for parents)
- Law Centres (legal action groups)
- Mencap (mental illness)
- MIND (mental illness)
- Minority Rights Groups
- Narcotics Anonymous
- National Advisory Centre on the Battered Child
- National Association for Maternal and Child Welfare
- National Association for Gifted Children
- National Association for Special Educational Needs
- National Association for Counselling Adoptees and Their Parents
- National Children's Bureau (needs of children)
- National Childbirth Trust (childbirth and child care)
- National Council for Civil Liberties

- National Council for the Divorced and Separated
- National Council for One Parent Families
- National Federation for Solo Clubs (loneliness)
- National Stepfamily Association
- Shelter (housing pressure group)
- Victim Support Schemes
- Volunteer Bureaux
- WRVS

A useful list can be found in *TIPS: The Teacher Information Pack – Support Services Guide* by Tricia and Ron Dawson (1988), or by reference to Citizens' Advice Bureaux or reference libraries.

This chapter concludes by listing some actual case studies, with altered identities, to illustrate the nature of liaison in problem behaviour, and perhaps to form the basis of discussion in college or in-service training groups.

CASE STUDIES

HARRY was a 15-year-old boy in an urban secondary school. After an uneventful and anonymous career in the lower forms, drifting along in the bottom sets and, sadly, hardly known by most staff, he was reported by the police for shoplifting in shops near the school. After a police warning and a fairly heated discussion between the headteacher and the shopkeeper (a parent of former pupils at the school), the staff discussed Harry at a 'committee of concern' reviewing Upper School pupils.

Gradually a fuller story emerged: Harry was intelligent but lazy and he could have had greater academic demands on him if anybody had been interested; he had for more than two years been associating with older pupils who had been great troublemakers at a neighbouring school; he was casually looked after by an aunt with whom he lived, his parents having separated and largely abandoned him; and his shoplifting had largely been for clothing and cigarettes.

For his final year at the school Harry was given more attention, given new youth club opportunities by a competent teacher–youth worker, sent on a residential activity weekend and given greater encouragement by his aunt and her family, who joined with his form teacher in giving greater attention and encouragement. When he left school it was with the beginnings of some ambition and a determination to join the armed services. The school pastoral system in the Lower School needed and was given revision and clearer leadership.

JOHN was a 10 year old attending a very good primary school in a middle class town setting. Excellent teachers and good liaison with outside agencies still left a gap in knowledge. It was only through a Victim Support volunteer contacting the school that two facts emerged: his long suffering mother had been continually assaulted by the father, with an eventual police intervention and a court case, and the boy and his sister had often been slapped and hit as well, with a resulting minor hearing defect in the boy. 'Good' families in fairly prosperous settings can at times conceal the same problems that more dramatic and less inhibited families display for the world to see. Good liaison between the school and John's new secondary school gave him good support and care.

The next two cases are given by an efficient and keen young teacher of some six or seven years' experience, in a large primary school on a disadvantaged urban estate.

KEVIN started school with very aggressive behaviour. He kicked, scratched, bit and swore if asked to do anything he didn't want to do, and my main worry was that he would seriously harm other children in the class. I had to spend most of my time sitting with him as one minute he would be stringing some beads and the next attempting to throttle another child. A major problem was that he didn't like any physical contact, and was big for his age so he was hard to handle in a tantrum. I wrote about his problems in my record book each week and the headmaster asked Kevin's mother to come to school after the first half term. Kevin was the eldest of four boys, mother in her twenties. She wouldn't admit to having any problems with Kevin at home, although it was local knowledge that he had set fire to his bedroom when he was three, and neighbours reported that he was tied to the garden fence during the summer holidays. The mother eventually agreed for the educational psychologist to see Kevin in the classroom situation and at home. The educational psychologist kept reviewing Kevin's case every six months and finally after three years in the infant department he was transferred to a special school. The Head there said Kevin should have been sent to him when he was four. In my opinion it was unfair on the children in the class and the class teachers to have to contend with the child as he required so much individual attention.

WENDY was a very unhappy little girl and when she entered school she had a very low opinion of herself. Her father had mistreated her and her mother. I was able to form a relationship with both Wendy and her mother, and the child responded to affection and praise, but it was impossible to give her all the attention she needed with twenty-four children in the class. Wendy never used to let me out of her sight or touch. She held my hand in assembly, sat on my lap in the classroom, and was very aggressive to other children who needed my attention. I told the head of my concern over Wendy and he asked her mother to come to school. The mother admitted she couldn't cope with Wendy's tantrums and stubbornness at home and she was quite willing for the educational psychologist to see her. The educational psychologist suggested that as Wendy was so attached to me would I be prepared to keep her in my class for an extra year. I didn't feel this was the answer for either of us. I felt under a strain all the time trying to meet Wendy's needs and at the same time to strike the right balance with the rest of the class. I was always worried that Wendy wasn't integrated with the rest of the class or forming friendships with other children. The educational psychologist reviewed Wendy's case every six months but it wasn't until she was 9 years old that she was sent to a special school. As Wendy progressed through our school she had personality clashes with some of her class teachers and grew more unhappy and alone, hence more anti-social behaviour. She suffered increased feelings of failure and isolation through her time in a mainstream school.

There are times when pressure from within the community is far more effective than even the strongest combination of other services!

MEG was a large woman, with a voice to match and language that was chosen to express her feelings immediately and clearly. One day the doors of the Family Centre burst open to admit Meg, with her two youngest trailing somewhat unwillingly in her wake. She stood for a moment, arms akimbo and with no denture in; then, with a motherly clip round each ear, sent her offspring to play. She sat for the rest of the session sternly surveying the scene. She accepted a cup of tea with a loud sniff and moved only once – to administer a sound cuff to her youngest, who was about to cover his sister in paint. At the end of the session, she gathered the two children up roughly and swept out.

The next week Meg came back – this time with teeth in and her knitting. We noted that the expression had softened just a little. It was only a couple of weeks later that Meg was to be found at the dough table with her own children and sundry others too – the teeth remained firmly in, but the knitting never appeared again. Furthermore her sister's child was added to her two and, on occasions, her sister was unceremoniously bundled into the Centre to 'do her bloody bit as well!'

Meg became a strong supporter of the Family Centre – she expressed her views strongly and loudly but was always there when help was needed. There were two families on her estate who all the local services and the Family Centre were trying their best to help and to get to regular sessions. One day in came Meg with the number three from one of those families, one hit hard by unemployment, illness, very bad living conditions and inconsistent parenting. This meant that she had two of hers, one of her sister's and now another under her ample wing.

The story did not end there. Meg managed to get the single mother of the other family to let her bring the youngest in. In this case there were suspicions of both drug and sexual abuse. The mother was extremely introverted and unwilling to come to the Centre herself. Meg now had five to collect, bring and get involved in Centre sessions, but the parents were not forgotten. Meg's sister put in appearances periodically, grumbling and swearing but occasionally admitting to some degree of enjoyment. The father of the first family was seen joining in a music session with one child, while mother looked on and bounced the latest on her knee in time to the music. As for the single mother, she began coming just inside the door to pick up her child at the end of the session, but she accepted a cup of tea at one point! It was Meg's strong and caring personality, coupled with her approval of the Centre, that got first the children, then the parents, involved – other services had tried but failed!

TRACEY AND GARTH were in the top class of an urban primary school, and caused concern to the staff because of wildly fluctuating behaviour, from being engaging and cooperative youngsters full of life, to a mood of sullen awkwardness. They were not twins, but behaved in similar ways. It was through the parents of other children in the class that the headteacher eventually found that the children were terrified of their father, who had legal access to them periodically. The mother was dead, and they were living contentedly with good foster parents.

Both had been treated badly by the father in their earlier years, when their mother was alive and before the family was broken up. The mother had been of low mentality and the father was often violent, and possibly abused the children sexually, though this was not certain.

There had been no contact between the school and social services over the children for some years, but contact was soon made after the discovery of the children's terror of their father, which was not known by social services and had not been reported by the foster parents, who had merely thought the children moody at times.

The father was eventually denied access to the children and the EWO and the foster parents kept closer liaison. Regular discussions with social services, the EWO and the staff were arranged.

A social services office received an anonymous telephone call one afternoon from a girl threatening suicide and complaining of sexual interference by her stepfather. She refused to give her name and eventually rang off. A social worker reported on this call at a regular case liaison meeting at the local comprehensive school, asking staff to try to identify the child.

The deputy head invited class tutors to have 'an ear to the ground' on the matter, and eventually a third-year tutor reported hearing from girls in the class that a girl, JEAN, had been complaining to friends about her stepfather.

After staff discussions it was decided to invite the parents in, with a pretext of discussion on a school medical examination. The parents were a quiet couple, clearly wishing to be cooperative with the school, though they had had little contact with the school before. They soon talked of the behaviour of Jean, the stepfather claiming he was 'at his wit's end' in knowing how to deal with her tempers and moods. After one example of teenage rebellion he had lost his temper and hit the girl, and had pulled her off balance by his hand catching in her loose jersey. The mother and he had then watched the girl storm out of the house, and clearly this was the girl's excuse for telephoning social services.

This story was volunteered by the mother and stepfather, who clearly had been worried by the girl's general behaviour, and further discussions with parents, with the EWO and the school doctor, and with Jean, indicated that the fault was the girl's.

The parents welcomed the possibility of help from the staff in coping with Jean, and a useful and helpful liaison was established with the class tutor and the EWO.

REFERENCES

Charlton, T. and David, K. (1990) *Supportive Schools*, Basingstoke: Macmillan.

Social Services Year Book, yearly, London: Longman.

Social Policy and Administration, quarterly, Oxford: Blackwell.

Dawson, R. (1985) *TIPS: The Teacher's Information Pack – Support Services Guide*, Basingstoke: Macmillan.

Smith, F. and Lyon, T. (1991) *Personal Guide to the Children Act*, Purley: Children Act Enterprises.

Wetton, J. (1982) 'Schools in the welfare network', *Child Care: Health and Development* 8: 271–82.

Chapter 10

Reflections and practices

Tony Charlton and Kenneth David

SCHOOLS AND TEACHERS DO MAKE A DIFFERENCE

In Part I of this book it was suggested, on the basis of substantial evidence from research enquiries, that much behaviour at school seems to be independent of home influences. In other words, children's behaviour at school appears to be strongly affected by 'within school' factors. In the broadest context these factors are concerned with *what* schools offer their pupils and *how* they offer it. While there is little doubt that aspects of school policy and organization, school ethos and the content/delivery of the curriculum make significant contributions to these offerings, we should not underestimate the impact of teachers' behaviour – particularly their classroom management skills – upon pupil behaviour.

A logical extension of the argument for a 'specific situation' cause of much behaviour, and the importance of 'within school' influences upon pupils' behaviour, is that much of pupils' classroom behaviour is less determined by wider school characteristics than by individual classroom influences. Schools (and homes) *do* affect behaviour in classrooms but we wish to emphasize that the behaviour which occurs in specific situations in the classrooms is largely determined by influences within those very teaching situations. It is difficult not to accept this if we recognize that the same pupils often behave disparately with different teachers.

In stressing the importance of the class teachers' role, and their classroom management skills in particular, we are not merely drawing attention to the good teaching and management skills which are evident in many classrooms, and suggesting that in other classrooms there are less successful colleagues who need to enhance such skills. None of us is perfect, and we do not all share common strengths and weaknesses. Rather, we recognize that:

1 the great majority of teachers make considerable efforts to succeed in their professional endeavours;
2 those efforts do not always lead to success; all of us, therefore, to a lesser or greater degree, benefit from continually evaluating and reflecting upon the efficacy of our efforts and making efforts to improve them – this is professionalism;
3 self-appraisal will most likely lead to success when it has the support of our school and colleagues;
4 efforts to enhance our management skills will be more likely to achieve success if we have guidelines to good practice for reference to, or comparison with.

In earlier chapters the contributors considered theories and practices which have relevance for the development and practice of teachers' classroom management skills. We now reflect upon, and highlight, some salient points from within those chapters and, with additional pointers of our own, assemble a tentative set of guidelines which may be helpful to practising and student teachers in their efforts to improve their skills in managing pupils' behaviour in classrooms and schools. This checklist is neither comprehensive nor in order of priority, but might be used by a teacher, or a school staff, to shape a personal or school plan for the better management of pupils' behaviour, learning and development.

USING REINFORCEMENT SKILLS

A knowledge of the reinforcement concept gives added meaning to much classroom behaviour and, with a healthy degree of self-criticism, we can appreciate the occasional errors of our ways when, for example, our *non-reinforcement of appropriate behaviour* and *reinforcement of inappropriate behaviour* can actively encourage misbehaviour.

While common sense often seems to guide us in our use of *positive reinforcements* it is useful to remember the following.

1 We need to be wary of an overzealous use of reinforcements which may lead to satiation.
2 Effort should be reinforced as frequently as actual achievements;

by doing so we encourage industry and persistence, without which achievement becomes less likely.

3 Similarly we should not be too niggardly in rewarding appropriate social behaviour. It is the responsibility of schools to help educate pupils not only in terms of their academic behaviour but also their social behaviour. However, research findings reported by Wheldall *et al.* (1989) found that teachers tended to give nearly five times more approval to academic behaviour, as opposed to social behaviour. Conversely an examination of disapproval rates administered to the two behaviours showed a tendency for teachers to administer twice as many disapprovals to social behaviour. Overall, the findings in the study by Wheldall and colleagues suggested an inclination for teachers to issue disapprovals to unwanted social behaviours and ignore wanted social behaviours. In behavioural terms these types of practices are counterproductive. They can encourage the behaviours we wish to discourage as well as discourage the very behaviours we should be seeking to promote.

4 With some individuals it may be necessary to search hard to find behaviours which warrant praise. Perseverance by the teacher in those instances is often crucial, for these may be the very pupils most inclined to misbehave because they have been reinforced so infrequently in the past.

5 Reinforcements administered publicly to some pupils may, in fact, be construed by the pupils as punishment. For a variety of reasons (e.g. shyness, and with older pupils a fear of ridicule from peers) some pupils dislike having public attention drawn to their efforts and accomplishments. Praise may need to be given privately and in confidence.

6 We are often misled into believing that reinforcements need to be given immediately following the occurrence of desirable behaviour. While this may be true in some instances (e.g. when working with children with mental handicaps or the very young perhaps) occasions become more frequent with increasing age and maturity when a delay between behaviour and reinforcement may be not only more convenient, but more effective and desirable. Many of the reinforcements we receive as we grow older (such as assignment grades, degree awards and promotion) may often be distant from some of the acts which earned them. As part of the maturing process youngsters need to learn to appreciate and accept this 'time gap'.

7 Reinforcements can be signalled in subtle ways, perhaps a wink or a smile. Where applied within large group situations they not only provide variety but can also be used in a 'confidential' manner. While young children may prefer a hug, it is a sad indictment of the age in which we live that we need to be especially guarded about using this physical contact.

8 What is reinforcing (e.g. attention and praise) *from one person* may not be so from another. Similarly, what is reinforcing *to one child* may not be so to another. An awareness of these differences provides a reminder of the complexity of the reinforcement concept.

9 Reinforcements can be given to small and large groups as well as individuals. They can work wonders for group morale.

10 On occasions we may need to make clear to pupils what has been reinforced, by drawing attention to behaviour-reinforcement associations. 'Good' may not necessarily indicate to the pupils 'what is good'. It may be more appropriate and beneficial to comment 'Good. You've worked hard this lesson.'

Negative reinforcements also have a contribution to make to teachers' management of classroom behaviour, but they should be used carefully and sparingly. Whereas positive reinforcers are applied to – and so encourage – good behaviour, negative reinforcers (e.g. threats) lead to improved behaviour only because pupils behave appropriately in order to *avoid* unwanted consequences. An example of negative reinforcement occurs when a teacher informs a class, at the onset of morning break, that they will remain in the classroom until their rowdy behaviour ceases; so to avoid the unpleasant experience of missing some of their break period, the class behaviour has to improve. However, not all children will regard remaining in the classroom as an unpleasant experience!

While negative reinforcers can make useful contributions to teachers' management skills, an over-reliance upon them can result in the frequent use of threats and warnings; conditions that make little, if any, contribution to a healthy classroom ethos and are inconsistent with good management practices.

CONSIDERING PUNISHMENTS

Punishment is a common and often effective occurrence in our lives. Undeniably, a variety of punishments are used in schools and classrooms including:

order-points

reprimands

detention

lines

time-out from positive
reinforcement

disapproval

ignoring

loss of privileges

suspension

on-report

token loss (within a token
economy)

sarcasm

cynicism

sanctions

Nevertheless aspects of its use in the classroom have aroused some concern and debate. There is evidence available showing that behaviour in some classrooms is controlled by a preponderance of punishments as opposed to rewards (Thomas *et al*. 1978). It is difficult to envisage a healthy classroom ethos where this type of control prevails.

Opposition against the use of some punishments is most frequently based upon the following arguments.

1 Punishments often serve only to help prevent a behaviour occurring in the future; by themselves they do not provide alternative acceptable behaviours which should be used.
2 They can generate fears and harmful anxieties which may encourage avoidance behaviours (i.e. the pupil may avoid places where, or people from whom, punishment has been – or is – given).
3 This avoidance of punishment areas (e.g. a particular teacher, subject or classroom) may generalize to other areas (e.g. other teachers, subjects, classrooms, school).
4 Their application may serve as an unhealthy model for pupils.

Clearly, where punishment is administered it should be recognized that it may not only prove unhelpful, in the sense that it does not provide positive guidance for miscreants' future behaviours and may provide unhealthy models for observers and recipients alike, but may also create unhelpful fears and anxieties which actively encourage avoidance behaviours such as truancy.

Nevertheless, it does not seem unreasonable to suggest that intervention attempts restricted to positive or negative reinforcements, building of self-esteem and good modelling may not always be in the best interests of children or teachers. At times it may be both expedient and helpful if pupils experience aversive consequences of their misbehaviour. This does not imply a wholesale usage of punishment, but rather that occasions may demand that it is used, though sparingly and effectively, for the very best of reasons.

Clarizio and McCoy (1983) consider arguments for the use of punishment, and offer the following guidelines for its administration.

1 Whenever possible the pupils should be given a signal or warning prior to potential punishment. This, by itself, may deter the misbehaviour. It also provides a degree of fairness where the punishment becomes inevitable (e.g. 'You were warned!').
2 Research evidence has consistently shown that it is usually better to punish early than to delay until the problem has become magnified.
3 Attempts should be made in the first instance to remove the rewards (antecedents, consequences) which elicit or sustain the misbehaviour.
4 It should be made quite clear why the punishment is being meted out.
5 Punishment should not be given unfairly and injudiciously.
6 It should be employed by teachers in a rational, systematic and 'mood free' manner. Its aim is to improve the pupils' present and future performance, and not provide a cathartic experience for the teacher.
7 It should not be administered through, or accompanied by, emotive screaming or yelling conveying an attitude of revenge which may, in fact, serve only to reinforce the very misbehaviour which is being punished.
8 It should not be too severe.
9 Its use over extended periods of time should be avoided. The length and nature of the punishment should match the offence (e.g. don't use a sledgehammer to smash a walnut), as well as the pupil's developmental level.
10 The punishment should not take up an inordinate amount of the teacher's time. A detention arranged for after school may be as punishing, if not more so, to the teacher as the pupil.
11 Wherever possible, related appropriate behaviour should be rewarded either side of the punishment of inappropriate behaviour; thus we reprimand the child when off-task but remember to reward when on-task; we reprimand (or try to ignore) unwanted social behaviour *and* reward desired social behaviour (i.e. catch the pupil being good).

MODELLING FROM TEACHERS' BEHAVIOUR

Modelling is an important way in which children and adults learn 'chunks' of behaviour. From a classroom management perspective modelling theory has much to offer. Children, in addition to that which they learn from the formal curriculum in school, learn much from observing their teachers and peers. Along similar lines Stott (1978) makes the pertinent comment that a small number of pupils in each class seem 'to set the tone either of studiousness or waywardness' (p. 133). It is common knowledge that they often find it easier to learn behaviours which they see practised, rather than only being explained to them: they tend to do even better when the two are combined. They will be more inclined to model the behaviours of those who have prestige in their eyes: while young children seem intuitively to assign prestige to their teachers, older ones are more discriminative and tend to require their teachers to earn such prestige. In general, teachers who are able to form good personal relationships with their pupils and earn their respect are more likely to earn prestige and therefore have their behaviour modelled.

It seems important, from a modelling perspective, that teachers behave in classrooms in ways which they wish their pupils to adopt. Where inconsistencies exist between the adult's own behaviour and the behaviours asked of the class, pupils can easily become either confused about which 'sets of behaviours' they should adopt, or imitate the wrong ones.

The following give only an indication of the wide repertoire of behaviours which prestigious teachers can demonstrate in classrooms and so encourage their pupils to model.

1 Recognizing, and respecting, the responsibilities of authority figures such as parents, colleagues, headteachers and police.
2 Respecting other individuals' rights by listening to them and responding with interest; refraining from using sarcasm and harsh criticism.
3 Acknowledging and accepting responsibility for personal errors, and failings, by accepting and responding appropriately to justifiable criticism, and apologizing to pupils where situations require it.
4 Demonstrating a sensitivity to, and concern for, individuals' problems and feelings (e.g. concerns, fears, unhappiness and anxieties), and a willingness to assist where practicable.

5 Refraining from over-reactions by practising control of their own emotions.
6 Exhibiting commitment, concern and personal respect which set standards which reflect positive expectations of pupil behaviour and attainment (Smith 1992).
7 Recognizing, accepting and responding responsibly to less, and more, obvious individual differences, such as children with special needs, those from ethnic minority groups and those in care.
8 Handling books, equipment and other materials with care.
9 Accentuating positive aspects of pupils, such as their attributes, achievements and efforts, rather than negative ones.

ENHANCING SELF-CONCEPTS

We are now more able, and willing, than in the past to recognize the role which the self-concept plays in helping to determine behaviour. We know, for example, that children who do not perform well academically often hold a more negative picture of their 'self' than their more successful peers. Similarly, there is evidence available suggesting that children experiencing a range of emotional problems such as anxieties, worries and concerns also tend to have low self-concepts. According to Charlton and David (1990) the self-concept is formed – in part – by a process of socialization by interactions with others and as a result of the feedback from those interactions. This feedback can include messages which depress the self-concept such as: 'you're not very bright' and 'we don't need you'. Instances such as these suggest an infinite number of ways in which low self-concepts may be associated with behaviour problems. Pupils who regard themselves as poor achievers, for example, may be conscious of, and sensitive to, their academic inferiority. If their inferior performance fails to attract desired teacher reinforcements, then they may resort to misbehaviour in order to 'succeed' in attracting teachers' attention. Equally important, the actual feelings of failure and inferiority may themselves constitute unhealthy emotional states.

What is clear is that classroom experiences may depress, as well as elevate, pupils' self-concepts. Teachers, understandably, have a key role in determining which of these two conditions predominate: their deliberate or unintentional actions help determine their pupils' concepts of 'self'.

Teacher characteristics such as *empathy, unconditional positive regard for pupils* and *genuineness* seem likely to encourage the growth of positive self-esteem in pupils. Empathic understanding implies that teachers can experience their pupils' 'inner world'. They know how they are feeling and, therefore, gain insight into their behavioural responses to those feelings. Unconditional positive regard suggests an interest in, and a liking and concern for, the youngster; feelings such as these actively demonstrate that the teacher 'cares' and wants to help. Genuineness is a teacher state which the pupil interprets as honesty and openness.

In combination these qualities illustrate the 'caring' concern on the teacher's part; one which is both sensitive to pupils' fears, worries and concerns and willing to support, or build up, pupils' skills and self-concepts. Given that such teachers are equipped with other appropriate skills they arrange classroom experiences for pupils which maximize opportunities for personal, social and academic success, yet make failure possible. Burns (1982) suggests that teachers can enhance a pupil's self-image by:

- making the pupil feel supported
- making the pupil feel a responsible being
- helping each pupil to feel competent
- teaching the pupil to set realistic goals
- helping the pupil to evaluate himself realistically
- encouraging realistic self-praise

More specifically, Canfield and Wells (1976) outline a hundred ways to improve children's self-concepts. They describe in detail a large number of teaching activities and teacher behaviours which can affect pupils' self-concepts in positive and negative directions. While there are too many to describe in detail – or even list – the following provide a cursory glimpse into those activities.

Social silhouettes

Daily, or less frequently, a pupil volunteers to become 'famous'. A full-size head silhouette of the child is drawn on a dark piece of paper, perhaps with the aid of the light from an overhead projector. It is cut out, mounted on a sheet of different coloured paper and pinned on the wall. For that day, the rest of the class are invited to write *complimentary* comments about that person on a piece of paper, and they attach them to the display. At the end of the day the teacher then reads the comments to the class, after which the 'head' is transferred to another prominent position elsewhere ('Hall of Fame'), perhaps in the hall. This type of exercise can work wonders! We would all like to hear the positive thoughts which people hold about us; but only infrequently do we have the opportunities.

Success sharing

Pupils are allocated to small groups and asked to volunteer to share some of their successes, achievements or accomplishments with the group. To give them some needed direction it may be helpful for the teacher to suggest that they first share the experiences they enjoyed, for example, before they started school; then before they were 6, then 9 and so on. Alternatively, the teacher could encourage them to talk about successes which happened recently, or within the last month, or the last year.

With some children, particularly those with low self-concepts, the teacher may need to draw attention to successes which *they* know the child has experienced – 'Your mother was telling me how helpful you had been in caring for the "new" baby.' This type of activity, correctly managed, can help children to recognize that they will have accomplishments of which they can be proud. In life it is so easy for all of us to become preoccupied with negative, rather than positive, aspects of our 'self'.

On my mind

Pupils each have a silhouette of their own heads. They then cut out pictures, words or sentences which represent their current thoughts and paste them on to the 'profile' to make a collage of their feelings. Later, if pupils are willing, these collages can be shared with others in the class. This activity not only may provide the teachers with helpful information about the pupils' feelings, but also may help some pupils to realize that some of their concerns, for example, are shared by others; they are not alone.

Killer statements

Here the teacher gives examples of how people can make comments which cause hurt to others:

- You're a thorough nuisance
- She's hopeless
- What a stupid boy. Can't you do anything right?

Drawing attention to the fact that other people have feelings that can easily be hurt can help pupils to become more helpful to, and considerate towards, their peers and others.

The goalpost

The teacher prepares a diagram of a football pitch, complete with a goalpost, on a display board. Children can elect to record their 'goal for the day' on a small piece of card and place it *beneath* the upper bar of the post. On the following day, the teacher invites only those who have achieved their 'goal' to discuss it with the class and then place their 'goal card' above the bar – assuming the 'referees' accept that it is a goal.

TO TEACHERS FROM THEIR PUPILS

Common sense often dictates, prudently and appropriately, how we should behave with – and towards – our pupils. The following list of 'guidelines' (source unknown) offers uncomplicated advice to teachers. Whilst many of the comments may have more relevance to younger children, others cross all age ranges.

1 Don't spoil me. I know quite well that I ought not to have all that I ask for; I'm only testing you.
2 Don't be afraid to be firm with me. I prefer it. It makes me feel more secure.
3 Don't let me form bad habits. I have to rely on you to detect them in the early stages.
4 Don't make me feel smaller than I am. It only makes me behave stupidly 'big'.
5 Don't correct me in front of people if you can help it. I'll take much more notice if you talk quietly with me in private.
6 Don't make me feel that my mistakes are sins. It upsets my sense of values.
7 Don't be upset when I say 'I hate you'. It isn't you I hate but your power to thwart me.
8 Don't protect me from consequences. I need to learn the painful way sometimes.

9 Don't take too much notice of my small ailments. I am quite capable of treading on them.

10 Don't nag. If you do, I shall have to protect myself by appearing deaf.

11 Don't make rash promises. Remember that I feel badly let down when promises are broken.

12 Don't forget that I cannot explain myself as well as I should like. That is why I am not always very accurate.

13 Don't tax my honesty too much. I am easily frightened into telling lies.

14 Don't be inconsistent. That completely confuses me and makes me lose faith in you.

15 Don't put me off when I ask questions. If you do, you will find that I stop asking and seek my information elsewhere.

16 Don't tell me my fears are silly. They are terribly real and you can do much to reassure me if you try to understand.

17 Don't ever suggest that you are perfect or infallible. It gives me too great a shock when I discover you are neither.

18 Don't ever think that it is beneath your dignity to apologise to me. An honest apology makes me feel surprisingly warm towards you.

19 Don't forget I love experimenting. I couldn't get on without it, so please put up with it.

20 Don't forget that I can't thrive without lots of understanding love, care/concern/understanding/listening/trusting, but I don't need to tell you that, do I?

EXPLORING 'BENEATH THE SURFACE' BEHAVIOURS

The needs of children (in mainstream as well as special schools) whose behaviour problems are more severe and long lasting may require teachers to be less concerned with changing *'surface'* behaviours than with exploring *beneath* these behaviours to identify, understand and provide for underlying difficulties the children may be experiencing. There is a range of techniques available which teachers can draw upon in order to provide appropriate help. By and large, these strategies and skills are of an order which requires specialist training. In general terms they include establishing classroom climates which provide *security, a degree of predictability, individual help, clear and realistic expectations* and *safety* for each pupil, in order to enhance individual personal, social and academic competencies and so help to erase the self-doubts and low self-esteem which often characterize these children.

These strategies and conditions are equally relevant to the needs of children without such serious and long-term problems. However, in more serious instances the use of these strategies requires protracted periods of time within which to develop chances of success.

Where teachers apply long-term strategies, they may well benefit from parallel initiatives which offer them skills to manage more immediate and challenging surface behaviours. Fritz Redl's (Redl and Wineman 1952) contributions to management techniques, rather surprisingly in view of his leaning towards psychodynamic approaches, have proved invaluable to mainstream and special school class teachers time and again. Working with children with severe emotional problems at Pioneer House in America, he stressed the residential community's long-term aims and strategies to assist pupils to establish 'controls from within', while recognizing that, in the short term, his teachers also needed management techniques which would provide 'controls from without'. His response was to construct a set of management skills, which he entitled *The Antiseptic Manipulation of Surface Behaviour*, designed to exercise control over pupils' surface (superficial?) behaviour. Like many effective techniques their apparent simplicity and common sense belies their impact. He talks, for example, about the following.

1 *Ignoring misbehaviours* as far as practicable, contending that some misbehaviours have only a limited 'charge' and, if ignored, they lose their charge and so disappear.

2 Using a *sense of humour* to exorcise bad feelings. For example, Jimmy, a petulant and aggressive adolescent, entered the classroom, sat down and placed his feet on the desk and announced to all and sundry that he was going to work at half-pace in future. The inexperienced, yet very sharp, young teacher immediately retorted 'Good; that will be an improvement'. The teacher laughed, the group laughed and Jimmy, somewhat less willingly, then joined in; a potentially volatile situation had been defused.

3 Using *signal interference* to exercise quiet (almost confidential at times) yet effective controls over minor misbehaviours –

raised eyebrows, a raised finger to the lips or a wink. Some teachers have achieved mastery with this skill. Where the class is working well apart from a single or small number of culprits, the teacher can practise such signals without disturbing the rest of the class, and without antagonizing the individual(s).

4 Giving *hurdle help*, where a teacher is alert to a situation which can develop unhealthily, such as pupils beginning to quarrel or becoming frustrated at not being able to do work. The teacher intervenes before the problem grows and helps the pupils to 'hurdle' or successfully deal with the problem situation.

5 Using *proximity or touch control*, where the teacher controls misbehaviour by physically moving towards it. Approaching the source of misbehaviour and, perhaps, touching a child's shoulder or hand is often sufficient to quell it.

6 The *involvement of interest relationships*, where a teacher notes that a child is losing interest in his or her work and is about to misbehave. By expressing an interest in that child's work the teacher can refocus the child upon the work and so prevent the misbehaviour.

7 *Restructuring*, where the activity being undertaken is beginning to generate unacceptable behaviour, and the teacher changes the activity to one which precludes 'disturbing' behaviour.

8 *Regrouping*, an activity where the teacher transfers the child to another seat, group or – in more extreme situations – another class in order to remove the child from situations in which he or she can either disturb, or become distracted by, others.

9 Providing an injection of *hypodermic affection* – giving praise or affection – so that teachers may encourage a pupil to cope with anxiety or frustration.

10 *Antiseptic bouncing*, which occurs for a number of reasons when the pupil has to be removed from a situation where he or she is either causing, or is on the receiving end of, behaviour likely to cause considerable harm to peers or himself or herself. Bouncing, or removal, takes place in order to give help to the pupil, and should not encourage feelings, on the child's part, of rejection or rewarding.

11 *Interpretation as interference*, where the pupil has 'misread' or misinterpreted a situation and the teacher intervenes to interpret the situation correctly to the pupil.

12 Using *direct appeal* for appropriate behaviour on occasions, appealing to a child's sense of fair play or justice.

13 Using *promises, rewards, punishments and threats* to encourage appropriate, and discourage unacceptable, behaviour.

Teachers, of course, will know that more severe emotional and behaviour problems demand help which, in terms of time as well as expertise, they are often ill-equipped to provide, and perhaps would be ill-advised to attempt. In these instances, if the severity of the problem was previously undetected or unsuspected, the teachers' primary function is to bring the pupil's difficulties to the attention of the relevant referral agencies, in accordance with the school's policy. Guidelines for such action have been reviewed in Chapter 9.

PREVENTIVE APPROACHES TO DISRUPTION

The preventive approaches to disruption (PAD) material (Chisholm *et al.* 1986) sensibly emphasizes a number of basic classroom rules which, though rarely given the recognition they deserve, help to keep pupils to their task, leaving little time for other activities likely to interfere with the smooth running of the class. The philosophy underpinning these 'rules' is as follows:

- pupils' behaviour is influenced by the teacher's behaviour
- teachers with effective classroom control are skilled at avoiding and de-escalating problem behaviour
- specific techniques of classroom management and control can be described, practised and acquired by teachers
- teachers should take responsibility for developing their skills and should be supported in doing so by their schools

The 'common sense' rules draw attention, for example, to the wisdom of teachers practising the following.

1 *Positioning* themselves, particularly at the beginning and end of lessons, where they have maximal opportunities to oversee and regulate pupils' behaviour. Similarly, when approaching a child to give individual attention there are obvious advantages in assuming a position which requires only an upward glance to monitor other pupils' behaviour.
2 Adequately *preparing lesson content*, making sure that materials and equipment needed are available in sufficient quantity and are easily distributed.
3 Using unobtrusive and *subtle management skills* such as proximity control by being near miscreants both to quell minor

misbehaviours such as talking, unnecessary fidgeting or 'fiddling' and to avoid giving them undue and possibly harmful prominence.

4 Refining and extending their repertoire of *non-verbal skills* in order to:

(a) avoid teacher behaviours likely to increase the likelihood of pupils misbehaving, such as:

- speaking in a monotonous way
- making little eye-to-eye contact with pupils
- using limited gestures
- communicating feelings of anxiety or tenseness to pupils

(b) practise behaviours likely to discourage pupil misbehaviours, such as:

- teachers being at ease with their classes
- using non-verbal gestures – eye-to-eye contact, rhythm and emphasis in their voices, and changes of posture

5 Organizing their classrooms in ways which motivate children to work well and so leave little time for misbehaviours. In this context the following seem important.

(a) Apparatus, materials and furniture should preferably be assembled and arranged prior to pupils' arrival.

(b) Lesson plans and content are prepared thoroughly, and additional work is prepared for those pupils who finish early.

(c) Work is made appropriate to pupils' age, ability and cultural background.

(d) Pupils' entrance to classrooms is supervised and orderly.

(e) Lessons commence in an enthusiastic manner and continue to attract and maintain pupils' attention.

(f) Instructions are given in a clear, audible fashion.

(g) Where lesson changes take place these are well organized and smooth.

(h) Vigilance or 'with-it-ness' is practised so as to enable teachers to monitor behaviour and intervene where potential difficulties arise so as to minimize disruptions.

(i) Where problems do arise, teachers intervene promptly.

(j) Teacher actions are perceived by pupils as being fair.

(k) Classwork and homework is marked promptly and thoroughly, and feedback is helpful and meaningful.

(l) Effective questioning techniques are developed to check whether pupils have assimilated learning and to help keep attention.

(m) Teaching techniques are varied so as to maintain interest.

(n) Anticipation of the timing of lessons is undertaken successfully so that the ending can be efficient and orderly.

(o) Attention is focused upon the potential dangers of narrow corridors and classroom seating arrangements that offer passageways which impede orderly movement by pupils and encourage rowdy and boisterous behaviours.

(p) Avoidance of:
- using physical means of governing pupils' actions
- ridiculing pupils

CONSIDERING THE CURRICULUM

We know only too well that it is important that pupils are in receipt of a curriculum which matches their present and future needs and arouses their interests and best endeavours. However, even the best tailored curriculum can be made to look shoddy if teachers of sufficient calibre are not available to administer it. Experiences have frequently shown us how one teacher, for example, can inject a 'breath of life' into a lesson, or subject, while another gives a similar lesson the 'kiss of death'.

Pupils' misbehaviour, therefore, may be a logical and not unreasonable response to a timetable which includes subjects and material which they have little or no interest in, and/or which is administered to them in a manner which depresses their interest and discourages healthy involvement.

Pupils' behaviour is also affected adversely or otherwise by the various ways in which schools organize their curriculum. Whether they stream, band or organize mixed ability groups, their policy for allocating teachers to classes and the range of options they offer, and truly make available, seem to be important considerations.

The main consideration, however, may not be *how* they organize the curriculum but *why*. Schools with similar organizational patterns and intakes often have differing impacts upon their pupils' behaviour as well as learning. An important factor in determining levels of success may be the extent to which senior management have adequately considered, and made informed responses to, the real needs of all their clients; how they have consulted with staff, parents and pupils and have consequently made sincere and successful overtures to convince staff, parents and pupils that what they offer and how they offer it is aimed to provide the 'best for all'. While perfection may not be practicable, and compromise may be necessary, *consultation, involvement, sincerity* and *informed decisions* work wonders.

Most good schools have sound policies for internal and external consultations and scrutinies when considering and implementing changes. While disparities will be evident in the ways in which they undertake such action, the types of questions which concerned parents may ask, on behalf of their children, could include the following.

1 How is the curriculum organized (e.g. setting/banding/mixed ability)? How is this arrangement justified in terms of meeting needs of pupils who are high fliers, average or low achievers?
2 Is the curriculum differentiated in order to meet pupils' present and future needs? What arrangements are undertaken to monitor this?
3 Are parents, pupils and staff consulted over curriculum matters, particularly where changes are being considered? Are meaningful attempts made to explain to staff, pupils and parents the rationale for the organization of the curriculum?
4 Are sexes separated for certain subjects? How is this justified?
5 Is there a homework timetable? Are pupils and parents given copies of this? Is there a school policy about staff adhering to it?
6 Is homework, and other work, marked regularly, adequately and promptly? Is feedback appropriate and adequate?
7 If children are absent what revision arrangements are available on their return?
8 Does the school have a whole-school policy on behaviour? Are copies of the policy document made available to pupils and parents?
9 What provision is available to help meet the needs of pupils with special educational needs?
10 Is there easy parental access to teaching/pastoral staff when problems/concerns arise?
11 How successful are the school's examination results?
12 How 'good' are the school's attendance rates?

LIFE-SPACE INTERVIEW

This term, originated by Redl (1959) and developed by Morse (1963), refers to effective support for a pupil being provided at a time and in a place where the child's problem is most relevant – in his or her own life-space, not in a more distant counselling setting. The immediacy and relevance of the support is then obvious to the child, even if referral to others is essential later.

Hamblin (1974) has also described such supportive therapeutic encounters between a troubled pupil and a helpful teacher, using the same principles as the life-space interview (LSI) theorists under the heading of school counselling. He provides a clear model for secondary-school counselling which has not been bettered in much school counselling literature in recent years. He describes life-space diagrams (p. 126) of the relationships between a pupil and other people with whom he or she has to live, including teachers, as part of a mutual analysis of a problem shared by a pupil with his or her teacher–counsellor. All teachers are inevitably counsellors to some degree, and within a secondary-school pastoral team or a primary-school staff there will be some teachers with extra pastoral or counselling training to support their colleagues.

Gobell (1980: 68), in describing a basic framework of LSI, writes of an inward first part of the interview, where the teacher listens, encourages and clarifies, and an outward second part where

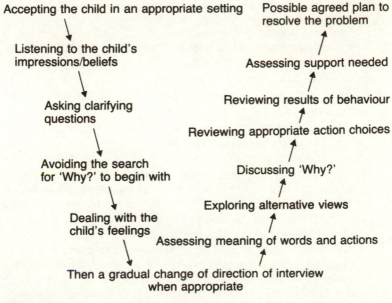

Accepting the child in an appropriate setting

Listening to the child's impressions/beliefs

Asking clarifying questions

Avoiding the search for 'Why?' to begin with

Dealing with the child's feelings

Then a gradual change of direction of interview when appropriate

Assessing meaning of words and actions

Exploring alternative views

Discussing 'Why?'

Reviewing appropriate action choices

Reviewing results of behaviour

Assessing support needed

Possible agreed plan to resolve the problem

Figure 10.1

alternative interpretations are discussed, other views put forward and appropriate action mutually sketched out. He suggests that this is possible even in the short time a teacher may have between lessons. The model of always listening attentively first, and then diagnosing and exploring possibilities (and perhaps allocating blame) later, is likely to be habitual to most successful and experienced teachers. More time is obviously needed when the problem is a major one, and when feelings have to be explored more fully, and when it may be necessary to 'squeeze' guilt issues into open awareness, using Redl and Wineman's (1952: 257) phrase.

As teacher and pupil mutually attempt to sort reality from fantasy, rage from apathy, aggression from helplessness, they may need more than a few moments between lessons to try to understand the feelings of others involved and to attempt to plan solutions and appropriate action. A school's system of pastoral care requires preparation for emergency or routine counselling.

The interview may appear as shown in Figure 10.1.

COUNSELLING SKILLS AND ATTITUDES

A class teacher's checklist of basic counselling (and for that matter much that lies in good teaching) skills and concepts might include the following.

1 The possession or development of congruence and empathy, of being 'in the child's shoes', of being able to hear and understand from the child's point of view.
2 Being able to offer undemanding and non-possessive warmth and genuine rather than forced interest.
3 Listening is a skill, not possessed by every teacher, and it can be developed in counselling training.
4 Many individual problems can be solved or reduced as a child listens within a group discussion to others talking on a theme that concerns him or her personally, and has relevance to his or her particular needs. Personal and social education schemes, with their discussion element, can reinforce counselling, as can appropriate study skills sessions and tutorial work.
5 Interviewing implies a child being sent for to discuss a problem, and implies a relationship between authority and a subordinate. Counselling implies more of a shared relationship, and a kind of equality between older and younger person; it has been well described as a reflective conversation.

6 There is need to keep a balance between cold detachment and too emotional an involvement.

7 The rule of parsimony suggests we do not labour the obvious, especially when the teacher presumes guilt, for this may deter honesty and may not reveal other underlying problems. There are often simple presenting problems which cover deeper needs.

8 Confidentiality is important, but may not be absolute, providing pupils know clearly (as part of the school's pastoral parameters) that there are limits; trusted teachers will not find this a major drawback.

9 Teachers have varying levels of counselling of which they are capable, and must refer to more expert help when their common sense warns them they are getting out of their depth. There is value in working as part of a pastoral team, where varying skills can be shared.

10 There are skills of clarifying and summarizing which help at appropriate times.

11 Too intensive a questioning by a teacher, or a reluctance to have silences for reflection at times, may inhibit counselling.

12 Problems can be cut down to size in skilful counselling, and pupils can begin to work on a problem in appropriate stages, as part of a mutually agreed 'action plan'.

13 We have to keep a balance between interference and intrusion into a child's personal autonomy, and necessary intervention.

REVIEWING PASTORAL CARE

Good pastoral care systems need regular review, but the basic principles do not appear to change as much as other aspects of education. It is difficult to believe that any school remains unaware of the need for a pastoral attitude in the management of behaviour in the school and the classroom, and only absence of leadership, or unusual apathy in a staff, will equate pastoral care just with basic discipline and simple welfare. Changes are happening in a tighter financial climate, and the appointment of experienced pastoral heads of house or heads of year in secondary schools is clearly reducing, or their roles are being diluted. One hopes that sufficient years of pastoral development and training have passed to have imbued school staffs with modern pastoral attitudes and habits, so that fewer pastoral appointments are essential.

Vision is not unreasonable; can we not still expect pastoral care systems to add to a school's ethos in developing an all-round education for living for pupils, in addition to the reasonable demands of the national curriculum and despite the difficulties of coordinating the cross-curricular themes, especially in personal and social education? One hopes that experienced teachers will not feel so browbeaten as to retreat only to league tables of examination results.

In considering his or her contribution to a school's pastoral care system a teacher might ask the following questions, and seek satisfying answers.

1 To whom am I responsible for pastoral and academic work, and is the support sufficient at my present stage of professional development?
2 Am I encouraged to share problems and skills with others in a staff team?
3 Have I developed the traditional tutorial skills of:
   (a) listening and discussing;
   (b) actively building feelings of security and trust;
   (c) being efficient in administration and in records of work;
   (d) being quietly effective in controlling behaviour;
   (e) constantly attempting to build contacts with parents;
   (f) observing in a relaxed and almost automatic way all that goes on amongst my pupils, including friendships, quarrels, moods, health and welfare needs, homework and academic results and steady all-round development;
   (g) knowing what is happening to my pupils' work and behaviour in other areas of the school?
4 What in-service development would best help me in my work, and how can I seek it?
5 What personal and social topics are appropriate for discussing with my pupils, and how can I prepare for this?
6 Have I developed diagnostic skills in dealing with behaviour problems?
   (a) When and where does misbehaviour occur?
   (b) Why does it occur?
   (c) What are the differences in the situations when misbehaviour occurs and does not occur?
   (d) What changes might be possible?
   (e) What support or advice do I need in dealing with these situations?

In continuing to reflect on changing times in pastoral care, one could list some questions a child might ask when considering the school's pastoral care system and attitude.

- Who can I talk to and trust?
- Who do they say I should go to in trouble?
- Which teachers do I like, and why?
- Who knows me best among the staff?
- Which teachers listen to me?
- Which subjects make me think about myself?
- Who checks me when I try it on?
- Who knows all my work?
- Who knows about the bullies?
- Who do my mum and dad feel they like talking to on the staff?
- Who gives me responsibilities in school?
- Am I going to contribute to my reports and assessment?

Finally, if our readers agree with us that vision is not unreasonable, and to complete this introspective review of pastoral care, is the school developing all its pupils to be adaptable in facing challenges and changes in work and in life, in being able independently to search for information and then to plan and take appropriate action, and in being capable of speaking his or her mind in an appropriate manner?

PARENT COOPERATION

Examples were given in Chapter 8 to illustrate how parents, teachers and other professionals can, through a sharing of educational responsibility, respond more effectively to problem behaviours. It was recommended that joint responses might best be developed through four stages of parent–professional involvement. The following questions are designed to help schools reflect upon their current practices within those stages and to consider the need for further developments.

1 *The introductory stage*
   (a) How are parents introduced to, and welcomed into, the work of the school? Are assemblies, displays, coffee mornings, concerts, information booklets and personal interviews useful?
   (b) Is there an agreed school policy for introductory events, or are teachers given a 'free hand'?

(c) Are parents introduced to, and encouraged to become active in, the life of the school *before* problem behaviours have been experienced?

(d) Who introduces new parents to the benefits of closer liaison? Are 'experienced' parents fully involved in this process, perhaps relaying accounts of successful liaison which was of clear benefit to their own child?

(e) How are hidden messages conveyed to parents? Is there a very formalized interview system or ready access via more informal methods? Are parents given a feeling that problem behaviours are 'their fault' and not a shared responsibility?

(f) Is the development of parent–professional liaison seen as a one-way process where the parent has to come to school, or should it be seen as a two-way process where professionals introduce the work of the school through home or community centres?

2 *The informative stage*

(a) How does the liaison process move from the stage of introducing parents to the school into more focused ways of discussing a particular child?

(b) What is the school's policy for giving and receiving information about a child?

(c) Is the process given above a procedure of information-giving or one which leads to improved forms of action which benefit the child? Is success consolidated through various complementary forms of controlled praise at home? Is the curriculum adjusted according to specific information regarding the child's interests and motivation?

(d) Is the informative process designed to lead, naturally, to the next stage of joint provision?

(e) Is the informative stage limited to formalized short periods of consultation on parents' evenings, or is this system extended via diary systems and opportunities for discussion at other informal events?

3 *The joint provision stage*

(a) To what extent do parents and professionals work together with whole classes, groups and individual pupils? Is there a consistent pattern of involvement throughout the school?

(b) How does this process help both partners to develop a better understanding of their respective roles and intentions towards pupils?

(c) Are there any whole-school initiatives for an active partnership through procedures such as paired and shared reading?

(d) Is advice given through short talks and seminars about particular aspects of the curriculum and ways of responding to problem behaviours?

(e) How do parents and professionals work together to provide for the particular needs of an individual pupil? Is this work clearly planned and coordinated?

4 *The sharing of responsibility stage*
When problem behaviours have been encountered the following questions should be asked.

(a) Do parents and professionals keep each other informed at a level which does *not* lead to jointly planned responses?

(b) Do parents and professionals join in the process of shared-information gathering so that they can arrive at a precise description of:

- the behaviour itself
- the factors leading up to and surrounding it
- the consequences which follow
- expectations about future behaviour?

(c) Is an attempt made by either party to dominate the process by advising the other person about the responses which *they* should make to problem behaviours, or are genuine attempts made to blend the knowledge and skills of both participants in providing for the pupil's needs?

(d) Is there a consistency of response at home and school?

(e) Are attempts made to evaluate the success of shared interventions?

ASSUMPTIONS AND EXPECTATIONS

We assume many things about our pupils; they will know, as we do, that hard work brings rewards, we assume. It is a clear and universal fact, we think – but in their particular world all the evidence of family history may have led them to know the opposite, which leads them to a blank incomprehension as to what we are on about. Attitudes and values can be influenced by a respected teacher, and can overcome the built-in assumptions of their neighbourhood and family, but it is skilled and committed work, and requires sensitivity and imagination on the teacher's part. Easy assumptions make life simpler; reflecting on our assumptions and keeping up a questioning and pragmatic attitude about our pupils and their ideas is harder. When we take the easier path and develop a reputation for not bothering to know their language and world, we alienate some pupils and behaviour problems easily arise. The disenchanted among our clients are likely to be cynical and watchful, and evidence that we do give thought to understanding (though not necessarily approving) their ideas may bring cooperation and a growing feeling of interest or curiosity in the teacher's attitudes and demands.

Parallel with this a consistency in terms of behavioural expectations gives a much needed security to pupils, both young and old. They become aware of teachers' expectations and are more able to respond favourably than where there is inconsistency. Arguably the best classrooms – and perhaps homes – have a limited number of essential rules and guidelines, and pupils are free to operate responsibly within these guidelines. Ultimately pupils need to regulate their behaviour from within rather than be controlled from without. If their teachers provide meaningful initial guidelines and provide freedom to exercise increasing control, most pupils benefit from this responsibility.

The Elton Report (DES and Welsh Office 1989) has been referred to already in Chapter 1. Whilst its findings and recommendations have been valued highly in many areas of education, the report also includes some exemplars of good practice for schools in their attempts to improve pupil (and staff) behaviour. Examples of those exemplars include the following. Relationships are vital: relationships between everyone at every level. Take the initiative:

- greet and be greeted
- speak and be spoken to
- smile and relate
- communicate
- use humour . . . it builds bridges
- keep calm . . . it reduces tension
- listen . . . it earns respect

Do all you can to avoid:

- humiliating . . . it breeds resentment
- shouting . . . it can be counterproductive
- over-reacting . . . the problems will grow

- blanket punishments . . . the innocent will resent them
- sarcasm . . . it damages you

CONCLUSION

The HMI (1987) report, *Education Observed 5: Good Behaviour and Discipline in Schools*, emphasizes many of the management skills and practices mentioned in this final chapter, and its summary provides a useful template for our conclusion.

In their report, HMI emphasize that good behaviour is both a prerequisite for effective learning and an important outcome of education itself, which society expects from its schools. Good behaviour in school not only minimizes the distractions and disturbances which interfere with learning, but is also a crucial part of the learning process within which pupils acquire the attitudes, values and skills which help to prepare them for the future.

HMI refer to the following principles of good practice which are influential in creating and sustaining high standards of behaviour in school.

A *school policy document* provides a small number of clear and defensible guidelines for behaviour. These guidelines make the school's expectations on behaviour clear, to pupils and parents, and are firmly, consistently and judiciously enforced. Linked to the formulation and enforcement of these guidelines is the type of *leadership from senior staff* that encourages good behaviour through example, holds healthy professional expectations of colleagues and pupils, is vigilant (and appropriately responsive) to behaviour in the school, and provides positive sources of support for staff as well as pupils.

The *school climate* or ethos both reflects, and influences, the general welfare of the school. The network of relationships and expectations amongst and between pupils, staff, parents and outside professionals, and the overall quality of pastoral care practices, are as influential in determining this climate as the impact of the formal curriculum and teaching skills of those who administer it.

Whilst teachers and their pupils derive benefit from the sparing and flexible application of *sanctions* for certain pupil misbehaviours, their use should be outweighed by the award of *rewards and privileges* for good behaviour. Such a policy actively encourages desirable behaviour whilst discouraging others which are less so.

These basic principles of good practice, and the plethora of highly developed professional skills which contribute to them, provide an insight into the nature of the influences which schools can put to good use to affect their clients' behaviour.

Schools are institutions; they are a microcosm, or inner world, of the larger outside world. As in the outer world, individuals' behaviour is fashioned by, for example, the manner in which they are regarded, valued and rewarded; the nature of the expectations held about them; the quality of the group and individual learning experiences made available to them; the examples set by those with responsibility and authority; and the adequacy of available caring provisions in monitoring and responding to individual and group needs.

The crucial differences between the two 'worlds' lie in areas such as *appraisal, accountability* and *involvement*. In the outside world we are continually having the quality of our lives *appraised* for (if not by) us and modified where there is a consensus of opinion amongst us that change is necessary, feasible and welcome. Those who are officially appointed to make decisions about our lives are *accountable* to – and often either elected or indirectly appointed by – us. They are also responsive to majority, or particularly strong, opinion. Most major decisions taken about us are made, therefore, with our *involvement*, directly or otherwise, or that of our elected representatives.

In the inner world, however, 'clients' are infrequently permitted to be actively, and effectively, involved in making decisions about matters which have a direct impact upon their lives.

There has been a strong wind of change blowing in education; one which threatens or heralds, depending upon your particular stance, more appraisal, improved accountability and enhanced involvement. Teacher appraisal, a national curriculum, the Education Reform Bill in general and The 1992 White Paper on Education present a plethora of exciting, innovatory, yet often threatening proposals. Although these changes may not always result in improvements, discussions about them place the 'ball in the school's court' to await their response. It is not practicable to legislate for good practice. The value of legislation is not that it prescribes good practice, but that *it makes clear where responsibilities lie*.

Many schools and their teachers provide an excellent service for their pupils, but the current climate of opinion, supported by research, is that some schools need to 'try harder to improve', 'pay more attention to', 'concentrate more upon' the content, range, administration and quality of their offerings. There is another opinion, which is attracting increasing recognition and acceptance; that teachers both individually, and collectively as a staff, can – and do – make a difference; they have considerable opportunities to make positive impacts upon their pupils' behaviour.

We hope that the information highlighted, and discussed, in this book will aid discussions as to how teachers can make a positive impact upon pupils' behaviour in school, and elsewhere.

REFERENCES

Burns, R.B. (1982) *Self-Concept Development and Education*, New York: Holt, Rinehart & Winston.

Canfield, J. and Wells, H.C. (1976) *100 Ways to Enhance the Self-Concept in the Classroom: A Handbook for Teachers and Parents*, Englewood Cliffs, N.J.: Prentice Hall.

Charlton, T. and David, K. (1990) *Supportive Schools*, London: Routledge.

Chisholm, B., Kearney, D., Knight, H., Little, H., Morris, S. and Tweddle, D. (1986) *Preventive Approaches to Disruption*, Basingstoke: Macmillan.

Clarizio, H.F. and McCoy, G.F. (1983) *Behaviour Disorders in Children*, New York: Harper & Row.

DES and Welsh Office (1989) *Discipline in Schools. Report of the Committee of Enquiry*, chaired by Lord Elton, London: HMSO.

Gobell, A. (1980) 'Three classroom procedures', in Upton, G. and Gobell, A. (eds) *Behaviour Problems in the Comprehensive School*, Cardiff: Faculty of Education, University College.

Hamblin, D.H. (1974) *The Teacher and Counselling*, Oxford: Blackwell.

HMI (1987) *Education Observed 5. Good Behaviour and Discipline in Schools*, London: DES.

Lawrence, J., Steed, D. and Young, P. (1984) *Disruptive Children, Disruptive Schools*, London: Croom Helm.

Morse, W.C. (1963) 'Training teachers in life space interviewing', *American Journal of Orthopsychiatry* 33, 727–30.

Redl, F. (1959) 'Strategy and techniques of the life space interview', *American Journal of Orthopsychiatry* 29: 1–18.

Redl, F. and Wineman, D. (1952) *Controls from Within*, London: Collier-Macmillan.

Smith, C. (1992) 'Keeping them clever: preventing learning problems from becoming behaviour problems', in Wheldall, K. (ed.) *Discipline in Schools, Psychological Perspectives on The Elton Report*, London: Routledge.

Stott, D.H. (1978) *Helping Children with Hearing Difficulties – A Diagnostic Teaching Approach*, London: Ward Lock Education.

Thomas, J., Presland, I., Grant, M. and Glynn, T. (1978) 'Natural rates of teacher approval and disapproval in Grade 7 classrooms', *Journal of Applied Behaviour Analysis* 11: 91–4.

Wheldall, K., Houghton, S. and Merrett, F. (1989) 'Natural rates of teacher approval and disapproval in British secondary school classrooms', *British Journal of Educational Psychology* 59: 38–48.

Appendix

Legislation and reports in recent years

RECENT EDUCATIONAL CHANGE

There have been seventeen Education Acts since 1979, including the following.

1 *Education Act 1980* – schools to have separate governing bodies, to include governors elected by parents and teachers; parents' right to information to help them choose schools; assisted places scheme.
2 *Education Act 1981* – responsibilities of local education authorities (LEAs) and mainstream schools for pupils with special educational needs.
3 *Education (No. 2) Act 1986* – governors' powers; end to corporal punishment.
4 *Education Reform Act 1988* – opting out; delegation of finances to schools; the National Curriculum; Schools' Examinations and Assessment Council.
5 *Education (Schools) Act 1992*– new chief inspectorate with private teams to inspect schools every four years; parents' charter and league tables.

Many improvements have come with these changes, and average and below average schools have in many cases been usefully tightened in their management and their academic work. As with so many changes so much depends on the quality (and health and stamina) of the headteacher, but a question also arises in the recruitment of governors. There may not be a rush to fill vacancies when local management of schools demands a great deal of time and responsibility from governors, especially those still at work and those with business and financial experience. Governors of modest ability and experience may be easier to find, but they may cause management to be left to the staff, which is not the purpose of governing bodies. The weakening of LEA services, advice and supervision is not as wise as present policy indicates, as not all grant-aided staffs will be repositories of all wisdom. We hope that teachers and parents concerned and knowledgeable in pastoral matters will be seeking election to governing bodies, especially with the weakening or disappearance of local government advisers and inspectors.

THE 1992 WHITE PAPER ON EDUCATION

This proposes radical changes in education, including:

1 a new funding agency to be linked with the expected growth of grant maintained schools, and 'opting out' methods to be made easier;
2 greater attention on truancy, including league tables of schools;
3 the new inspectorate to complete a survey of all schools within four years;
4 specialization and diversity in schools to be encouraged, and changes in selection or non-selection to require approval of the Secretary of State;
5 a moral dimension in the ethos of schools;
6 strong leadership and better management to be encouraged;
7 greater efficiency with surplus school places;
8 education associations to take over 'at risk' schools if LEAs fail;
9 combining of the National Curriculum Council and the School Examinations and Assessment Council;
10 improvements in meeting all pupils' needs, including assessments and statements and methods of appeal;
11 groups of smaller schools being able to apply to become grant maintained;
12 an enhanced role of churches and voluntary bodies in education.

The effects of these proposed changes will be debated for some time to come, and many will be popular, but objections have already been strongly voiced. It has been suggested that specialization may lead to the return of greater selection, and will ignore the developing and changing nature of pupils' abilities. Critics also claim that it will lead to local confusion and fragmentation of education, with the slow death of many good LEAs, often popular with their schools and needing less drastic surgery than they are threatened with. The idea of introducing education associations (the 'hit squads' of the popular press) to deal with schools that are unsatisfactory seems to bristle with problems, including local reaction to imposed strangers: these changes appear misconceived and the plans are confused. It has also been suggested that we are seeing further strengthening of central government powers and the reduction of local democratic control of education as deliberate policy decisions, with the possibility of greater political interference in the way education is managed and in the details of curriculum.

Our view, particularly with the subject of this book in mind, is that the main critical reaction to this proposed Act should be, 'What is the effect on average and below average pupils and their parents?' We feel that the more articulate, intelligent and educated parents will continue to look after their children well in every type of school, as they usually have in the past. It seems likely, therefore, that capable and above average pupils and parents may well gain from the opting out of schools, and the worry must remain at present that less capable and less articulate families and their children (who may well have slowly developing intellectual or technical potential needed by the economy) may find reduced opportunities and resources, especially in the special educational needs and pastoral care areas of education. There are already the first signs of this happening. Responsible governors and headteachers will presumably be vigilant and vocal.

PERSONAL AND SOCIAL EDUCATION FROM 5 TO 16 (DES), 1989

This *Curriculum Matters 14* gives an authoritative view on fostering personal and social development and responsibility. 'PSE refers to those aspects of a school's thinking, planning, teaching and organisation explicitly designed to promote the personal and social development of pupils.' It is concerned with 'qualities and attitudes, knowledge and understanding, and abilities and skills in relation to oneself and others, social responsibilities and morality', and it brings 'relevance, breadth and balance to the curriculum'. It refers to the effect on pupils of styles of learning and of the school as a community. It commends:

1 pupils taking responsibility for their learning, exercising choices;
2 opportunities to achieve;

3 everyone's contributions deserving attention;
4 opportunities to work in groups differing in size and purpose;
5 exploring personal and social experience through role play;
6 opportunities for pupils to use their imagination.

It states that 'every subject has a moral dimension', and asks that 'teachers are concerned to ensure that what pupils learn is not trapped within the confines of a particular subject but leads to the exploration of broader understanding'.

The useful objectives listed (pp. 13–17) range widely from the general (independence of mind) to the particular (how to react if bullied or abused) and may be useful for teachers coordinating personal and social education schemes within the cross-curricular themes of the National Curriculum.

THE CHILDREN ACT 1989

This far reaching Act is addressed to parents, LEAs and anyone who works with children and aims to encourage good parenthood, to clarify the responsibilities of child services, to ensure a fairer and more efficient legal framework and to benefit the child by more consistent decision-making principles. The child's welfare is paramount, and the child's wishes have influence on a court's decisions. Parental responsibility aims to create a partnership with parents, to keep families together, to speed up decisions and to reduce custody cases. Implementation of the Act will take up to five years.

Children suffering 'significant harm' or likely to suffer 'significant harm' are to merit intervention, but 'significant harm' is not defined as it will be different for every child.

Parents have the right to see all records about them and their children, though names of third parties involved are private. Anyone can act to protect a child considered to be at risk, but clear proof is required. Social services must have a written plan for all children they are involved with and parents can see and discuss changes in these plans. The parent is to be presumed to know best unless it is proven otherwise.

Divorce situations may have four orders involved: a variable contact order appropriate for a particular child; a prohibited steps order against unwelcome persons; a residence order detailing where and with whom a child is to live; and specific issue orders.

Educational supervision orders from a Family Proceedings Court will enable educational welfare officers (EWOs) to attempt to enforce attendance.

A child of 'an age and understanding' can apply for orders in divorce situations, and may not be forced to have medical examinations in abuse cases. The definition is not clarified further yet.

Parents cannot now put their children into care voluntarily, and a 1992 Criminal Justice Act will permit fines on parents who do not take care of their children or have control over them.

The Act will have many future developments and praise or criticism is premature: the aim of securing family life must be good, though the worst types of families will still scuttle all good intentions and add grey hairs to EWOs. For the social services it may give a clearer picture, for the courts and magistrates will now have the responsibility for assessing risks. The police may be even more reluctant to be involved in family situations, for they have to be responsible for their own actions. Schools on the whole should benefit from a clearer legal picture, but difficult decisions on exclusion from school and on suspected abuse cases will still have to be made, hopefully now with easier liaison with social service departments. It seems probable that problem behaviour pupils will be more likely to remain with their families and in their mainstream schools (or out of school and on the streets), and less likely to be placed in custody. One hopes that in schools a senior teacher (as well as a member of the governing body, perhaps) will be asked to study the provisions of the Act, and to liaise with social workers over the future development of the Act.

THE ELTON REPORT OF 1989

Lord Elton was chairman of a committee of enquiry on behaviour and discipline in schools which provided a variety of recommendations to LEAs and schools on behaviour management, discipline and pastoral care. It reported that incidents of verbal abuse and physical violence to teachers were comparatively rare, but that stress for teachers from behaviour management was considerable. The links between behaviour problems and under-achievement were noted, as was the absence of preparation of new teachers for the constant 'stream of relatively minor disorders'. Few LEAs had policies for supporting teachers in dealing with difficult pupils. Some recommendations were as follows.

1 LEAs should provide comprehensive in-service training and support, and should monitor disruption.
2 Schools should provide 'clear statements on behaviour', balancing rewards and punishment and serious and minor offences, and should provide a positive setting for all pupils.
3 Pupils should be consulted more on school policy regarding behaviour, and should contribute directly in their records of achievement.
4 Parents should be more responsible for their children's behaviour and should cooperate with school policies on behaviour.

In their submission to the Elton Committee, the National Children's Bureau submitted points which we listed in some detail in the first edition of this book. Since they reinforce the findings of the Elton Report and represent our own views, some can usefully be repeated briefly here:

1 the need for a 'whole-school policy' in viewing behaviour;
2 the need in initial teacher training for more advice on classroom control and management, and for more practical experience;
3 the need for schools to find ways to listen to and heed the views of pupils more;
4 the need for schools actively to involve parents in the formulation and review of their policies;
5 the need for schools to give higher priority to the teaching of personal and social education and the preparation for parenthood.
6 the need for government to improve morale and job satisfaction for teachers as part of reducing 'an unsettledness which has undermined confidence'.

The Elton Report now provides a better basis of careful evidence for debate on the management of behaviour in schools, has reduced some of the more anecdotal evidence of physical assault and abuse and has reinforced the picture of the 'minor' but distressing offences which harass teachers. It should enable classroom behaviour management, and 'whole-school' approaches, to have greater attention; this expectation was reinforced by the government's decision that management of pupil behaviour was to have national priority in the LEA training grants scheme for in-service training of teachers.

Index